Seeing the City

Interdisciplinary Perspectives on the Study of the Urban

T0342112

Edited by:

Nanke Verloo

Luca Bertolini

Amsterdam University Press

Volume 6 of the Series Perspectives on Interdisciplinarity

Cover illustration: Photo by Nanke Verloo
Cover design and lay-out: Matterhorn Amsterdam

ISBN   978 94 6372 894 2
e-ISBN   978 90 4855 309 9
DOI   10.5117/9789463728942
NUR   740

Contents

Acknowledgments   10

1 Introduction   12
Nanke Verloo and Luca Bertolini
Seeing the city   15
Seeing Amsterdam   18
Seeing this volume   19
References   21

2 Quantitative data collection: A meta view   22
Willem Boterman
Introduction   22
Origins of quantitative data collection and uses: the census   23
Collecting survey data   24
Administrative data   28
Big data   31
Conclusion   33
References   34

**3 Urban ethnography and participant observations:
Studying the city from within**   37
Nanke Verloo
Why studying the city from within?   37
'Thick description', limitations, and underlying assumptions   39
Preparing for ethnographic fieldwork   40
Doing fieldwork   44
Representing and interpreting ethnographic data   47
Reflectivity and positionality   50
Conclusions   52
References   53

4 Sensing the city through new forms of urban data   56
Achilleas Psyllidis
Introduction   56
Physical sensor data   58
Mobile phone data   59
Social media data   61
User-generated & POI-based web data   63
Summary   64
References   67

5 Interviewing in urban research   70
Fenne M. Pinkster
Introduction   70
The purpose of interviewing   71
Developing the methodology: research sample   72
Constructing an interview guide   73
Ethical considerations and interview protocol   78
Going into the field   78
The art of interviewing   80
Processing your data while in the field   82
Conclusion   83
References   84

6 Digging in the crates: Archival research and
historical primary sources   85
Tim Verlaan
Introduction   85
What is an archive, and what lurks inside?   86
Setting foot in murky waters   88
Conclusion   93
References   94

7 Reading spaces: A cultural analysis approach   96
Daan Wesselman
Object selection, research questions, and analytical toolkit   99
Analyzing aesthetics and discourse   101
Reflection   106
General conclusion   107
References   108

8 The practice of institutional analysis in urban contexts 110

Federico Savini

Objectives and motives of institutional analysis 110
Distinguishing and connecting levels of analysis departing from institutional tensions 112
Setting operational grids to set up the analysis 115
Gathering and analyzing data in a targeted way 117
The challenges of institutional analysis 121
References 122

9 Household preferences and hedonic pricing 124

Hans R.A. Koster and Jan Rouwendal

Introduction 124
Micro-economic foundations 128
Econometric estimation of hedonic price functions 136
Summary 141
References 141

10 Urban research in another dimension: methods for modelling historical cities 145

Claartje Rasterhoff

Introduction 145
Mapping and modeling methods 146
From dusty old archives to fuzzy new data 148
Urban mapping and models 151
Conclusion 157
References 158

11 Mapping the city: Geographic Information Systems and science in urban research 160

Rowan Arundel

Introduction: space matters 160
Geographic Information Science and Systems 161
Applying a GIS approach to research 164
Conclusion 174
References 174

12 Methods for studying urban biodiversity   177

Gerard Oostermeijer

Introduction   177
Describing biodiversity   181
General conclusions   190
References   192

13 Action research in the city: developing
collaborative governance arrangements for the urban
commons   196

Joachim Meerkerk and Stan Majoor

Introduction: Making the city together through action research   196
Performing action research: Becoming a contributive actor   198
Using a conceptual model to foster systemic transformation   206
Conclusions   209
References   209

14 Streetlabs as a co-creative approach
to Research Through Design   212

STBY (Nina Stegeman, Geke van Dijk, Bas Raijmakers)

Introduction   212
Streetlabs: a co-creative and collaborative approach   213
Initial exploration and reframing   214
Streetlab Facilitation   216
Orchestrating conversations around current situation (AS IS)
and future situation (TO BE)   218
Documentation and analysis of the stories and ideas collected   221
Delivering the results   222
Implementation & Reflection   223
Recommendations for further reading   225

15 *Too many cities in the city?*
Interdisciplinary and transdisciplinary city research
methods and the challenge of integration   226

Machiel Keestra and Nanke Verloo

Introduction: Interdisciplinary, transdisciplinary and action
research of a city in lockdown   226
Setting the stage: establishing an ID/TD research team   229
Integrating disciplinary perspectives   231
Interdisciplinary research as an iterative process
of mutual learning   238
References   241

16 Exploring city science   243
   Caroline Nevejan
   Introduction   243
   The need for city science   244
   Current collaborations between cities and universities   246
   Research, Policy and Design   249
   City science, the research process   249
   Research design   253
   Discussion and future research   263
   References   264

17 Conclusions   266
   Luca Bertolini and Nanke Verloo
   What did we see and understand?   266
   How did we progress?   268
   What did we miss?   269
   Agenda for Urban Research   271

Glossary   272

List of contributors   287

Acknowledgments

This edited volume is the product of a long journey that brought together a wide variety of Amsterdam-based scholars, all of whom study the city within their respective disciplines. Inter- or transdisciplinary work is only possible if we allow ourselves to open our minds to different views and interpretations: it demands that we look beyond boundaries that are often taken for granted, and on top of that it requires us to engage with others and form collaborative networks. In the first place, we are therefore indebted to our authors, who brought such open-mindedness to their participation in the various author workshops, and whose knowledge and efforts were indispensable for making this volume a success. We are more than grateful to them for helping us to develop a collaborative community of scholars who were willing and able to engage in all these facets of inter- and transdisciplinary work.

This book is part of the University of Amsterdam (UvA) Institute for Interdisciplinary Studies (IIS) series 'Perspectives on Interdisciplinarity', which has made significant contributions to scholarship on interdisciplinary studies and beyond. The book would not have seen the light of day without the knowledge and experience of the IIS, and specifically the efforts of Yorike Hartman and Lucy Wenting, who supported us throughout the process and contributed constructive feedback every step of the way. And we would like to acknowledge Katusha Sol from the IIS who first initiated the idea.

We are also grateful for the contribution of the interdisciplinary Scientific Board, who provided us with ideas and critical commentaries at various points in the process and who reviewed drafts and gave useful feedback on individual chapters. Each session with the academic board replenished our thinking and helped us move forward. Its members are Prof. Dr. Ir. A. Bozzon (Professor of Human-Centered Artificial Intelligence, Department of Design Engineering, Faculty of Industrial Design Engineering, TU Delft); Prof. Dr. J. Grin (Professor of Policy Science, Department of Political Science, University of Amsterdam); Prof. Dr. R. Jaffe (Professor of Urban Geography, Department of Human Geography, Planning and International Development Studies and the Centre for Urban Studies, University of Amsterdam); Prof. Dr. C.I.M. Nevejan (Professor by special appointment, Amsterdam School for Social Science Research, University of Amsterdam, and Chief Science Officer of the city of Amsterdam); Prof. Dr. J.J. Noordegraaf (Professor of Digital Heritage, Department of Media Studies, University of Amsterdam); Prof. Dr. K. Pfeffer (Professor of Infrastructuring Urban Futures, University of Twente); Prof. Dr. P.M.A. Sloot (Professor of Complex Adaptive Systems and Scientific Director Institute for Advanced Studies, University of Amsterdam); and Prof. Dr. E.T. Verhoef (Professor of Spatial Economics, School of Business and Economics, Free University Amsterdam).

Finally, we would like to recognize the IIS and the Centre for Urban Studies (CUS), who provided us with the resources to work on this edited volume, and the team at Amsterdam University Press, whose support in finalizing the manuscript and preparing it for publication is greatly appreciated.

1 Introduction

Nanke Verloo and Luca Bertolini

Figure 1.1: Amsterdam streetscape.

I see a man on a bike pulling up his legs to avoid the water staining his pants. He is not using the bike lane, but instead takes the risk of cycling over the rather slippery tram track. Behind him, a tram stops at a station near the Waterloo square in the city center of Amsterdam. I see the historic architecture of the Zuiderkerk that was built in 1611 as the first reformed church. The green trees reveal that this picture must have been made in spring or summertime, when Amsterdam is usually crowded with tourists, but none are portrayed in this picture. The biker's aesthetics – the skinny tie, low but colored socks, vintage glasses and a nonchalant beard – remind me of what some would call a 'hipster'. The crate on his bike is a typical Amsterdam artifact. The picture also hints at a world that cannot be observed with the naked eye: the network of pipes and cables that supply the city's population with water and electricity, or the pollution in the air threatening biodiversity. The same picture also awakens more critical considerations: is this a representative picture of the Amsterdam population? Who belongs in Amsterdam? May the detour from the bike lane reveal a lack of cycling infrastructure? How does the local government maintain its infrastructure and balance between trams, bikes, boats, pedestrians, and cars? And what about the historic architecture in the back – who is able to afford the city center since the rise in tourism and property developments? Which species are inhabiting those leafy trees? Are they threatened?

These observations and subsequent questions could be asked by urban researchers from a wide variety of fields. The field of urban studies is an **interdisciplinary** field by nature. Cities around the globe are dealing with complex challenges like rapid expansion, increasing crowdedness, intersecting forms of diversity, and staggering inequality between the rich and the poor. These processes take shape in the context of a climate emergency, biodiversity loss, globalization, and unprecedented urbanization. These multifaceted and complex challenges require researchers to move beyond disciplinary boundaries and approach urban problems and solutions via interdisciplinary approaches.

An interdisciplinary approach is uniquely positioned to inform urban governments who are up to the complex task of developing policies and designing interventions that are inclusive, multifaceted, intelligent, and sustainable, but also resilient and adaptable to unexpected change. Urban scholars can contribute to these tasks by unravelling complexity, revealing unequal power relations, or identifying potential solutions using technological or social innovations. Such cooperation with governments and other societal stakeholders pushes the interdisciplinary nature of the field to a **transdisciplinary** approach that urges scientists to take responsibility for contributing to societally relevant questions, to step outside of academic boundaries and engage professionals and citizens in their research projects.

The persistent and urgent problems cities currently face demand both scholars and practitioners to make better sense of what is going on in the city. To do so, they need methodologies that help them to collect and analyze a diversity of urban data in a diversity of ways, and to integrate and combine these different analyses. This book offers a wide variety of quintessential urban methodologies developed, used, and reflected on by Amsterdam-based researchers. As the editors of this volume, we curated a selection of methodological approaches that we believe will help urban researchers but also practitioners to better understand the multifaceted problems and opportunities of the urban environment.[1]

---

[1] This book includes a selection of methodologies that we believe provide a broad and multidisciplinary overview of the dominant methodologies used in urban studies. We realize that the book is by no means exhaustive of all urban methodologies, and indeed that it cannot be. In the concluding chapter, we return to this point.

Some research starts with a theory or concept that provides a possible explanation or a hypothesis. Other research starts with a methodology. Often, researchers use a combination of these things: they have a certain methodological and theoretical expertise and observe what is going on in the city, they see real-world problems that they care about and start imagining a research project based on those observations and their specific background. To structure the process of setting up a research project, we propose four central questions:

1   What do I see?
2   How can I understand?
3   What do I miss?
4   Why does it matter?

The first and last questions are highly interrelated, since what we see is usually strongly related to what we care about. The text box above gives a range of possible answers to the first question. Starting with figure 1.1, the question 'What do I see?' moves the viewer through various disciplinary avenues that all provide a different view and observe different aspects of an urban streetscape. The final question could be answered personally – why do you care about this topic? But a good research proposal also includes a broader discussion of the societal and academic relevance of a certain research question. The academic relevance of a question is related to other research in and beyond the field. What does the research add to the current state of knowledge? The societal relevance of a given project is highly dependent on contextual factors. How does the research distinctively contribute to making that place, process, or socio-economic or political dynamic – and perhaps other places, processes, or dynamics – better? In the conclusion to this volume we reflect more on the relevance of various forms of urban research.

The first section of this volume answers the question 'What do I see?' by providing various methodologies to gather data. It offers ways to decide which methodologies are most suitable for collecting the data that you need to answer your questions. The second section of the volume answers the question, 'How can I understand?' Here you'll find methodologies for analyzing your data in the context of the city. We distinguish between methodologies for data collection and methodologies for data analyses, to prevent repetition. The same methodologies for data collection – statistical data, ethnographic data, interview transcripts, archival data, sensory data – can be used for various methodologies of data analyses. The distinction, however, is not so easy to make in reality because the processes of collecting data and analyzing data overlap and go hand in hand as the research progresses.

The third question, and third section of the volume, requires researchers and professionals to critically reflect on their approach and data. It asks to reflect on what it is that you do *not see* when you use a certain methodology. Any methodology is a tool that helps to see something in detail but will also and inevitably overlook something else. The clearest example of this is between qualitative and quantitative studies. Qualitative research aims at detailed insights into the *why* and *how* of processes. A qualitative study could, for example, help develop deep understanding of the everyday experiences and unintended practices of institutional racism. This could make visible why and how institutional racism still jeopardizes the full participation of other ethnic or racial groups in a society or organization. The same study, however, would be missing the actual numbers of instances of institutional racism. These numbers might be necessary to convince leaders that racism is taking place in their organization at a significant scale. Quantitative analysis can provide those numbers. Quantitative research aims at statistically identifying relationships. Quantitative data analysts could provide the necessary numbers and may even prove a relationship between the number of colleagues of color and the lack of promotions among them. Those statistics alone, however, do not explain how and why this is the case. Qualitative analysis can help here. Although it often occurs in a more nuanced way than in this example, all methodologies focus on something and leave out something else. We therefore asked each author of the volume to reflect with us on the question 'What do I miss?' when applying their methodology. Next, we invited them to think how their different approaches could complement each other and be integrated towards new forms of knowledge. Section three is the result of that journey and offers practical guidelines for researchers and practitioners who are willing to cross disciplinary boundaries, and boundaries between academic disciplines and non-academic knowledge.

Seeing the city

Before we can proceed to the methodologies discussed in this volume, we must reflect on the way we see – that is, that crucial first question. First, because the kinds of observations we make as researchers are closely related to the disciplines in which we are educated. Second, because the way we see the city and formulate problems and methodological solutions is closely related to the paradigm we employ. Being aware of those is key for being able to position and value a particular view relative to other possible views.

Seeing the city through different disciplines

A discipline could be explained as a pair of glasses. If the shades are red, they emphasize the red tones in the picture and the viewer would have more difficulties seeing the yellow or the blue, and the other way around. If we put on these metaphorical glasses to view the image above as urban anthropologists, we see a man employing a tacit cycling practice; it could tell us something about the unwritten rules of cycling culture in Amsterdam. Such observations are usually the product of ethnographic research that builds on in-depth and real-time experiences. If the ethnographer did not research infrastructure management, her uninformed eye might believe that the image portrays a flood. It might make her wonder whether Amsterdam is the victim of quickly rising water levels and climate change. To understand the picture better she needs to include the knowledge of an infrastructure planner who knows that, in the summer, local infrastructure management pumps water out of the canals onto the bridges so that they do not expand due to the heat. Infrastructure planners, however, might not notice the tactics of the biker pulling up his legs and instead focus only on the streetscape and interconnection of bike lanes, water ducts, tram tracks, street markings, and traffic signs. Triggered by the peculiar tactics of the biker, a data analyst would critically wonder why and how often people detour from the bike lane, and employ sensory data to calculate how many accidents might be avoided with a better street design.

Looking at the same picture from a historical perspective would reveal the story of the first Protestant church in the city, the burial of Rembrandt van Rijn's first child and the baptism of his fourth, or the church's relevance to the care for orphans mid-seventeenth century. A cultural heritage expert might research its architectural value, an economist the increase in surrounding properties after the investment in cultural heritage. Geographers might use similar quantitative data to analyze the more general process of **gentrification** these areas of Amsterdam underwent in the past few decades. The eyes of cultural studies experts would be drawn to the aesthetics of the man and his bike, which may be used to critically read the discourse of this picture. Meanwhile, the biologist would sharpen her eyes and ears to observe and listen to the variety of birds singing in the trees. Action researchers and designers might be drawn to this rather confusing site to engage in a **streetlab** or experiment with municipal actors and citizens using this space to learn about effective and inclusive interventions.

As this carousel of viewpoints suggests, the discipline in which researchers and practitioners are educated shape their way of seeing the city and the problems they identify. Seeing something beyond your discipline is a challenge – usually it does not come naturally and thus requires work and perseverance. That challenge is even stronger if you try to look from the perspective of a discipline that uses a different paradigm to make sense of the world.

Seeing the city through different paradigms

All research projects and questions are embedded in a certain paradigm. A **paradigm** is a set of beliefs that shape the way you make sense of the world. It represents a worldview that defines, for its holder, the nature of the 'world' (Guba & Lincoln, 1994, p. 107). Guba and Lincoln (1994) distinguish between four basic paradigms in the sciences: **positivism, post-positivism, critical theory,** and **constructivism**. These paradigms, albeit often unconsciously, shape the way researchers understand the nature of the world (**ontology**), how we think we can know that world (**epistemology**), and finally the way we formulate questions and organize to research the world via methodologies, the purpose of the project, and the relationship between the researcher and the field. (For further reading on ontology, epistemology, and methodology see Guba & Lincoln, 1994). The main tension between these four paradigms exists between positivism or post-positivism on one side, and critical theory or constructivism on the other.

In a nutshell, positivist or post-positivist paradigms present a worldview that assumes that the world is an external objective reality that is apprehensible via objective findings that explain how things 'really work'. The difference between positivism and post-positivism is that the latter still assumes an objective reality, but grants that the understanding and study of that reality is always imperfect and approximate. The methodologies used by positivist and post-positivist researchers are often, but not always, quantitative. In this paradigm, the researcher is seen as independent from what is researched, and it is assumed that the researcher does not influence the field of research. The outcomes of this type of research usually verify or falsify a hypothesis in order to prove, predict, or control something. Chapters 2 and 4 provide a more in-depth discussion about quantitative data collection.

Researchers employing a critical or constructivist paradigm, on the other hand, see the world as inseparable from themselves: they refuse an 'objective' truth, and assume that our world is constantly subject to change. For critical theorists, that change is shaped by historically situated structures, while for constructivists the world and all its related meanings or structures are a product of human intellect, and thus always under construction and often contested. They assume that there is no single truth that can be known and that knowledge itself is value-mediated and therefore dependent on the researcher, the historical context, or the interactions among researchers and the field. They often, but not always, use qualitative methodologies that represent conflicting interpretations, dialogical and dialectical constructions. The goal of this type of research is not to prove or predict something, but to critique and transform (in critical theory) or to understand and reconstruct (in constructivism) a given process or phenomenon. Chapters 3 and 5 delve deeper into the collection of qualitative data, and chapter 6 into collecting historical data.

Paradigms also shape the ways in which the quality of research findings ought to be assessed. The main criteria for determining the quality of findings are objectivity, reliability, and validity, as derived from experimental-statistical hypothesis testing (Flick, Kardorff & Steinke, 2004, p. 183). There is much debate about whether or not these positivist, quantitative criteria should be transferred to critical, qualitative research. Positivist, quantitative research is based on the premise that there is one objective reality (developing objectivity), the relationship between the researcher and the object is independent (strengthening reliability), and the nature of truth to a finding can be assessed (validity of findings). On the other hand, critical, constructivist, qualitative research rejects the idea of an objective reality and thus does not aim at developing objectivity. The relationship between the researcher and the object can never be objective since data is developed in close interaction with the field and the people in the field. Finally, the outcomes are oriented to providing descriptions, analyses of processes or behavior, or critical reflections, rather than one truth. To assess the trustworthiness of qualitative research, some qualitative scholars use **triangulation**. Some propose using criteria such as the credibility of the findings and argumentation; transferability (to rethink how the findings hold in some other context); and dependability and confirmability (by auditing the research process via fieldnotes, interview transcripts, data analysis decisions) (Anney, 2014; Flick, Kardorff & Steinke, 2004). Because paradigms are so radically different, researchers should rethink which quality criteria can best be applied to their projects. They argue that a misuse of criteria or the application of quantitative criteria to qualitative research – or the other way around – poses critical problems and curtails the development of credible and valid outcomes (Leininger, 1994, p. 96).

In this volume we do not favor one paradigm over another: the methodologies discussed in section two have qualitative and quantitative roots and employ all paradigms discussed by Guba and Lincoln. We also do not take a stance in the debate on which quality criteria to use, but we urge all researchers to reflect on this issue and actively choose which criteria you will apply to your findings. Quality criteria, trustworthiness, and limitations of each methodology are discussed in the context of each methodological chapter. For a more general discussion of how quantitative data is verified you can continue reading chapter 2, and for qualitative data you can read chapter 3. For further reading on this debate see Anney (2014); Flick, Kardorff and Steinke (2004); van de Port (2017).

Paradigms and research questions

The paradigm a researcher or practitioner adopts also shapes the way they ask questions. From the description above it might be clear that positivists and post-positivists usually ask questions that allow them to test a hypothesis. That means that they often formulate research questions that aim to generate an objective and often statistical outcome. Common formulations of such research question start with 'To what extent...?' or 'What share of ... leads to ...?' or 'What is the impact of ... on ...?' Chapters 2, 4, 9, 11, and 12 of this volume provide examples of methodologies using these kinds of research questions.

Researchers using a critical or constructivist paradigm are more prone to ask questions that generate an analysis of the reasons behind a certain process or phenomena, formulated as a 'why' question. They may also try to understand the unfolding of or the dynamics within a process using 'how' questions. Or, when they seek to understand things that are rather uncommon or unknown, they might use descriptive questions that are often formulated as 'what' questions. Chapters 3, 5, 6, 7, and 8 describe research projects that used these kinds of questions.

Finally, there are research questions that are oriented to making an intervention and creating change. These applied questions often include a certain normativity of what could or should be improved and the projects are focused on researching how these interventions can take place, and to what effect. Chapters 4, 13, and 14 in this volume illustrate such change-oriented research projects.

Seeing Amsterdam

The city of Amsterdam is the case study that runs through this volume to illustrate the way researchers execute their methods, make choices, and develop insights. The choice of Amsterdam has practical as well as more principled reasons. First of all, the Center of Urban Studies (CUS) at the University of Amsterdam brings together a broad group of interdisciplinary scholars using a wide variety of methodologies to study the city. We wanted to tap into this existing network and make use of the knowledge and practices that these scholars have to offer to the field of urban studies. Second, we set out to establish more cooperation between CUS and an even larger group of scholars and professionals from related universities, research institutes, and the municipality of Amsterdam. Our search led to a transdisciplinary collection of authors who are at the forefront of urban research, theory and practice. The authors are all situated in Amsterdam for either work, life, research, or a combination of these things, and know the city by heart. By seeking local contributors, we were able to facilitate a process of workshops in which authors developed a transdisciplinary community of urban research.

We believe that seeing and understanding the city can never take place through only one perspective. The main purpose of the volume is to provide hands-on practices to view the city and its real-world problems from various points of view. The book offers 15 unique ways of seeing and understanding the city and each chapter offers another perspective on the city of Amsterdam. That way, the added value of seeing one city through a multitude of perspectives becomes visible and tangible in the case of Amsterdam.

We hope that these reflections on Amsterdam inspire both urban scholars and practitioners to apply these methodologies to their own urban context.

Seeing this volume

The four main questions that structure this volume – 'What do I see?', 'How can I understand?', 'What do I miss?', and 'Why does it matter?' – also provide an approach to setting up a problem-based urban research project. Section one includes chapters on quantitative data gathering (via **census**, **survey**, or **big data**), **ethnography**, **sensory data**, **interviewing**, and **archival research**. Section two provides chapters on **cultural analysis**, **institutional analysis**, **economic analysis**, **historical simulation**, spatial analysis using **Geographic Information Science and Systems**), analysis of **urban biodiversity**, **action research**, and **research through design**. All these chapters explain the goals, techniques, choices, and limitations for gathering data or analyzing those data. Each chapter in the volume provides two types of text; the main text explains the respective methodology in general terms and the textboxes discuss how the researcher has applied these methods to the case study of Amsterdam.

While developing this volume we became aware of the multiple audiences this book might have. We did our very best to cater to these different audiences and devise a volume that could function as a work of reference for readers with different needs. Therefore, we offer our various readers a guide for how to use this book.

If you are an urban scholar or professional looking for methodological avenues to study the city, we invite you to carefully think through what it is you see, consider how you approach what you see through paradigms, and start imagining a research question about what you see. Sequentially, you can read all relevant methodological chapters and the textboxes to learn how the various methods are applied, how choices were made, and what results came out of these studies.

If you are a professional from the municipality of Amsterdam, another local organization, or a citizen and you are mostly interested in the outcomes of various research projects that took place in Amsterdam, you could decide to focus your reading on the textboxes that illustrate each methodology and provide an array of findings, ranging from studies of gentrification (chapters 2 and 6), to the question of **ownership** (chapters 3, 5, 7, 8, 11, and 12), and the analyses of **spatial flows** and designs (chapters 4, 11, 13, 14, and 16).

If you are a scholar of interdisciplinary studies and your key interest is to understand the process of developing such an interdisciplinary book, we propose you start reading chapter 15, in which myriad possible forms of integration between methodologies are discussed. This discussion reveals the possibilities and difficulties of interdisciplinary processes but also offers hands-on practices to successfully mediate such process. Based on your interest, you can work your way back to the various methodological chapters in the volume. And finally, you could read our own reflections on establishing this volume and the missing methods in the conclusion.

If you are an urban professional or citizen and you would like to better understand how the city, the municipality, and other organizations can work together in a transdisciplinary team, we propose that you start by reading chapter 16, which discusses the potential and difficulties of such an endeavor. After that, you might be interested in reading chapters 13 and 14, which also provide engaging examples and practical strategies for transdisciplinary research.

For all other readers who do not fit in one of these categories, we hope that this introduction has provided you with some ways to navigate our volume. We wish you much inspiration and welcome you in the ongoing dialogue about the complex but endlessly engaging environment that we call the city.

References

Anney, V. N. V. (2014). Ensuring the quality of the findings of qualitative research: Looking at Trustworthiness Criteria. *Journal of Emerging Trends in Educational Research and Policy Studies (JETERAPS), 5*(2), 272-281.

Flick, U., Kardorff, E. von., & Steinke, I. (2004). *A companion to qualitative research.* London: Sage.

Guba, E. G., & Lincoln, Y. S. (1994). Competing paradigms in Qualitative Research. In N. K. Denzin & Y. S. Lincoln (eds.), *Handbook of Qualitative Research.* London: Sage, pp. 105-117.

Leininger, M. (1994). Evaluation criteria and critique of qualitative research studies. In J. M. Morse (Ed.), *Critical issues in qualitative research methods.* London: Sage, pp. 95-116.

van de Port, M. (2017). The verification of ethnographic data: A response. *Ethnography, 18*(3), 295-299.

2 Quantitative data collection: A meta view

Willem Boterman

Introduction

Quantitative research is first and foremost concerned with the measuring, indeed, the quantification of the object of study. However, quantifying observed phenomena of our social world, such as segregation, is not merely a particular way of measuring that differs from (and complements) other ways of measuring, which are placed in the 'qualitative' domain that will be discussed in chapters 3 and 5. As discussed in the introduction to this volume, quantitative methods are associated with specific epistemologies that do not just refer to data collection and analysis, but also – and perhaps even more so – to the types of questions asked and the interpretation of research findings. Quantitative methods are generally, though not exclusively, associated with positivist epistemologies, in which theories about the social world are tested rather than inferred. Quantitative methods are generally applied in research that aims to know the world *as it is*. Measuring the world will reveal bits and pieces of its reality. However, apart from the sheer difference between the types of data through which meaning is expressed in numerical terms versus qualitative data, whose meaning lies in representations and construction of reality, quantitative methods are part of a broader cluster of research strategies, epistemologies, and ontologies. Notwithstanding this often iterated dichotomy, quantitative methods are also used by researchers that do not adhere to orthodox positivist and objectivist academic approaches. Quantitative methods can also be used to infer theory, to be critical of the possibility of knowing the 'real world', and to work from other epistemologies than positivism. Quantitative data and methods are indispensable for urban research as they are better equipped to address questions related to the **aggregated** level (e.g. region, city, (sub)population) than qualitative data and methods. To make sense of an urban and urbanizing world we need to be able to generalize for, but also beyond specific urban contexts. To address the question 'What is the urban?' (Castells, 1977) quantitative data and methods are a crucial element of our research.

This chapter will focus on different types of quantitative data and how they can be collected and used. I will start by sketching a brief history of quantitative data collection, then discuss the main forms in which quantitative data appear: census data, survey data, administrative data and so-called 'big data'. I will discuss its uses and limitations and then briefly look into the future of quantitative data.

Origins of quantitative data collection and uses: the census

The history of measuring social phenomena is intrinsically linked to state formation. For any political body, whether headed by a chieftain, monarch, or aristocracy, the questions 'How much, how many?' were indispensable to ruling. How many subjects, how much tax? How many soldiers, how far is the enemy? Quantifying the economy and demography of a territory are crucial for governing. The State has therefore been always engaged in collecting data, but typically with distinct purposes. James Scott (2017) in his research about early state formation in Mesopotamia argues that the transition from hunting and gathering to agriculture was enforced by ruling parties to make it easier to measure resources and to control those resources. When the main food source was in the form of grain (wheat, barley) rather than simply collected when needed, this introduced the possibility of measuring the amount of grain and monitoring its harvest, and finally taxing these resources for a certain share of the total yield. Tax collectors were managing the economy and administering the demographics *through quantitative measurement*. The collection of quantitative data is literally as old as (the concept of) time. The idea of a **census** originally referred to the enumeration of the population, including men older than seventeen in ancient Rome, the *civium capita* (Lo Cascio, 1994). In later periods, however, the population was defined differently, including all free subjects, or *capita libera*, while still excluding enslaved people (Frank, 1930). The measuring of the population for military and taxation purposes was thus contingent on the definition of what constituted the population and the use of the data. The definition of the census was therefore not stable.

So what were the methods of conducting the census in the classical period? Obviously, enumerating the whole population by making them walk through one central gate (as was sometimes done in smaller political entities) was impossible in the vast Roman Empire. Instead, local officials were made responsible for collecting information by gathering people at different locations throughout the empire (legend has it that Joseph and Maria were on their way to a Roman census in Bethlehem). A significant element of the census thus consisted of actual observations and headcounts, as well as collecting additional information about estates through direct inquiry. Other methods, such as those reported for the Roman province of Egypt, included the writing down of 'a declaration to local authorities containing the names, ages, and other identifying information of all co-residents' (Claytor & Bagnall, 2015, p. 639). By relying on self-reporting, the ancient census therefore already contained elements of a **survey** of the population.

Collecting survey data

Surveys are a method for understanding a social phenomenon in a population by looking at a sample of the population. Surveys have a very prominent place in the recent history of social science and policy research. There is a vast literature on sampling and method books always reserve ample space for sampling methods and their problems (see e.g. Bryman, 2016; Altmann, 1974). As outlined above, sampling methods arose out of the desire to gauge and enumerate populations. To do this it is important to first establish the **population** about which the researcher wants to make (general) statements. The population is also the sum of all units from which the **sample** will be drawn. If the sample is complete and the whole population is enumerated, it is a census, but usually the sample is used to *stand for* the whole population; it is intended to be a **representative sample**. The general idea is that if a sample is randomly drawn from the population and there is no (or only a small) **sampling error**, it is more likely that the sample is also representative. To estimate the size of the sampling error, the difference between the sample and the population must be known.

For instance, in my PhD research on residential and school choice I did a survey among highly educated women in the inner-city of Amsterdam who were expecting their first child (Boterman, 2012a). To judge whether this sample was representative of this group, I needed information about the population I wanted to generalize about, concerning the share of highly educated women, populations of women of child-bearing age in the inner city, the number of first-born children, etc. This kind of data for the population was not completely available, which possibly meant my sample was not fully representative. Nonetheless, the fact that the sample contained approximately a third of the total population of highly educated women expecting a first child, and no significant bias in the sampling could be expected, it is likely that it is a representative sample.

To gauge the population, the State uses a special kind of survey: the census. The census is a very large survey based on a complete sample that, however, also increasingly relies on probabilistic statistics to correct biases due to over- and under-sampling. The modern census also aims to enumerate and gauge the entire population, relying on indirect methods, such as surveys, for collecting data. The first modern census, which was conducted in the US in 1790, was based on handwritten answers to a small number of questions initially gathered by US Marshals, who supplied paper and pens to their respondents (Census.gov, 2019[1]). In the UK, the first census was collected in 1801 by 33,000 literate enumerators, who presented the

---

[1] https://www.census.gov/history/

head of household with a schedule in which information about the household had to be filled out. The enumerator helped respondents to fill them out when necessary, thereby introducing mistakes, for instance due to difficulties in understanding local accents (Taylor, 1951). Although neither uncontested nor flawless, in most modern states the census emerged as a primary source of data, used for official statistics informing policy, which is conducted every five to ten years.

To explain procedures for increasing the validity of the census, the British census uses the analogy of estimating the number of fish in a pond (Benton, 2011). The analogy is used because it is not directly observable how many fish there are (the population is unknown). A system of catch, release, and re-catch is used to estimate the actual population. Modern census bureaus apply Dual System Estimation (DSE) to validate the reliability of the first enumeration round. A second round is a **survey**, which is used to correct biases against those who might have been missed in the first enumeration round. To do this, the census is stratified: the population is divided into groups that are expected to differ in terms of how many are missed and therefore not counted. These expectations are based on earlier experiences but also revealed through comparison with existing registers and additional surveys. Although the census reflects the ambition to obtain a complete sample of the whole population, it is important to realize that it is still a –highly probable– *estimation* of a population. This is even more true for data that is collected by the State for addressing specific policy questions. Often this type of data collection takes the shape of a survey based on a sample. From the late nineteenth and early twentieth centuries, the sample-based survey became one of the key forms of collecting quantitative data about a specific topic, both for policy purposes but also for (social) scientific purposes.

Surveys depend on at least some knowledge of the population prior to the survey research. In addition, other errors may further compromise the generalizability of the findings of the survey – for instance, when there is a discrepancy between the population and sampling frame, or incongruity between the sampling frame and the final sample due to a factor such as biased non-response (if one group of people responds more than another). Despite the difficulties associated with the sampling process, surveys are extremely valuable for collecting data for policy and scholarly questions. Data on the labour market, for example, what kind of job people do or whether they try to find a job, can only be obtained through surveys such as the Dutch EBB (enquete beroepsbevolking). When discussing surveys, many people might immediately think of questionnaires, which are structured lists of questions, often a mix of questions with pre-structured answers and (more) open answers. **Questionnaires**, whether sent out to a home address, taken at a specific sampling location, or web-based, are indeed a key method for collecting survey data. Other forms of data collection are also considered surveys. **Structured interviews** (chapter 5), structured observations (chapter 3) and – when the aim is to collect quantitative data – even archival or document research (chapter 6) can be viewed as methods to collect survey data (Bryman, 2016).

Using survey data

The forms in which survey data are used can be roughly divided into categories, which are a) primary or secondary data; and b) processed or raw data. The first and most processed (and least useful) form in which survey data are available and appear is as secondary sources, often issued as statistics by official institutions, but also by media and businesses. These kinds of data can be found in public repositories such as CBS.nl; CPB.nl or Kadaster.nl. Private businesses, such as marketing companies and banks, also publish reports in which they show tables and graphs – for example, relating to the housing market (Rabobank; CBRE; Vereniging voor ontwikkelaars en bouwondernemers) – which are often based on survey data. Likewise, many reports from different government agencies present statistics based on large probability samples that are typically intended to be representative of a particular population (national, urban, young people, refugees, etc.).

Many scholars, including myself, rely on secondary data. Even if you do your own survey or other kinds of data collection, secondary data from reliable sources such as national statistical offices are often indispensable. For instance, if you do research on mechanisms of school choice in gentrified neighborhoods, you need to first define where gentrification can be found based on existing data. Even if they are not the key form of data you use for your analysis, secondary data are still needed for case selection, and also for contextualizing your findings. In my research, I made typologies of neighborhood change based on secondary survey data, which then served as input for my qualitative and quantitative data collection.

Most of the survey data that are used by researchers are (partly) processed secondary data sources. National statistical offices, government agencies, and local municipal department are important sources of this type of data. The major advantages with using the data is that they are high quality as they have been systematically collected and generally use large and representative samples. Typically the surveys have also been verified through different robustness checks and are easily accessible by the public. Disadvantages are that often only the polished and processed form of the data is available and decisions concerning, for instance, the cleaning of the dataset and corrections for under- and over-sampling are obscured. The same applies to a second category of survey data, which are the 'raw' and unprocessed data of surveys that underlie the published statistics. They are more flexible in their use because it is possible to do your own analyses with them, but they are still secondary data, which means that many of the definitions are pre-structured. For instance, many data on migrant backgrounds are based on official definitions as decided by the Statistical Office, which were used as categories in a questionnaire. It is therefore often impossible to use your own definitions, that fit your research question. Although somewhat more transparent than processed data, for raw secondary data it can also be hard to assess the validity of the data. For instance, knowing the methods that were used in collecting the data and different potential errors (face validity; sampling bias; processing issues) are difficult to gauge.

A third category of data are primary data, which means data collected by the researcher who is using the data. This category is most extensively discussed in social science textbooks, but as it is very laborious (and expensive) to collect large samples of primary data, most researchers work instead with secondary data. The advantages of self-collecting survey data are, however, obvious. By constrast with secondary data, primary data collection allows the researcher to much more precisely define their concepts and how they are measured.

For instance, a concept widely used in urban research, such as '**gentrification**', could be measured using solely secondary data about average income or educational level, or real estate values within specific **spatial units**, such as neighborhoods (see for instance Boterman, Karsten & Musterd, 2010 and Teernstra & Van Gent, 2012). Using this data guarantees that the methods for collecting data about real estate value and income are systematic across neighborhoods, endowing greater validity to the findings. However, to define a concept as richly theorized as gentrification requires an **operationalization** that goes beyond pre-defined definitions of social status and also measures other aspects such as cultural capital in the neighborhood. A self-constructed questionnaire or other survey methods, such as structured face-to-face **interviews**, could include questions about, for instance, cultural preferences, consumption, or knowledge, which are measurements of the concept that do not exist in secondary data sources (see for instance Boterman, 2012b). In general, primary data are much better for aligning theory, concept, and measurement, but the degree to which findings can be generalized for the population of which a sample is taken is generally lower, too. This may have to do with the smaller sample size, although this is mainly due to the costs of collecting a large sample of primary data. Depending on the resources of the researcher, making sure the sample is randomized and accounts for the diversity of the sampled population is generally more of an issue for primary data. Furthermore, it is also difficult to assess sampling bias since often the population is unknown. Whether or not primary data gathering is warranted therefore depends on the type of research question and the size and type of population one seeks to make statements about. Of course, the availability of secondary data and how well existing data could be used to measure the concepts as intended are also important for assessing which kinds of data should be used (Swanborn, 1994).

Administrative data

The census is in many countries still held on a regular basis, most often decennially, but is gradually being replaced by other sources of data. Although the census was the foundation of the most important sources of official statistics, many countries are now seeing the rise of much richer forms of quantitative data: administrative or register data, produced and collected, managed and processed by different levels of government.

In the course of the nineteenth and twentieth centuries, in parallel with the expansion of State bureaucracy (Weber, 1978) the types of administrative data collected by the State increased rapidly (Anderson, 2010). For instance, not only were data on household size and income collected, but also vast amounts of economic data, public health data, labor market data, and data on education.

In the study on gentrification and school choice I draw on various kinds of administrative data from different registers, such as neighborhood data about housing values and population from the municipal registers, as well as school registers from the Ministry of Education. The interlinking of different registers makes it possible to couple neighborhood data with school data, allowing me determine where children from different backgrounds go to school and how this differs between neighborhoods (Boterman, 2019). The different registers in the Dutch System of Social Databases are a great data source, which enables unique coupling of data at the individual level. Unfortunately, access is still highly restricted and usually only possible when embedded within institutional research institutes. For students, access to this type of data is generally only possible through collaborations with embedded researchers or through internships at CBS or OIS Amsterdam.

Most administrative data is collected with a purpose related to the activities of government, while some data is generated or collected without a direct objective related to State affairs but is nonetheless administered and stored. In the Global North, but also in China, Korea, and other emerging economies, the amount of data stored in a vast number of registers is astonishing. Most administrative data is either economic data or demographic data. Economic data might include amounts and prices of traded commodities and services; individual income, company profit, collective and individual debt; and government revenue and expenses. Demographic register data concern data from public civic and church registers of place of birth/ residence; birth/death; marriage/divorce; immigration/emigration; nationality/ naturalization, etc. Additionally, other domains in which the State has a key controlling and administrative role, such as the judiciary, health care, education, and social services, also keep records for the purpose of tracking and monitoring but also because of accountability.

Administrative data is almost always collected and managed and made available in the interest of its administrative purpose. Administrative data are always 'contaminated' and compromised by the power structures under which they were collected, managed, and ultimately shared. This clearly applies for private businesses but also for the State. The literature on governmentality argues that statistical politics of the State shapes its subjects through the administration of data, and the concomitant creation and reproduction of social facts (Murdoch & Ward, 1997; Uitermark, Hochstenbach & Van Gent, 2017; De Wilde & Franssen, 2016). The question of which data are collected and categorized does not simply register reality, it also creates it. In fact, looking at which categories of data are defined and collected can tell us a lot about the power relations at that time and place. Studies in the Dutch context, for instance, reveal how the administrative term 'allochtoon' became part of everyday discourse and became mobilized in processes of boundary making (Uitermark, 2005; Bonjour & Duyvendak, 2018).

Using administrative data

Administrative data is thus often collected with a policy or business related purpose, but only seldom with the objective of answering an academic research question. Quantitative researchers have to recognize the fact that categories and definitions have been pre-structured, delineated by their (political) purpose and by logics of classification that developed historically. While this is not necessarily or always a problem for research, it is something that requires critical reflection from researchers when they use the data collected for another purpose besides doing research. To work with administrative data requires reflexive scholarship that deconstructs the categories *imposed* onto the data and takes the wider social and political context into account. This could be achieved by actively using other categories – for instance, ethnic background – that are either self-reported or allow for greater diversity by not using generic categories (such as 'non-western').

In particular, Nordic European countries and the Netherlands have facilitated access to register data for researchers, although privacy requirements and high costs highly restrict access, making them less suitable for students. Within the social sciences register data are used for addressing questions that were difficult to address prior to its availability. Register data have major advantages over census data, on the one hand, and sample-based surveys, on the other: First, administrative data are not based on a probabilistic sample but on registers containing data of entire populations, which means that it is possible not just to infer but to actually describe the statistics of populations. Second, administrative data in one register can often be coupled with other registers, which allow for much more refined multivariate analyses (see chapters 9, 11). Third, administrative register data are often **longitudinal** instead of **cross-sectional**, which makes it possible, for instance, to analyze trajectories and study the effect of life course events. Fourth, contrary to other secondary data, with register data it is possible to define how certain concepts are operationalized. While many data are still pre-structured in registers, too, they generally allow for a greater degree of tailoring of one's categories. For instance, income categories such as 'low income' are typically pre-defined when a researcher uses official statistics, but register data allow a researcher to set their own boundaries, which are in line with their research questions.

So what kinds of registers exist? Wallgren & Wallgren (2011; 2014) identify four types:

1   population registers (persons and households);
2   activity registers (jobs and studies);
3   registers of businesses/organizations;
4   real estate registers.

Dutch register data are also organized by object (person, household, activity, organization, and buildings) (Bakker, Van Roiijen & Van Toor, 2014). Of special interest for urban scholars and practitioners are, of course, the registers that also contain geocoded information. Registers on properties (homes, businesses, schools), especially if they are coupled with population registers, are very useful for addressing questions in urban social sciences.

The spatial quantitative data that are most relevant for urban social research are typically related to spatial units as larger containers of individual units (persons, businesses, schools, etc.). Often these data exist as secondary data, containing averages (and sometimes distributions), such as the mean or median housing price in an area, and proportions of particular groups, such as the share of low-income households in the neighborhood. Inherently, scale becomes an issue here. For much urban research it is important to have 'spatial container data' at the lowest possible level. This allows for aggregation at a higher level if desired. Often, however, spatial data is supplied only at higher levels, which may make spatial analyses coarser than we might like. Again the distinction between raw and processed data applies here: if the researcher has access to the raw data, the level of aggregation is typically lower, albeit still dependent on the level of measurement. This allows for tailor-made grouping of a lower level variable with a higher level, such as the numbers of high income families within a census tract within a multifamily building or within a postal code area. In particular, the combination of having geo-information (as in chapter 11) and other information from registers at the individual level enables the construction of new spatial data that is generally not provided in processed secondary data sources. For instance, while the share of low-income individuals, or highly educated individuals, or social renters in the neighborhood of a city may be provided by the Statistical Office, the combination of low-income highly educated individuals in different tenure positions in a neighborhood is never provided. Geocoded individual level register data enable urban scholars to answer new questions that were previously difficult or almost impossible to address, certainly with a greater scope. It is also indispensable for GIS analyses, which are hugely advanced by individual spatial data.

For instance (school) segregation has been explored using data from surveys or census. The pre-definition of the categories used to calculate segregation levels and map patterns, however, often only allowed for the analysis of specific pre-defined groups. In my research I have used register data to create other more nuanced categories at the intersections of different dimensions such as combinations of income, level of education and occupation (see Boterman et al., 2017). Furthermore, register data are also geocoded, which I have used to calculate segregation in schools and neighborhoods putting children into their nearest school (Boterman, 2019). Comparing the real and hypothetical situation was only possible through the use of register data. Finally, the longitudinal structure of register data also enables the study of people in time. In my school segregation study it is therefore possible to see how residential mobility and school choice are interlinked.

Big data

A fourth category of data that are increasingly discussed and used are what is referred to as **Big Data**. Big data is a relatively new term which, despite the fact it does not have a clear definition, seems ubiquitous and unavoidable in public and academic debate. In the emerging literature describing the rise of big data (McAfee et al., 2012; Ward & Barker, 2013) it is characterized by four V's, starting with its *volume* and its lack of structure (*volatility*). The vast amounts of data require a different type of management and, moreover, analysis. In addition, big data is also fast data, the *velocity* of its genesis and its analysis separating it from traditional large-n datasets. In some definitions of big data, the uncertainty or unreliability (*veracity*) of the analysis is also mentioned (Ward & Barker, 2013). Big data are sometimes deliberately created but are also created as byproducts of the use of, among other things, email, electronic money transfer and payment, online clicks and views, mobile phone data, but also several forms of sensing, such as camera footage and monitors of pollution, light, smell, etc. (Törnberg & Törnberg, 2018) (see chapter 4 in this volume). Sources of big data can be categorized into three types: directed (targeting specific places or people), automated (generated thorugh the use of devices) and volunteered (gifted by users with active consent) (Kitchin, 2013). The boundaries, however, are not clear. Social media data, for instance, which are partly voluntarily provided by users, also 'automatically' generate data, which are deliberately created for commercial purposes and even may become used to actively surveil people, and thereby also become 'directed'. Most of the automated data generated by the automatic function of the system, the device, or the application, can also be used to track people, whether voluntarily offered or not. For instance, fitness apps are voluntarily installed onto a smartphone but this generates different kinds of data, both automated and user-input data.

Another key aspect of big data is that it is often, but not exclusively, generated by and for commercial enterprises. The most discussed applications and usages are therefore related to the knowledge businesses need to have to respond to and influence their customers. According to Davenport and colleagues (Davenport, Barth & Bean, 2012), big data should be seen as a continuous stream of newly generated data, which also originate from interaction with its analysts. This is referred to as streaming analytics, and it 'allows you to process data during an event to improve the outcome' (Davenport et al., 2012, p. 23). Here, big data differs from other large data sets, which is also one of the reasons why academics should be cautious about using big data. The lack of structure and the sheer volume encourage people to go **mining the data**, that is, look for patterns in the vast piles of data that are available. While one could see this as a form of **inductive** research, it usually occurs without any clear theoretical focus. Some have even called big data the end of theory, as the sheer volume 'let[s] the data speak for themselves' (Anderson, 2008). In a way, big data analysis is inductive research without grounding, which makes it vulnerable to various criticisms. For example, significant effects are easily found in big datasets, a problem that is referred to as **false positives**. Also, more fundamentally, if one looks for patterns one will always find them (Lin et. al., 2013; Becker, 2017). Big data's lack of structure is therefore a big challenge for scholars working with it. Nonetheless, there are clear examples of big data that are hugely beneficial for urban scholars, especially data that are geocoded allow for addressing new questions that were previously very difficult to answer.

Using big data

Big spatial data is very relevant for urban research because it enables the mapping of the time–space behavior of individuals (as discussed in chapter 4). As time–space behavior is generally not kept in any register, its study used to rely on either self-reported time–space diaries or small-scale observations. Big spatial data may be generated through mobile phone networks or other sensing data (see chapter 4 in this volume). Additionally, all online data are spatially and temporally referenced (via IP address or otherwise). Large social network sites such as Twitter, Facebook, and Instagram may reveal some of this geocoded information, which then may be cropped through software that downloads the data from the internet. Several studies in urban research have used this source of information to combine social and spatial dimensions in their analysis (see for instance Boy & Uitermark, 2017). Platform companies, such as Airbnb and Uber, also generate and collect vast amounts of spatial data. Although access to this kind of data is limited, as much of its collection and ownership lie with the private enterprises, researchers are sometimes able to acquire data directly or indirectly from these platforms, enabling new lines of research. Big data may therefore become part of the set of sources social scientists can draw on to address urban questions.

For example, the study of (school) **segregation** could benefit from new types of data. The character of big data, beyond classical variable-based analysis, might allow for a dynamical approach to segregation akin to studies in the natural sciences (Törnberg & Törnberg, 2018). While precise definitions and operationalizations of background variables are clearly more difficult with this type of data, the almost real-time generation of data and the continuous flow in which they may be processed enable, for instance, a dynamic and relational analysis of school segregation in which the process itself is studied, rather than the outcomes. The tracking of people in time and space also makes it possible to expand studies of segregation based on activity spaces rather than static places of residence, school, or work. There is already an emerging literature that draws on mobile phone data for segregation (Silm & Ahas, 2014; Kwan, 2016), but there is still great potential for utilizing the networked character of much of the data that comes from the rapid digitalization of social data.

Conclusion

This chapter has provided a brief and introductory overview of different types of quantitative data and how they are collected or generated. Further, I have tried to point to some of the weaknesses and caveats with not only the collection but also the epistemologies of quantitative data collection and analysis. Nonetheless, for urban research gauging the size of subpopulations and how they develop is indispensable knowledge. The census and other smaller surveys will, certainly in combination with the increasing use of administrative register data, continue to play a central part in urban research. The enumeration of populations remains a central task and precondition for the functioning of the State. However, the rise of big data will transform the nature of doing quantitative research to address relevant questions – not only because big data allows us to address *new* questions but, moreover, because it challenges the epistemologies and the legitimacy of social sciences research as we know it (Törnberg & Törnberg, 2018). Paradoxically, this challenge does not lie in the inevitability of rendering traditional quantitative data sources obsolete. Rather, big data and its promise may reduce the salience and the legitimacy of traditional data. The politics of big data may therefore prove to be a greater challenge for traditional quantitative data than the quality of big data itself. This is further complicated by the fact that many big data are not public data. The critique this chapter has sought to advance about the interests that are inherently connected to the generation and interpretation of data in relation to the State is even more relevant to data generated by commercial enterprises.

Table 1:   *Summary of types of quantitative data*

Type	Scope	Sources	Order	Operationalization	Questions
Census data	Whole population; cross-sectional	Questionnaires, structured interviews	Secondary data	Based on pre-defined definitions	Exploratory/ Descriptive
Survey data	Sample; cross-sectional or longitudinal	Questionnaires, structured interviews, structured observations	Primary/ Secondary data	Theory-driven definitions/ Based on pre-defined definitions	Exploratory Descriptive/ Explanatory
Administrative data	Whole population; cross-sectional or longitudinal	(Public) registers	Secondary data	Pre-defined definitions, with more space for tailor-fitting	Descriptive/ Explanatory
Big data	Population not clearly defined; Real-time/ longitudinal	Directed systematic monitoring Automated sensoring Volunteered tracking	Secondary data	Lack of definitions	Exploratory/ Descriptive/ Explanatory

References

Altmann, J. (1974). Observational study of behavior: sampling methods. *Behaviour, 49*(3-4), 227–266.

Anderson, C. (2008). The end of theory: The data deluge makes the scientific method obsolete. *Wired magazine, 16*(7), 16–17.

Anderson, M. (2010). The Census and the Federal Statistical System: Historical Perspectives. *The ANNALS of the American Academy of Political and Social Science, 631*(1), 152–162. https://doi.org/10.1177/0002716210373721

Bakker, B. F., Van Rooijen, J., & Van Toor, L. (2014). The system of social statistical datasets of Statistics Netherlands: An integral approach to the production of register-based social statistics. *Statistical Journal of the IAOS, 30*(4), 411–424.

Becker, H.S. (2017) *Evidence*, Chicago, University of Chicago Press.

Benton, P (2011) Trout, Catfish & Roach. the beginners guide to census population estimates, Census UK, https://www.ons.gov.uk/ons/guide-method/census/2011/the-2011-census/census-coverage-survey/trout-catfish-and-roach-the-beginner-s-guide-to-census-population-estimates.pdf

Bonjour, S., & Duyvendak, J. W. (2018). The 'migrant with poor prospects': racialized intersections of class and culture in Dutch civic integration debates. *Ethnic and Racial Studies, 41*(5), 882–900.

Boterman, W. R., Karsten, L., & Musterd, S. (2010). Gentrifiers settling down? Patterns and trends of residential location of middle-class families in Amsterdam. *Housing Studies, 25*(5), 693–714.

Boterman, W. R. (2012a). *Residential practices of middle classes in the field of parenthood*. Amsterdam: Universiteit van Amsterdam

Boterman, W. R. (2012b). Residential mobility of urban middle classes in the field of parenthood. *Environment and Planning A, 44*(10), 2397-2412.

Boterman, W. R., Manting, D & Musterd, S. (2018). Understanding the social geographies of urban regions through the socio-economic and cultural dimension of class. *Population, Space and Place, 24*(5), e2130.

Boterman, W. R. (2019). The role of geography in school segregation in the free parental choice context of Dutch cities. *Urban Studies, 56*(15), 3074-3094.

Boterman, W. R., & Van Gent, W. P. C. (2014). Housing liberalisation and gentrification: The social effects of tenure conversions in Amsterdam. *Tijdschrift voor economische en sociale geografie, 105*(2), 140-160.

Boy, J. D., & Uitermark, J. (2017). Reassembling the city through Instagram. *Transactions of the Institute of British Geographers, 42*(4), 612-624.

Bryman, A. (2016). *Social research methods*. Oxford: Oxford University Press.

Castells, M. (1977). *The urban question: A Marxist approach* (No. 1). London: Hodder Education.

Claytor, W. G., & Bagnall, R. S. (2015). The beginnings of the roman provincial census:: a new declaration from 3 BCE. Greek, *Roman and Byzantine Studies, 55*, 637-665

Davenport, T. H., Barth, P., & Bean, R. (2012). How'big data'is different. MIT Sloan Management Review, 54(1), 21-24.

De Wilde, M., & Franssen, T. (2016). The material practices of quantification: Measuring 'deprivation'in the Amsterdam Neighbourhood Policy. *Critical Social Policy, 36*(4), 489-510.

Frank, T. (1930). Roman census statistics from 508 to 225 BC. *The American Journal of Philology, 51*(4), 313-324.

Kitchin, R. (2013). Big data and human geography: Opportunities, challenges and risks. *Dialogues in human geography, 3*(3), 262-267.

Kwan, M. P. (2016). Algorithmic geographies: Big data, algorithmic uncertainty, and the production of geographic knowledge. *Annals of the American Association of Geographers, 106*(2), 274-282.

Lin, M., Lucas Jr, H. C., & Shmueli, G. (2013). Research commentary-Too big to fail: Large samples and the p-value problem. *Information Systems Research, 24*(4), 906-917.

Lo Cascio, E. (1994). The size of the Roman population: Beloch and the meaning of the Augustan census figures. *The Journal of Roman Studies, 84*, 23-40.

McAfee, A., Brynjolfsson, E., Davenport, T. H., Patil, D. J., & Barton, D. (2012). Big data: the management revolution. *Harvard Business Review, 90*(10), 60-68.

Murdoch, J., & Ward, N. (1997). Governmentality and territoriality: The statistical manufacture of Britain's 'national farm'. *Political Geography, 16*(4), 307-324

Scott, J. C. (2017). *Against the grain: a deep history of the earliest states*. New Haven, CT: Yale University Press.

Silm, S., & Ahas, R. (2014). Ethnic differences in activity spaces: A study of out-of-home nonemployment activities with mobile phone data. *Annals of the Association of American Geographers, 104*(3), 542–559.

Taylor, A. J. (1951). Taking of the Census, 1801-1951. *British medical journal, 1*(4709), 715-720.

Teernstra, A. B., & Van Gent, W. P. (2012). Puzzling patterns in neighborhood change: Upgrading and downgrading in highly regulated urban housing markets. *Urban Geography, 33*(1), 91–119

Törnberg, P., & Törnberg, A. (2018). The limits of computation: A philosophical critique of contemporary Big Data research. *Big Data & Society, 5*(2), 2053951718811843.

Uitermark, J (2005). 'The Genesis and Evolution of Urban Policy: A Confrontation of Regulationist and Governmentality Approaches', Political Geography 23(2): 137-163.

Uitermark, J., Hochstenbach, C., & van Gent, W. (2017). The statistical politics of exceptional territories. *Political Geography, 57*, 60–70.

van Ham, M., & Tammaru, T. (2016). New perspectives on ethnic segregation over time and space. A domains approach. *Urban Geography, 37*(7), 953-962.

Wallgren, A., & Wallgren, B. (2011). To understand the possibilities of administrative data you must change your statistical paradigm. *Joint Statistical Meetings. Section on Survey Research Methods*, pp. 357–365.

Wallgren, A., & Wallgren, B. (2014). *Register-based statistics: Statistical methods for administrative data*. Hoboken, NJ: John Wiley & Sons.

Ward, J. S., & Barker, A. (2013). Undefined by data: a survey of big data definitions. *arXiv preprint arXiv:1309.5821*.

Weber, M. (1978). *Economy and society: An outline of interpretive sociology* (Vol. 1). Berkeley, CA: University of California Press.

3 Urban ethnography and participant observations: Studying the city from within

Nanke Verloo

Why studying the city from within?

Urban ethnography allows us to understand the city from within by engaging in the multiple perspectives and experiences of the people inhabiting, planning, building, policing, organizing, contesting, or using it. It is especially equipped to study the impact of large socio-political and economic developments like **segregation**, **gentrification**, migration, **urbanization**, ghettoization, and democratization on the real-life experience of diverse people.

Ethnography draws insights through the use of participant observations over a long period of time and repeated engagement with the field. The method has its roots in anthropology and sociology, where scholars from the Chicago School of Sociology adapted the method to study specific urban phenomena like urbanization, industrialization, and immigration (Parks, Burgess & McKenzie, 1925; Wirth, 1938).[1] They approached the city as a 'laboratory' in which people, places, and institutions could be studied through observation. The premise was that 'learning' takes place via the observation of action in its local context. They combined observations with life histories, statistical information, and maps, and were some of the first to develop mixed-methods case studies. Seeing the city as a laboratory thus urges students and scholars to leave the library and bring their bodies out into the city.

Ethnographic findings can shake up ideas we might take for granted about the way the city is lived and used, who belongs and who doesn't, and stereotypical images of neighborhoods and their inhabitants (Jaffe & Koning, 2016). It is especially equipped for projects seeking to understand cultural expressions, urban life, and subgroups. It may also have a strong spatial focus when it is used to study the routines, **aesthetics**,

---

[1] For further reading on the ongoing relevance of CSS see the volume *Standing on the Shoulders of Giants: The enduring relevance of the Chicago School of Sociology* (Jones & Rodgers, n.d.)

use, or design of urban space and place. Urban ethnography is also used to study policy processes and the ways in which the city is governed, planned, and designed (Schatz, 2013; van Hulst, 2008). By scrutinizing the practices of those responsible for governing the city and juxtaposing them with the perspectives and experiences of clients and citizens, urban ethnography provides welcome insights into the politics of welfare, police, policy, and planning *in action*.

An important goal of urban ethnography is to reveal hidden processes, for example forms of inclusion or exclusion that do not show up in statistical data or unexpected forms of agency by people who are usually described as passive. It offers a welcome 'eye-level' perspective of spaces in a world that is dominated by maps and plans drawn from a 'helicopter view'. Ethnographers look beyond policy documents and evaluations and approach policy making as a discursive practice that should be understood as enacted and embodied and that is highly contingent on its local context (Baiocchi & Connor, 2008; Wedeen, 2010; Ybema et al., 2009). All research that is concerned with the complex and multiple meanings of the city and that seeks to look beyond conventional understandings of socio-spatial, political, or cultural issues could benefit from an ethnographic approach.

Good ethnographies are usually developed through in-depth conversations with and guidance from supervisors or peers. But ethnographic fieldwork is something that researchers first and foremost have to *do*. The job of ethnographers is to go out in the streets, parks, bars, community homes, or institutions of the city and engage with everyday life. This requires researchers to trust their own sociological instincts and communicative skills. Researchers have to become skilled at listening and seeing what is relevant. They have to be able to construct a fieldwork plan but also stay open to unexpected events and opportunities.

This chapter describes a set of skills, strategies, and underlying knowledge that are necessary for any urban ethnography. While other chapters in this volume discuss **interviewing** (chapter 5), document analyses (see chapters 6 and 8), and **mapping** (see chapter 11) which are all key methodologies used in urban ethnography, here, I focus on one specific, distinctive methodology in ethnography: participant observation.

First, I will discuss the opportunities of ethnographic fieldwork, its limitations, and the underlying assumptions that ethnographers have to consider while developing the aims of a research project. In the next section, I lay out strategies to prepare for fieldwork. I focus on strategies for making qualitative fieldnotes during fieldwork. I follow with a discussion of the representation and interpretation of ethnographic data after fieldwork. Finally, I discuss issues of credibility and ethics that are especially relevant to arrive at convincing conclusions.

Introducing the case study[2]

In one of my own projects, I studied how citizens, tourists, local policymakers and politicians, police officers, and other street-level professionals negotiated **ownership** of public space in the Red Light District of Amsterdam. The period of research marks the aftermath of a policy called the 1012 project, which sought to upgrade the area, establish a more diverse range of functions, and diminish criminal activities. The policy was honed and criticized by various people and institutions, and many evaluations contradicted each other. My project started in 2014, in the period after the 1012 policy was implemented and when new challenges emerged. The area became more attractive to tourists, leading to increased crowding in the very limited public spaces. Between 2014 and 2020 the number of visitors to the city increased from 5 to 20 million, of whom the majority visited the Red Light District (Couzy, 2020). Functions that catered to local residents disappeared as rents quickly increased. A large number of residential buildings became vacations rentals with the increasing popularity of Airbnb. My research is not meant to evaluate the 1012 policy, but aims at analyzing how citizens, policymakers, and other public professionals negotiate ownership in the context of these changes. I used urban ethnography to study the multiplicity of perspectives and experiences of ownership as well as the efforts to (re)establish ownership through local interventions and policies.

'Thick description', limitations, and underlying assumptions

Studying the city from within requires a specific type of writing that is based on detailed fieldnotes and diary excerpts. Clifford Geertz called ethnographic writing '**thick description**' (Geertz, 1973: 27) referring to the detailed descriptions of what researchers see, hear, smell, and sense in order to describe situations, events, and behavior of people in such detail that the reader can be transported to the situation at hand.

Participant observation is an embodied practice that includes the experience of the researcher as an important source of information. The interactions between the researcher and the researched are fundamental as they shape the way ethnographers interpret what they observe (DeWalt & DeWalt, 2011: 11). A common critique of ethnographic research is that it is subjective, biased, and seemingly lacks the validation criteria of predominantly quantitative studies. As discussed in the introduction of this volume, the **ontological** and **epistemological** nature of ethnography is not more or less trustworthy than quantitative research, it simply has a different form of reasoning (usually **abductive** or **inductive**), and different purposes and underlying assumptions. Its epistemology rejects the notion of a fixed truth. It is based in the **constructivist** idea that researchers are always engaged in a dialogue with what they research and that social realities are actively constructed via social interactions. By entering the field, the researcher thus changes the field itself.

---

2   An early analysis of this case study was published in *Rooilijn* (Verloo, 2017).

As in any methodology, there are limitations to what can be done with ethnography. These are mostly related to the specific goals of an ethnographic approach. An ethnographic approach does not enable us to predict future developments; for example, it cannot predict voting behavior or housing prices. Nor is it intended to prove causal relations, such as the likelihood of youth to turn away from crime after a policy intervention. It does not usually provide data that is generalizable for a larger unit than the unit of analysis; insights about a specific culture, place, or group can usually not be generalized for all such places or groups. But where studies that prove a correlation often cannot explain why it exists, ethnography is all about the why.

Ethnographers study *why* people behave the way they do and *why* processes unfold in a certain way. Ethnographic data provide insights in the *process* of producing culture, identity, and space or place. To deal with the limitations and specific challenges of ethnography, researchers are transparent about the ways in which they are involved in the production of knowledge. A fieldwork plan and transparent techniques of note keeping, representation, interpretation, and reflection are necessary for conducting convincing ethnographies that shed new light on old issues.

Preparing for ethnographic fieldwork

The decisions fieldworkers make in designing their projects play a key role in the type and quality of the data they collect and analyze. In the following I list a set of considerations that help researchers to prepare their fieldwork.

Unit of analysis

As in any study, defining a **unit of analysis** is closely related to the research question and sub-questions. Ask yourself, 'what is part of my study and what is not?' A **unit of observation** within what is being studied provides an **empirical** focus for participant observations. It may be a particular subgroup, a space or place, an organization or policy/planning process or, often, a combination of these things. Ethnographers usually start with a unit of observation but expand this focus throughout the fieldwork based on experiences that draw attention and moments of serendipity that provide unexpected opportunities.

A spatial unit of analysis – a neighborhood, square, street, café, market – seemingly provides a clearly defined boundary. On the other hand, what citizens consider to be 'the neighborhood' usually does not overlap with administrative boundaries (Madden, 2014). Since urban ethnographies' main goal is to overcome stereotypical meanings, researchers must be flexible in their definitions and allow themselves to adjust their units of analysis based on empirical insights.

When studying a particular subgroup, ethnographers usually choose to do participant observations in social situations and/or interactions as 'temporally and spatially bounded series of events' (Garbett, 1970: 215). This means that researchers can prepare their fieldwork by rethinking what kinds of social situations or interactions they should observe and participate in, in order to answer their research question.

When studying an organization or (policy) process, the unit of analysis is often not a place or a group, but the socio-political relations among members of an institution, between public officials and citizens, or professionals and clients. This means that positions are explored within a complex set of interrelated processes. For this purpose, 'shadowing' someone is a particularly suitable data collection strategy because it allows the researcher to closely follow a subject over a period of time to investigate what they actually do in the course of their everyday practice, not what their role dictates (Pickering, 2010)[3].

Whether researchers decide to focus on a place, particular group, organization, or process, it is important to note that we can only understand them in relation to other spaces, people, and processes. Although these units of analysis seem bounded in space and time, their meaning should be understood in a wider context.

An important question is thus, how can we decide what the boundaries of our unit of analysis and unit observation are? Which events that are external to the situation have to be taken into account in order to understand the behavior of actors within them (Garbett, 1970: 217)? The answer to this question has to be given in relation to each particular field and specific research question.

> During my fieldwork, I did participant observations in the social situation of a local celebration. Citizens, civil servants, and politicians celebrated, presented, and discussed the outcomes of the annual 'Schouw'. The Schouw is a community activity that neighbors organize each month in order to collectively walk a route through the district and observe various forms of nuisance: dirt, graffiti, crime, cabs that are parked illegally, overcrowded streets. The municipality facilitates this annual gathering - a social situation that provided insights in the relationship between citizens and local politicians.

Understanding exactly what was going on during the event required me to relate the meeting to the broader context. My fieldnotes said, 'During the dinner I noticed some tension; some eyes were rolled, citizens gazed at each other and locked eyes while the borough mayor gave his speech.' I could only make sense of these interactions because I attended a series of meetings some weeks before in which the organizers of the Schouw complained that not enough was done with the outcomes of the Schouw in local policies. These prior meetings had set a tone that affected the relationship between citizens and local officials during the celebration dinner.

---

3   For further reading on the particular method of shadowing, see Gill, Barbour & Dean, 2014; Quinlan, 2008.

Fieldwork plan

In advance of fieldwork it is useful to make a fieldwork plan that includes a strategy for collecting relevant data from primary sources – fieldnotes, diary, interviews, etc. – and secondary sources – policy briefs, leaflets, flyers, etc. – that provide input for better understanding the unit of analysis.

Very few urban ethnographers nowadays are able to do what cultural anthropologists did by living with communities for years. Instead, many urban ethnographers combine what some have called 'appointment ethnography' and 'deep hanging out'. The latter is referred to as ethnographic fieldwork in which the researcher is aware of what she sees, smells, hears, and senses. Appointment ethnography is characterized by moving in and out of the lives of participants by the help of appointments (Lindegaard, 2017).

A fieldwork plan answers the following questions:

1   What is my unit of analysis and why?
2   In what kinds of places, groups, processes, or interactions should I do participant observations and why?
3   Whom should I interview, shadow, or observe and why?
4   What will I do and focus on during participant observations and why?
5   How often should I observe certain events, or at what times should I do participant observations at specific sites, and why?
6   Where will I start my fieldwork, and why?
7   How will I introduce myself to the people in the field?
8   How can I stay focused and open for unexpected changes, people, events, places?

Notice that I ask 'why' after almost all questions. The answer to this question is important because it connects a fieldwork plan to the **operationalization** of the research question. Questions 3 and 5 require the ethnographer to reflect on the representativeness of the data. Although ethnography does not claim to be generalizable of a larger group beyond the unit of analysis, it should try to be as representative of the object of study as possible. That means that if you study a site, participant observations take place repeatedly and at enough moments in time to be able to say something about that site at different times of the day, week, or even year. When studying a group, researchers have to think how to represent that group in its multiplicities without reifying or stereotyping its members. A process needs to include various moments in time and various activities or struggles. All of this requires ethnographers to strategically identify spaces, moments, events, or meetings that allow them to observe (inter)actions repeatedly.

Fieldwork plan

1 My units of analysis were the practices of citizens, civil servants, politicians, and other stakeholders, aiming to develop a sense of ownership in the Red Light District.

2 Because this was a longitudinal ethnography (i.e. unfolding in time), there were many events and interactions that could not be foreseen, so I made a typology of events that should be observed: meetings between citizens and local officials, community activities, everyday life in public space.

3 I did participant observations with a limited group of approximately 10 citizens, 5 public officials, and 3 politicians. I decided to reduce the number of people to enable myself to follow them in-depth throughout their activities and routines and interview them at different moments in time.

4 My focus during observations of public space was the behavior of people in relation to the public space and facilities, my focus in meetings was on the interaction between citizens and public officials; what they said, their body language, and the dramaturgy of the meeting itself. I participated in walking the Schouw with residents, and in community events organized by the municipality. I observed meetings between citizens and civil servants at the municipality, I shadowed a local police officer for one day. I was present in the neighborhood as much as possible, I walked the routes of tourists during daytime and nighttime, hung out with neighbors, tourists, and café owners, and took walks with various people through the neighborhood. I attended council meetings about the district, participated in public debates, did interviews, and always kept notes and archived secondary sources.

5 I observed meetings and activities that took place in autumn 2014 and spring 2015 and in spring and autumn 2019. In between these more intense fieldwork periods I attended the most important meetings and activities. I made observations of public space on various mornings, afternoons and evenings on various days of the week, and in various sites in the neighborhood throughout the whole period.

6 I started my fieldwork by contacting active citizens who were managing a community organization that seeks to influence local decision making and organized community activities. Because I was studying issues that generate tension, I decided to start out with key interlocutors in the field. Trust would have been more difficult to build if I had started with public officials because then citizens would have thought my research was a municipal assignment.

7 I introduced my research by stating that I was interested in the ways citizens and the municipality were dealing with the increasing crowdedness in the district and what kinds of activities citizens organized for the community.

8 I remained alert and prepared for unexpected changes by maintaining my network with local people involved and urging them to invite me when something important came up.

The personal nature of ethnographic fieldwork requires a high degree of transparency from researchers. In order achieve this, anthropologists have developed a particular technique of note taking that differentiates between fieldnotes, diary, and logbook (DeWalt & DeWalt, 2011; Emerson, Fretz & Shaw, 1995).

Fieldnotes

Fieldnotes are the main source of ethnographic data. They are the raw data that describe what ethnographers see, hear, smell, and taste in events, rituals, meetings, public spaces, or during policy practices. The main challenge of writing fieldnotes is to make them as descriptive as possible; try to not infer meaning, values, interpretation, or analyses from the fieldnotes. I often see my students describe people as 'poor' or 'typical Dutch', their behavior as 'friendly', places as 'busy' or 'full', and policy practices as 'dominant'. This is not very helpful because these terms are multi-interpretable and these descriptions do not reveal what is going on. Fieldnotes are more useful if they describe the details of how people dress, what they say, how they move, and what they do, and how people behave when they are being 'nice' or 'friendly'. Places are better described by specifying exactly what 'busy' looks like, how many people are present, or how many buildings, houses, benches, etc. there are. Counting specific elements or people in public spaces is an important aspect of making fieldnotes. Policy practices are best described in terms of how people act, what they say, and how others respond.

Interaction-rich ethnography rests on and incorporates microscopic, detailed accounts that feature local particulars and variations (Emerson, 2009: 536). This means that ethnographers have to become equipped in minutely describing sequences of events, actions, and spatial arrangements. Describing in such detail immediately begs the question, 'when do I have enough detail?' In the same way, the focus of participant observations should be understood in relation to the research question and the wider context, decisions of which details should be included in the descriptions should be made in relation to the research question and in reference to aspects of the wider context that are necessary to include in order to make sense of what is observed. A common strategy is to start out with general descriptive observations to get to know the field. Only when the field becomes more familiar can you decide to focus on a particular aspect that is then described in relation to other events and contexts. Finally, when the context is clear and you, the researcher, are familiar with local meanings and behavioral cues, you can identify detailed aspects to make selective microscopic observations of one person, interaction, meeting, or place, and record these in written, photographed, and recorded fieldnotes.

Diary

The second type of note keeping is the **diary**. Ethnographers differentiate between their diary and their fieldnotes so that the personal experiences and initial interpretations are not mixed up with actual observations. In their diary, ethnographers write down their first impression and personal experiences or senses (smell, feelings, tastes, etc.). It is important to not ignore emotions in the diary, because these experiences provide informative resources and points of reflection about the field.[4] In the diary researchers can also write down their initial interpretations that, although prematurely, relate the observations to theory.

Logbook

The last document that ethnographers keep is a **logbook**: this lists everything the researcher has done, where, when, and with whom. The logbook provides a basic overview of the whole research process. It also provides a place to reflect on the ongoing fieldwork and techniques, to write down successes and failures of the methodology as well as insights on unfolding relationships with people in the field. The logbook offers important input for any methodological chapter in a thesis or paragraph in an article. I will return to the importance of this in the final section of this chapter.

Logbook

What follows is an excerpt of a thick description of a quarterly meeting about the Schouw, office Municipality, November 2014.

Fieldnotes:

At the entrance we (three citizens and I) receive a visitor pass to enter the building. Once inside we go up the stairs to the room that was announced in the email. The room is light and sterile and we sit around a square table with 10 chairs. The three citizens and I on one side, two civil servants and the consultant who does the statistical analysis of the results of the Schouw on the other. One civil servant starts by stating that they are currently working on three topics: how to spread tourists, the physical structure of the neighborhood, and the use of public space. These topics, in his perspective, "go beyond the everyday nuisances of dirt, wrongly parked bikes, hotdog vendors, and crowdedness".

Diary:

By making the above statement the civil servant is positioning (Harré & Langehove, 1999) himself above the everyday experience of the citizens. He invites them to speak about issues in more abstract and general terms, but in doing so, he diminishes the everyday experience of the citizens and makes them seem of less importance. Since this is the very beginning of the meeting, it creates a tension between the topics that are observed in the Schouw (everyday forms of nuisance) and the interests of the civil servant. Furthermore,

---

4   An influential work that reveals the importance of diary notes is the classic literary non-fiction work by Claude Lévi-Strauss called 'Triste Tropique', in which he used his diary notes to reflect on his fieldwork expeditions in the interior of Brazil (Lévi-Strauss, 1955).

since the ritual of entering the building gave us an embodied experience of being a visitor in the space of the civil servant, the clash between the formal topics he introduces and the informal experience of the Schouw seems deepened.

Fieldnotes:

The citizens smile, two change their position from arms crossed to a more open posture. One responds by emphasizing that they would like to discuss the way the information in the Schouw is used in making policies about those topics. They add two things; first, the spread of tourists and the use of public space are one and the same topic and it is the most important form of nuisance in they experience: "Crowdedness makes us prisoners in our homes. At the weekends we leave the city. At the same time, this is not included in the Schouw so we would like to discuss how we could include it?" Second, they think that municipal enforcement agents, who are in charge of controlling livability, should cooperate more with citizens to know what is going on and what to focus on. "Based on the outcomes of the Schouw we know exactly where and when the problems arise on an average night."

The civil servant nods and responds, "Yes, we should start a participation monitor."

One of the citizens says, "The city feels like a festival terrain without any control. We don't need another monitor, we already know what is going on and when and where the issues happen, we could just work together."

Diary:

While the civil servant is trying to listen and provides the citizens with space to talk, they seem to not have the same conversation, their responses mismatch. The citizens want answers about what is going to happen with the Schouw results, practical steps of including crowdedness in the Schouw, and more and better-informed enforcement agents at night. The civil servant's responses remain abstract, he does not respond to the question of including crowdedness in the Schouw. And in response to more cooperation between citizens and enforcement agents he proposes to establish a formal tool for doing research instead of using the practical knowhow of the citizens around the table. The meeting, although well intended, seems to end in more frustration on both ends.

Representing and interpreting ethnographic data

The next stage of doing ethnographic research is to move from fieldwork to 'thick description' that represents observations in written text and interprets findings to reach an analysis. Ethnographic data may consist of everything from verbal **transcripts** of interviews, other physical artefacts such as photographs or lists, to the memories and impressions of the ethnographer (Pool, 2017: 282). Ethnographers thus come back from the field with a wealth of data that needs to be represented in a coherent narrative and interpreted in a credible and convincing analysis.

Representation and interpretation often happen via an iterative process that moves back and forth between concepts and empirical observations (see for example the chapter by Federico Savini and Daan Wesselman). Grounded theory scholars start out with empirical findings and build up their analyses by using insights from the field (Glaser & Strauss, 1999). Others have hypotheses or existing theories that they apply to their empirical material. No matter which method of analysis the researcher uses, interpretation always moves back and forth between representation and interpretation.

Interpreting meaning is difficult because meaning is often contested. People give contradictory meanings to events, places, meetings, others, and even the self. Different people apply different meanings to the same thing, but people also often contradict themselves. Instead of deducing one truth, the goal of ethnographic writing is to allow conflicting realities to exist side by side.

It is therefore important to analyze the unit of analysis from various perspectives and by using various data sources **(triangulation)**. Relying too much on observations alone runs the risk of inferring meaning from the behavior of people. Meanings, background experiences, and emotional currents cannot be directly expressed and are not readily visible in particular interactions (Emerson, 2009: 537). Thus, researchers need to not only observe but also talk to people about what they are doing with others and how they experience these interactions. Ethnographers thus combine participant observations with formal and informal interviews (see chapter 5) and document analysis (see chapter 6).

Conversely, participant observations complement research based on interviews because people often do things differently from what they say they do. There is an attitudinal fallacy in inferring situated behavior from verbal accounts (Jerolmack & Khan, 2014). Therefore, ethnographers do not simply draw conclusions about people's behavior based on what they tell us (for instance in an interview or **survey**), but observe and participate in actual behavior (participant observations).

Interpreting data

I was interested in understanding the various ways in which citizens, public officials and other stakeholder negotiate ownership. To operationalize the negotiation of ownership I used De Certeau's theory about the 'practices of everyday life' (1984). This theory helped me to differentiate 'tactics' of ownership that are usually more ad hoc and improvised from 'strategies' by which ownership is practiced through more formal and planned interventions. To understand how these practices affect the meaning of space I used theories of space like Lofland's theory of the parochial realm (Lofland, 1998).

The strategic practice of the Schouw represents a strategy to create ownership by producing knowledge of where, when, and how the experience of ownership by citizens is jeopardized. The meeting in which the outcomes of the Schouw are negotiated with public officials reveals that, although the Schouw is supported by the municipality, the local and everyday knowledge creates a mismatch with general policy terms that public officials use. The difficult negotiation of local and conventional knowledge leaves citizens in the dark about the impact their strategy had on local policies.

Figure 3.1: Tactics of ownership (photo by author).

To reclaim public space, citizens can only resort to the domain of tactics where they must utilize the 'gaps and circumstances that open in the sphere of control and create surprises' (Certeau, 1984: 6). They do so by tactically appropriating public spaces in the neighborhood, for example, by placing flowers in a circle on the sidewalk to informally designate and claim space (see figure 3.1).

Other tactics are informal signs in windows that instruct tourist behavior (figure 3.2).

Figure 3.2: Tactics of ownership (photo by author).

While the Schouw offers knowledge that seeks to have a long-term effect on policy, these tactics provide an immediate physical experience of ownership. These acts of placemaking (Friedmann, 2016) communicate to visitors that this is a parochial domain – something in between the private and the public that brings together a sense of 'commonality between neighbors who are involved in interpersonal networks that are located in communities' (Lofland, 1998: 10). The parochial exists in between private spaces that are characterized by 'ties of intimacy among primary groups members who are located in households or personal networks' (Lofland, 1998 10) and the public that is 'inhabited by persons who are strangers to one another or who 'know' one another only in terms of occupational or other non-personal identity categories' (ibid: 9). The tactical spatial practices create a space where ownership is renegotiated and directly produce a parochial space. These tactics, however, are not supported by the municipality and when enforcement agents see the flowers they ask citizens to take them away. To them, these practices jeopardize the public meaning. They ignore the in-between meaning of parochial spaces.

Credibility & verification

Ethnographers' deep engagement with the field allows them to develop knowledge from within the city that reveals how meanings are produced, how inclusion or exclusion takes shape through everyday interactions, how power is discursively practiced, and more importantly, why these processes unfold the way they do. Ethnographic data is by nature not replicable nor generalizable, nor does it claim to be, because the goal is to understand the how and why of a certain phenomenon or process. The deep engagement with the field requires deep reflection on the relationship between the researcher and the field, particularly because these aspects of research aid or interfere with data collection (Ocejo, 2013: 7).

Recent debates address three ways of ensuring transparency to strengthen ethnographies' verification (see Pool, 2017; van de Port, 2017). First, ethnographers must be transparent regarding the process of fieldwork: providing information about the number of people they worked with, the number of observed meetings and spaces, the timespan and strategies of fieldwork. Second, final reports should give more voice to the people in the field by generously providing quotes, original utterings, or observations. Third, the final analyses must make clear where the argument of the researchers and the analyses coincide with the voice and interpretations of people in the field, and where it doesn't, demanding that researchers be transparent about the method of analysis.

The trustworthiness of the data increases with honest reflections on the process of fieldwork, its failures and successes. The diary can be a place to provide input for such reflection and the logbook might show how the data was collected. To increase credibility further, the diary could reveal how interpretations are embedded in empirical data via quotes and observations, and where and how theories can be applied to empirical observations, or where and how concepts should be extended and adjusted to make sense of complex realities.

Reflection on ethics

Ethnographies' intimate nature also requires special reflection on ethics. Ethical guidelines are developed in order to protect the wellbeing of participants and researchers. Specific ethical considerations need to be made in relation to each particular project, but for the purpose of this chapter I categorize the two most important: procedural ethics and ethics regarding the intimate relationship with others and the self.

In general, the guidelines for procedural ethics are the same as for any type of qualitative data. Procedural ethics include informed consent, anonymity of people and situations, confidentiality and privacy agreements, the safeguarding of information, identification of conflicting interests, and preventing potential misuse of data (see for further reading Atkinson, 2009; Bourgois, 2007; Johnson, 2014).

Ethics regarding the intimate relationships with others and the self should help researchers to make ethical decisions before and during fieldwork. Ethical challenges that may emerge during ethnographic fieldwork can range from becoming too close or remaining too distant from people in the field, having to deal with a culture shock, or concerns about personal safety.[5] All of these might affect the ability of the researcher to collect trustworthy data, and therefore demand reflection. Although the best advice is to discuss these issues with supervisors or peers who are familiar with the particular field, I want to pay attention to two general ethical challenges that are particularly important to ethnographers.

Ethnographers usually develop intimate relationships with people in the field. Often, this means that they become so familiar and friendly with informants that they start to identify themselves with their grievances and struggles.[6] In such moments, it is important to reflect on your relationship with 'the other'. Ask yourself, 'Am I able to represent all sides of the story or did I become an advocate for one group?' If the latter, that does not by itself pose a problem; it does, however, change the aim of the research and the kinds of claims that can be made based on the findings. The ethnographer's role as an advocate has to be transparent in the research plan (see the discussion on applied ethnography in Hammersley & Atkinson, 1994: 253).

I am a citizen of Amsterdam with an existing local network. On the one hand this puts me in a privileged position to do fieldwork, on the other hand it requires me to reflect on my own positionality in doing this research and to be transparent about the process of data collection and analysis. To balance my positionality as a citizen, I had to do more work engaging with the perspective of municipal actors and owners of companies catering to tourists. It goes beyond the confines of this chapter to include materials from all interview transcripts; what I present here is a selection. To create equal opportunity for all parties to discuss their perspective on ownership publicly, my team and I organized a public debate where all parties engaged in a dialogue about the neighborhood's future.

---

5   Some urban fieldwork may pose safety concerns; if that is the case, researchers should always include this in their fieldwork plan and discuss their safety among peers. For further reading on safety related questions in ethnographic fieldwork, see Lindegaard, 2017; Rodgers, 2007.

6   For further readings on blurred boundaries between ethnographic fieldwork and personal life see McLean & Leibing, 2007.

Another important ethical concern is the commitment not to 'glamorize', 'exotify', 'objectify' or 'orientalize' (Said, 1978) people in the field. Staring at people who are different from ourselves is not what ethnography is about. Many of my students confuse participant observation with obscurely gazing at 'others' in the street. This type of covert observation, however, does usually not lead to helpful insights that inform a research question. At best, it produces superficial descriptions of behavior without any contextual or analytic purpose; at worse, it deepens stereotypes, reifies cultures or identity, or is straightforwardly racist. Ethnographers preparing for fieldwork should reflect on these aspects of their research and make a comprehensive fieldwork plan that is sensitive to reification and stereotyping and prevents it.

Conclusions

Researchers preparing for fieldwork are encouraged to read existing ethnographies related to the topic or case study they intend to study. In this chapter I discussed possible units of analysis and the preparation of fieldwork via a fieldwork plan. When entering the field, researchers can rely on strategies of note keeping that differentiate between fieldnotes, diary, and logbook. Finally, ethnography is all about finding your voice in order to understand, analyze and communicate about the city from within.

The excerpts presented here reveal how citizens and public officials use different definitions of 'public' space, resulting in contrasting practices to produce ownership. To residents, the publicness of the space in the Red Light District is jeopardized by the large amount of visitors, and their tactics of placemaking offer an informal response with immediate effect. Public officials cannot accept these tactics because in their view they claim public space and turn them into private spaces. The parochial meaning of public space is overlooked in that view, as is the importance of public familiarity that refers to a sense of belonging in a locality through the distant recognition of familiar faces in public space and local neighborhood shops (Blondeel, 2006).

While residents are trying to (re)develop public familiarity through their tactics, the local government approaches ownership as a management problem. Formal interventions aim at reducing criminal activities and managing crowds of tourists by spreading them more equally over the city. Although public officials recognize the impact of nuisance and crowdedness on livability and provide support for the Schouw, they are unable to embed local knowledge into formal policies and interventions. Even though they intend to include the knowledge of citizens, it seems difficult to translate small, contextual, and detailed knowledge into strategic policy making.

Recognition and support for the efforts of citizens are no longer enough in the context of growing nuisance, dirt, crowdedness, and the overall lack of public familiarity and parochial space. Citizens need tangible interventions that empower them to regain ownership over their living environment and strengthen the identity of an urban community over an exotic tourist attraction. From 2019 onwards, strong interventions have banned short term rent of apartments in the area and sought to support neighborhood functions. Further research will shed light on how these policies impact the negotiation of ownership in the district.

References

Atkinson, P. (2009). Ethics and ethnography. *Twenty-First Century Society, 4*(1), 17–30.

Baiocchi, G., & Connor, B. T. (2008). The Ethnos in the Polis: Political Ethnography as a Mode of Inquiry. *Sociology Compass, 2*(1), 139–155. https://doi.org/10.1111/j.1751-9020.2007.00053.x

Blondeel, P. (2006). *'Als het werkt, komt de samenhang vanzelf': Hoe burgers omgaan met wat niet verandert en wat steden kunnen*. R4R.

Bourgois, P. (2007). Confronting the ethics of ethnography: lessons from fieldwork in Central America. In A. C. G. M. Robben & J. A. Sluka (Eds.), *Ethnographic fieldwork: an anthropological reader* (pp. 288–297). Oxford: Blackwell.

Certeau, M. de. (1984). *The practice of everyday life*. University of California Press.

Couzy, M. (2020, January 5). Het Amsterdam van 2020: vol, druk en gewilder dan ooit. Achtergrond, Parool. https://www.parool.nl/amsterdam/het-amsterdam-van-2020-vol-druk-en-gewilder-dan-ooit~b0b5bc3b/

DeWalt, K. M., & DeWalt, B. R. (2011). *Participant observation: A guide for fieldworkers*. Altamira Press.

Emerson, R. M. (2009). Ethnography, interaction and ordinary trouble. *Ethnography, 10*(4), 535–548. https://doi.org/10.1177/1466138109346996

Emerson, R. M., Fretz, R. I., & Shaw, L. L. (1995). *Writing ethnographic fieldnotes*. Chicago: University of Chicago Press.

Friedmann, J. (2016). Place and Place-Making in Cities: A Global Perspective. *Readings in Planning Theory: Fourth Edition, 9357*(November), 503–523. https://doi.org/10.1002/9781119084679.ch25

Garbett, G. K. (1970). The analysis of social situations. *Man, 5*(2), 214–227.

Geertz, C. (1973). *The interpretation of cultures: Selected essays*. Basic books.

Geertz, C. (2005). Deep play: Notes on the Balinese cockfight. *Daedalus, 134*(4), 56–86.

Gill, R., Barbour, J., & Dean, M. (2014). Shadowing in/as work: ten recommendations for shadowing fieldwork practice. *Qualitative Research in Organizations and Management: An International Journal, 9*(1), 69–89.

Glaser, B. G., & Strauss, A. L. (1999). *Discovery of grounded theory: Strategies for qualitative research*. Transaction Publishers.

Hammersley, M., & Atkinson, P. (1994). Ethnography and participant observation. In N. Denzin & Y. Lincoln (Eds.), *Handbook of qualitative research* (pp. 248–261). London: Sage Thousand Oaks, CA.

Harré, R., & Langehove, L. van. (1999). *Positioning theory*. Blackwell Publisher Ltd.

Jaffe, R., & Koning, A. de. (2016). *Introducing Urban Anthropology*. Routledge.

Jerolmack, C., & Khan, S. (2014). Talk Is Cheap: Ethnography and the Attitudinal Fallacy. *Sociological Methods & Research, 43*(2), 178-209.

Johnson, B. (2014). Ethical issues in shadowing research. *Qualitative Research in Organizations and Management: An International Journal, 9*(1), 21-40. https://doi.org/10.1108/QROM-09-2012-1099

Jones, G., & Rodgers, D. (n.d.). *Standing on the Shoulders of Giants: The enduring relevance of the Chicago School of Sociology*. Cambridge University Press.

Kirk, J., & Miller, M. L. (1986). *Reliability and validity in qualitative research* (Vol. 1). London: Sage.

Lévi-Strauss, C. (1955). *Tristes tropiques*. Atheneum publishers.

Lindegaard, M. R. (2017). *Surviving gangs, violence and racism in Cape Town: Ghetto chameleons*. London: Routledge.

Lofland, L. H. (1998). *The public realm: Exploring the city's quintessential social territory*. Aldine Transaction.

Madden, D. J. (2014). Neighborhood as spatial project: Making the urban order on the downtown Brooklyn waterfront. *International Journal of Urban and Regional Research, 38*(2), 471-497.

McLean, A., & Leibing, A. (2007). *The shadow side of fieldwork: exploring the blurred borders between ethnography and life*. Blackwell Publisher Ltd.

Ocejo, R. E. (2013). *Ethnography and the city: readings on doing urban fieldwork*. Routledge.

Parks, R., Burgess, E. W., & McKenzie, R. D. (1925). The city. In *Chicago, IL*. University of Chicago.

Pickering, A. (2010). *The mangle of practice: Time, agency, and science*. University of Chicago Press.

Pool, R. (2017). The verification of ethnographic data. *Ethnography, 18*(3), 281-286.

Quinlan, E. (2008). Conspicuous invisibility: Shadowing as a data collection strategy. *Qualitative Inquiry, 14*(8), 1480-1499.

Rodgers, D. (2007). Joining the gang and becoming a broder: The violence of ethnography in contemporary nicaragua. *Bulletin of Latin American Research, 26*(4), 444-461.

Said, E. (1978). *Orientalism*. Pantheon.

Schatz, E. (2013). *Political ethnography: What immersion contributes to the study of power*. University of Chicago Press.

van de Port, M. (2017). The verification of ethnographic data: A response. *Ethnography, 18*(3), 295-299.

van Hulst, M. (2008). Quite an experience: Using ethnography to study local governance. *Critical Policy Studies, 2*(2), 143-159.

Verloo, N. (2017). Strijd om de straat in de Amsterdamse Wallen. *Rooilijn, 50*(1), 8-17

Vidich, A., & Bensman, J. (1954). The validity of field data. *Human Organization, 13*(1), 20-27.

Wedeen, L. (2010). Reflections on ethnographic work in political science. *Annual Review of Political Science, 13*, 255–272.

Wirth, L. (1938). Urbanism as a Way of Life. *American Journal of Sociology, 44*(1), 1–24.

Ybema, S., Yanow, D., Wels, H., & Kamsteeg, F. H. (2009). *Organizational ethnography: Studying the complexity of everyday life*. Sage.

4 Sensing the city through new forms of urban data

Achilleas Psyllidis

Introduction

Different data sources and the methods that turn the generated data into insights have hitherto largely shaped how we conceptualize urban phenomena. Coarse-grained or **aggregate data** allow us to understand the evolution of a phenomenon (e.g. traffic flows, **gentrification**, etc.) within a specific and predefined area – or *spatial unit* – at a larger scale (e.g. neighborhood, postcode area, etc.). Fine-grained or **disaggregated data** offer the possibility of gaining insight into processes at a smaller scale. One example could be the daily commuting behavior of a group of individuals from home to work, or the amount of people visiting a shop over the course of a day.

Traditionally, the study of cities has been based on both quantitative and qualitative data with various granularities, from coarse to more fine-grained. The primary sources of information have been – and continue to be – **censuses**, **interviews**, and statistical **surveys**, usually designed and implemented by governmental authorities (see chapters 2 and 5). **Observations** at a finer level (e.g. household income, employment status per person within a household) are often aggregated into higher-level spatial units (e.g. rates in a postcode area or electoral unit) to ensure privacy. However, aggregation into coarser units had also to do with the limited analytical capabilities of computer systems in previous decades. Until recently, it was almost impossible to store and process urban data at fine resolutions. Lately, however, the exponential increase of storage and processing capabilities of modern-day computational systems has not only allowed the analysis of very disaggregated data: it has also given rise to a whole new range of data sources about cities, and an extended arsenal of analysis techniques that can turn them into actionable information.

The current landscape of urban data comprises two general categories, based on how the data are generated: (1) the traditional, *designed* **data** such as censuses, interviews, and surveys that I referred to previously, and (2) the contemporary, *organic* **data** about cities that are generated either through technologies embedded in the **urban fabric** (e.g. sensors, cameras, etc.) or are the byproduct of people's online activities (e.g. tweets, blog posts, reviews, etc.) (Singleton, Spielman, Folch, 2017). This chapter focuses specifically on the second category of urban data, given that – unlike the ones belonging to the first category – they have only recently been introduced to and considered in the analysis of cities. For this reason, I will collectively refer to them as *new forms of urban data.*

Sources that generate new forms of urban data may vary substantially. From the perspective of devices and technologies embedded in the urban fabric, these could include various types of sensors, cameras, Wi-Fi networks, GPS receivers, and card-based ticketing systems in public transport. Regarding online sources, examples include geo-enabled social media (e.g. Twitter, Instagram), mapping applications (e.g. OpenStreetMap, Google Maps), travel and tourism-related platforms (e.g. Airbnb, TripAdvisor), through which people actively provide and generate new data. Spatially-tagged user-generated reviews, textual descriptions, ratings, and other media (e.g. photos and videos) could further enhance our understanding about people's experiences, sentiments, and overall behavior in cities. Moreover, information is being updated dynamically, often in real time, and therefore offering insight into aspects of cities and city life that have not been recorded before.

New forms of urban data do not, by any means, replace the conventional, well-established sources of information in city analytics. Instead, they may ideally complement them with features that are latent or absent in designed datasets. To do so, however, new approaches to the processing and analysis of emerging data are needed. As opposed to traditional, *designed* data, the newly emerging datasets are generated *organically*, sometimes even spontaneously, without a carefully defined purpose and scope in mind. For example, social media records could facilitate our understanding of human mobility over time, but this comes, in fact, as a byproduct – that is, the original purposes of social media are different than the ones we could eventually use their data for. The resulting datasets are, therefore, messy, often uncertain, and conceivably unrepresentative of a population. Statistical (spatial) analysis techniques developed originally for structured datasets of limited size and variety of types are, hence, not suitable for the analysis of new (unstructured) urban data. Instead, new methods and tools are needed. Moreover, in making the most of heterogeneous and messy datasets, it is important that clear research questions and goals drive the data collection, processing, and analysis.

This chapter sheds light on emerging forms of data about cities, as complementary sources of information to conventional urban data. It presents their main categories, outlines their limitations and uncertainties, and introduces a range of new methods suitable for turning new data into actionable insights. I classify new urban data into four categories: *physical sensor data*, *mobile phone data*, *social media data*, and *user-generated and POI-based web data* (other than social media). The characteristics, limitations, and suitable methods for each data category are described in the corresponding sections.

Physical sensor data

Physical sensors were the first of the new data sources that complemented conventional urban data with real-time measurements of the urban environment. The first application concerned the measurement of traffic flows (Batty et al., 2012). **Sensors** are miniaturized computer systems that can be embedded and deployed in the urban fabric. Of course, there exist several types of sensors used in the measurement of indoor environments (e.g. in buildings), yet in this section we will focus only on sensors and sensor networks deployed in public spaces and/or at city-wide scales.

There is currently a wide range of sensor types, usually classified based on the measured property. Examples of the latter may include *environmental properties* (e.g. natural light, temperature, humidity, CO_2-levels, atmospheric particulate matter, etc.), *urban mobility* (e.g. car flows, pedestrian flows, cyclist flows, etc.), *transactional dynamics* (e.g. purchases of goods, demand-supply dynamics, etc.), *transport transactions* (e.g. taps in or out on public transport), and *satellite measurements* (e.g. positioning, electromagnetic radiation, vegetation remote sensing, etc.).

Sensors may exist as individual entities, measuring a property at a targeted location, or – as is increasingly more common in cities – comprise sensor networks. In this case, each sensor is a node in a wider network, which collectively measures a given property in a collaborative fashion (Verdone et al., 2010). The interconnection of sensors in a network enables simultaneous monitoring at city-wide scales. This would have been close to impossible with individual independent sensors, given their limited spatial coverage. Communication among the nodes is usually achieved wirelessly, using Wi-Fi modules and various wireless communication protocols, such as the long-range wide-area network (LoRaWAN). Such connectivity enables devices to form an Internet of Things (IoT). Most of sensor devices have **geolocation** capabilities and, thereby, generate data that are spatially referenced, making them valuable in the study of cities. **Open access** to sensor data is increasingly made possible through dedicated online portals, maintained by public authorities[1] or private organizations. The case of SAIL 2015, discussed in the box, exemplifies some of these possibilities.

Sensor observations are transmitted continuously and can be collected in real time. Such high frequency updates introduce new ways of measuring and understanding urban phenomena. Whereas traditional urban analysis and planning approaches put

---

[1]   An example of this is the Sensoren Crowd Monitoring Systeem Amsterdam: https://maps.amsterdam.nl/cmsa/.

emphasis on long time intervals – given the low update frequency of conventional urban data – sensor technologies allow us to focus on very short time horizons (Batty, 2013; Psyllidis, 2016). In fact, they enable us to study the *dynamics* of urban phenomena (e.g. human mobility, crowd monitoring, traffic etc.) at higher spatial and temporal granularity.They also provide the opportunity to simulate the evolution of a phenomenon at fine-grained scales.

However, there is a range of challenges related to the collection, analysis, and interpretation of sensor data. Observations derived from sensors (or sensor networks) are of quantitative nature. Measurements are translated into, usually, numerical values of the studied property (e.g. temperature degrees in Celsius or Fahrenheit scales, sound levels in decibels, number of taps in or out, etc.). The accuracy of these measurements – although dependent on the technical aspects of the sensor device – is generally considered high. What they lack, however, is semantic expressiveness. That is, it is often difficult to distinguish any qualitative aspects of the measured property. For instance, in the case of ticketing systems in public transport, although we might be able to acquire an accurate picture of the flow volumes of passengers, it is often difficult to obtain additional demographic information, such as gender and age (with the exception of personalized cards). This could already limit the interpretation potential of sensor data and, subsequently, their transformation into actionable knowledge.

Besides semantics, sensor data often suffer from issues of representativeness. Each sensor device has the capacity to measure a given property within a limited spatial range. As mentioned above, this limitation can be mitigated by deploying a network of sensors that collectively cover a wider area. Yet due to high deployment costs, coverage of entire cities or wider urban areas is often cumbersome, leading to partial coverage of city regions or population groups (e.g. people who use public transport to commute). The extent of **representativeness**, the level of semantic expressiveness, and device-related measurement errors are aspects that need to be considered in the process of analysis and interpretation of sensor data. Combining sensor measurements with other types of data – presented in the following sections – could mitigate these issues, as also shown by the SAIL 2015 example. Notwithstanding these limitations, physical sensors and sensor networks introduce a valuable source of information, especially in studying the dynamic evolution of urban phenomena.

Mobile phone data

A special class of sensors relates to the ones that are embedded in handheld devices, such as mobile phones. Modern-day cellular devices comprise several sensor technologies, including gyroscopes, Wi-Fi modules, and cameras that, in turn, generate an abundance of spatially and temporally tagged data. In a broader sense, data generated by mobile phones can be classified into two main categories: (1) call detail records (CDRs), and (2) user-generated application data. This section focuses on the former, whereas user-generated content deriving from social media and installed applications on mobile phones will be covered in the following sections.

Call detail records refer to the documentation of telecommunication transactions, such as phone calls and text messages, derived from cell tower pings. These data records are usually structured in tabular formats, which contain various attributes relating to the phone call or text message. Examples of such attributes include caller and receiver IDs, geolocations of both the caller and receiver, timestamps marking the starting time of the call (or the transmission time of the text message) in date/time format, and duration of the call, among others. Already from the types of attributes listed previously, one can easily realize that CDRs could contain valuable information on where, when, and how people communicate with each other, as well as with whom.

In short, the main novelty that mobile phone data, and especially CDRs, bring to urban analytics pertains to the study of *social interactions*. The ubiquity of mobile phones around the globe enables us to study these interactions *at scale*, as opposed to traditional surveys that rely on population samples. Moreover, the spatial and temporal features of CDRs give us the opportunity to respectively analyze the *geographical footprint* of social networks and their *dynamics*. For these reasons, CDRs have been gaining in popularity in scientific research over the past 15 years, and have found application in various domains relating to cities. Application domains include social analysis (networks, communities, relationships, interactions), human mobility, planning, epidemics, and crime detection. For a comprehensive overview of research and applications using CDRs, we refer to Blondel, Decuyper and Krings (2015). Indicative research in the context of cities and wider urban regions explore person-to-person activity over space and time (Calabrese et al., 2011), the behavior of individual human trajectories (González, Hidalgo & Barabasi, 2008; Gao et al., 2013), and the delineation of urban regions, based on the interactions between users (a class of problems, which in urban analytics and quantitative geography is referred to as *regionalization*) (Blondel, Krings & Thomas, 2010; Ratti et al., 2010). The combination of CDRs with traditional data, such as the census and travel surveys, further allows for comparative analyses of human activity dynamics across cities (Grauwin et al., 2015), and between nations (Amini et al., 2014).

The geolocation of a user in CDRs – either caller or receiver – is relative to the closest cell tower in an area, and its corresponding range. In other words, the exact location of a person remains relatively unknown. In their simplest form, CDRs are represented as networks, consisting of nodes that represent people (callers and receivers) and links between them. Network analysis techniques, in combination with statistical measurements of graph properties (e.g. clustering coefficients, centrality, coherence, community detection, etc.), are the prevalent methods in analyzing mobile phone data. More advanced techniques intertwine social networks with physical (urban) space, leading to complex geo-social networks, to explore the behavioral characteristics of mobile phone usage over geographic space (Hristova et al., 2016; Andris, 2016).

Of course, working with mobile phone data, and especially CDRs, comes with various challenges and limitations. The most prominent restriction is that of data access. Depending on privacy protection laws and internal operator policies about data sharing, access to CDRs may vary significantly across countries and mobile phone operators. Although the content of phone calls or text messages is not recorded, raw mobile phone data contain sensitive information, such as demographic information of the caller and receiver (e.g. home address, gender, date of birth, etc.). In ensuring privacy preservation, *anonymization* and *aggregation* techniques are used. A customary **anonymization** technique consists of replacing users and their phone numbers with a unique ID, or disassociating users from individual geolocations. The latter can be achieved by means of spatial aggregation that preserves the possibility to identify general patterns, without uniquely identifying individual users. Other limitations of CDR data relate to the relatively low precision of a user's location (which is relative to the range of the closest cell tower), as well as the limited semantic richness of the data, given that the actual content of phone calls or text messages is generally not recorded. Despite these challenges and limitations, the analysis of mobile phone data has led to novel insights into human mobility and activity behavior, as shown in the referenced research examples.

Social media data

Besides CDRs, mobile phones produce a wealth of data from applications installed in and running on the devices. By leveraging on the built-in global positioning system (GPS), these applications passively generate real-time streams of **geo-referenced data**. A prominent example of this is the case of Google Maps, in which traffic congestion estimates are calculated on the basis of pooled geo-data from cellular devices.

Aside from these passively generated datasets, a set of online social networking applications has introduced an entire new class of data sources about cities and human behavior, with unprecedented characteristics. On platforms such as Twitter, Instagram, Facebook, and Foursquare, content is created actively by the application users themselves, and consists of various data formats, as will be explained further in the following paragraphs. Access to such data is usually obtained through Application Programming Interfaces (APIs), offered by the corresponding platforms. This section focuses specifically on user-generated data derived from online social media, while other types of user-generated web content will be described in the next section. The case of SAIL 2015 illustrates some of these applications.

Although the characteristics of social media data may vary among the different platforms, there exist some general common features. Most of the platforms contain information about demographic characteristics of the users such as gender, age, hometown, and place of residence, among other things. Users generate posts, frequently accompanied by texts expressed in natural language (and often with Internet-specific writing styles, including abbreviations, emoticons, and other symbols), and other media such as photos and videos. Much of these posts contain a spatial tag – either in the form of exact geo-coordinates or in reference to a named location – and a timestamp. Lastly, they include information about relationships between users, which can help build social networks. This multiplicity of information embedded in social media data has opened new avenues in gaining insight into aspects of urban life that are otherwise hardly observable and measurable. Indicative examples include insights into the attitudes and behaviors of people regarding specific activities in cities over time (e.g. relating to leisure, mobility habits, social interactions, etc.), and into their experiences and sentiments. One can thus easily ascertain that social media data are by far the most *semantically rich* data of the types I have discussed thus far. Analysis of such high-dimensional (i.e. with numerous attributes) datasets could reveal how people interact with the places they visit and with each other, how their activities are distributed through space and over time, and how they communicate about places through opinions, perceptions, and sentiments.

Before delving into commonly used analysis techniques, it is important to explain in further detail the concept of *point of interest* (POI), around which many user-generated data sources revolve. From a computational perspective, **POIs** are digital proxies of real-world places (e.g. restaurants, theaters, squares, etc.), represented as geometric point entities. In early phases of social media platforms, geolocations (i.e. geographic coordinates of latitude and longitude) were the prevalent way of spatially tagging user posts. More recently, however, much of georeferenced social data are in fact associated with a POI instance, picked from a predefined list of places (a prominent example is that of Foursquare). Subsequently, the activity described in the post is linked to the geo-coordinates of the associated POI. This creates an unprecedented interlinkage between real-world places and the way people communicate about and experience them over time, through textual descriptions, photos, videos, ratings, and reviews. Also, the interconnection of POIs allows us to study the dynamics of place-to-place relationships. In other words, social media – and other user-generated web – data give new opportunities to studying the concept of *place* (examples to follow) – a long-standing issue in urban studies – as opposed to *space*, represented by a generic geolocation.

The variety of data types that comprise social media data requires a set of new analytical methods that are designed to address their specific characteristics. Integrating textual descriptions in natural language with images, videos, and spatiotemporal references can be a challenging process. Many of the techniques applied to social media analytics derive from various fields of data science. These range from machine learning techniques for natural language processing (e.g. part-of-speech tagging, named entity recognition, topic modeling, sentiment analysis, etc.) and image analysis techniques (e.g. scene detection, object recognition, etc.) to spatiotemporal analysis methods (e.g. spatial regression, point pattern analysis, spatial clustering, etc.) (Janowicz et al., 2019). Social network analysis techniques, as described in the previous section, are also useful in understanding dynamic interactions between users and between places. Each of these techniques targets a specific type of data included in a social media record. More advanced techniques aim to simultaneously take into account the various dimensions (i.e. spatial, temporal, thematic, social) of social media data. The use of these data in urban studies implies that the spatial aspect plays an important role. Yet it is important to consider that, given the high-dimensional nature of social media data, the focus on spatial aspects is not so much on distances, topology, and directions. Instead, it is more about deriving semantic relationships with and among places, through spatially and temporally referenced linguistic descriptions and human interactions with the (urban) environment.

The new avenues that user-generated social media data open to capturing, understanding, and representing urban life in various places have led to a wealth of related research over the past ten years. An extensive overview of these works falls outside the scope of this chapter. A few indicative examples include the comparative analysis of human mobility patterns across cities (Noulas et al., 2012), the classification of venues in cities based on users' activity profiles (Silva et al., 2013), the study of the segregation extent between urban neighborhoods (Shelton, Poorthuis & Zook, 2015), the investigation of city attractiveness factors (Sobolevsky et al., 2015), the regional variability of human activities over time (McKenzie et al., 2015), and the discovery of functional regions within cities, based on the social interactions of people at various places (Psyllidis, Yang & Bozzon, 2018; Gao, Janowicz & Couclelis, 2017).

The very nature of social media data poses, however, several challenges to urban analytics. Being user-generated, they possess several biases related to culture, context, technology penetration, and personal habits (Mislove et al., 2011; Olteanu et al., 2015). The use of natural language, and especially Internet-specific writing styles, could lead to misinterpretations of the actual content relating to a human activity. Moreover, the possible difference between the time a post is created and the actual time the activity it refers to took place could give a wrong impression about the distribution of human activities over time. Text analysis plays an important role in disambiguating posts that refer to places generically from those that concern a real activity happening at a place. Finally, given that social media data are generated predominantly by population groups with specific characteristics, the representativeness of the collected data should be given careful consideration in the generalizability of the analysis results. Again, this further strengthens the need to collect and link data from various sources to mitigate the drawbacks and biases present in individual data streams.

User-generated & POI-based web data

In addition to social media data, there is a wealth of online sources in which users contribute, directly or indirectly, geographic information about the places they visit. Integral to these sources is the concept of POI, as described in the previous section. In principle, each of the platforms relates to a specific function. Examples of the latter include mapping applications (e.g. OpenStreetMap, Google Maps), travel and tourism platforms (e.g. Airbnb, TripAdvisor), photography sharing (e.g. Flickr), discussion forums (e.g. Reddit), among others. Each source contains different information and contributes to a variable understanding of POI-related aspects. For instance, OpenStreetMap focuses on geometrical and locational characteristics of POI footprints, Foursquare concentrates on the number of users that have checked in to a place, whereas Google Maps further provides temporal occupancy profiles, especially for retailer and entertainment stores. The POI concept across these data sources is constant, though the attributes that describe it may vary significantly. A POI can thus be characterized by several features, besides its point-based geometry and geographic location. Such features include a name, address, function, opening hours, website, and phone number. In addition, as in the case of social media data, POIs could be linked to textual descriptions, ratings, photos, and videos. The challenges relating to these data are similar to the ones described in the previous section.

Another data source with great potential for urban studies is **street-level imagery**. This is a more recent addition to the spectrum of POI-related sources. Unlike the well-established satellite imagery, this source provides panoramic views of – primarily urban – environments at ground level. Street-level imagery can be extracted from both proprietary (e.g. Google Street View) and user-generated public (e.g. Mapillary) online repositories, usually through APIs. This new type of data gives a novel perspective on how we represent urban environments. In fact, it simulates the process of a person walking along the streets, thereby providing a three-dimensional overview of visible spatial elements (e.g. building facades, trees, lamp posts, etc.), while highlighting their morphological characteristics (e.g. height, color, materials, geometry, etc.). For this reason, an increasing number of recent studies have used street-level imagery to analyze various aspects of the urban environment. Examples include the estimation of city-level travel patterns (Goel et al., 2018), the classification of land uses (Zhu, Deng & Newsam, 2019), the quantification of urban perception (Dubey et al., 2016), crowd-mapping of physical objects in the urban environment (Qiu et al., 2019), and the inference of business-related POIs, combining visual and text analytics (Sharifi Noorian, Psyllidis & Bozzon, 2019; Sharifi Noorian et al., 2020). In line with the recent advancements in deep learning, the combination of street-level imagery with other user-generated data allows for the extraction of latent city-related characteristics that are otherwise hard to observe or measure (e.g. perceptions of urban public spaces).

Summary

In this chapter, I have presented an overview of new forms of urban data that can complement conventional data sources about cities, and could offer new insight on modern-day urban life. The case of SAIL 2015, discussed in the box, is an illustration of potential applications. Although the potential of emerging data sources has been leveraged in scientific fields, such as data science, their incorporation in urban studies and implementation into planning/design tools is still at a nascent stage. In making the most of these data, it is required that new dedicated methods and analytical frameworks are applied and developed, catering to the unique qualities of emerging data sources. I have outlined the main characteristics, the latest methodological advancements, and the limitations that should be considered in the analytic process. I have further provided indicative references to a variety of application examples from recent research work, with emphasis on aspects of the urban environment. This new paradigm of urban research has given rise to a new generation of burgeoning scientific fields, such as urban analytics, spatial/urban data science, and location intelligence, which lie at the intersection of urban theory, planning, and information sciences.

Crowd management at city-scale events – the case of SAIL 2015

The emergence of new forms of urban data has opened new avenues in analyzing, understanding, and explaining the behaviors and activities of people during large-scale events. Music festivals, sports events, and national festivities are examples of events that attract large numbers of people, and often lead to re-organizations in the city infrastructure (e.g. transportation adjustments, closure of streets and other public spaces, etc.). In that sense, they are exceptional cases of everyday city life. Real-time measurements of visitor density and estimates of visitors' movement and activity patterns across space are integral to emergency support and crowd management. Such measurements can hardly be inferred from conventional data, yet emerging urban data could prove valuable in this regard. To illustrate this, I use the case of the SAIL 2015 nautical event in Amsterdam as an indicative example of crowd management application, informed by insights that are retrieved from various new forms of urban data.

SAIL is the largest free nautical event in the world, and takes place every five years in Amsterdam. With a total duration of five days, it attracts more than two million visitors from the Netherlands and abroad. The 2015 version of SAIL took place from August 19 to August 23 of that year. Vessels sail across the river IJ, and visitors have the chance to attend the event through various pre-defined walking routes and observation areas along the river. The main event is further enhanced by concerts, markets, and exhibitions, taking place in the streets and selected buildings surrounding the main attraction areas. Getting a better understanding of attendees' movement behavior during such large-scale event is of vital importance for the safety of visitors, the supply of services, and emergency support. To that end, the Municipality of Amsterdam assigned a crowd management task to a group of researchers (including the author) at Delft University of Technology (TU Delft).

Various sources of emerging urban data were employed to address this task. More specifically, data were collected from 20 Wi-Fi sensors (forming a sensor network), 100 GPS trackers, 8 camera-based counting systems, and social media posts from Twitter, Instagram, and Foursquare. Access to the already installed sensing infrastructure and counting systems was granted by the Municipality. The GPS trackers were distributed to attendees, who consented to carry them throughout their visit. To enrich the location-based track records, the attendees who volunteered also provided additional demographics (e.g. age range, gender, whether they were local visitors or foreign tourists) by means of signing a consent form. Social media data were crawled, processed, integrated, and analyzed using the *SocialGlass* platform (https://social-glass. tudelft.nl); a platform for real-time urban analytics developed by the author and his team at TU Delft (Psyllidis et al., 2015).

Wi-Fi sensors recorded signals from mobile phones within a given radius. These measurements were used to approximate the density of visitors in different places during the event. Records of adjacent sensors were matched to provide a picture of pedestrian flows in the entire area covered. Sensor records were complemented by individual headcounts from the camera-based counting systems. The latter provided flow measurements on a minute basis in both directions (i.e. inflow and outflow), using computer vision algorithms. To preserve privacy, different mobile phone **signals** were assigned unique anonymized identifiers to allow for density calculations of attendees, while counting systems only provided the amounts of unique users passing by.

Sensing devices, as also explained throughout the chapter, provide precise quantitative estimates of human flows, yet have no semantics attached and cover limited areas. To mitigate this, sensor data were combined with data from various social media. Each social media dataset has been created using a different crawling mechanism. Typically, this was a combination of *geo-fencing* (i.e. retrieval of tweets and Instagram posts annotated with a geolocation, within a pre-defined bounding box covering the event area and its surroundings) and *keyword matching* (i.e. retrieval of tweets and Instagram posts that contain keywords directly relating to the event). All social media datasets were collected through publicly available API calls, offered by the corresponding platforms, and covered the entire period of the event. Additionally, the spatial coverage of social media was larger than the one of sensing devices, yet with varying fluctuations in terms of the density of posts within pre-defined spatial units. For each post, the longitude, latitude, timestamp, and post content (text and accompanying media) were collected. To preserve anonymity, each post was assigned a user ID (posts generated by the same user were assigned the same user ID), expressed in hexadecimal code. Using **user modeling techniques** that have been implemented in the *SocialGlass* system, additional demographic characteristics of the visitors were retrieved, including age range, gender, and the type of visitor (i.e. resident, local visitor, foreign tourist). The demographics collected through the consent forms of the GPS trackers were used as reference indicators to compare them with the characteristics inferred by the analysis of social media data. Additional text analytics (e.g. natural language processing, named entity recognition, and topic modeling) and spatial analysis techniques (e.g. spatial autocorrelation, density-based spatial clustering) were used to gain further insight into activity patterns in space and time, movement flows, indications of crowdedness, and sentiments (for further details, see Gong et al., 2018).

The case of crowd management during SAIL is an indicative example of urban analytics, where various new forms of urban data were used in a combined fashion. On such occasions, such as city-scale events or emergency situations, where near real-time information and insights are of vital importance, conventional urban data may prove inadequate. Emerging urban data are particularly useful in the study of human activity patterns, flows of goods and people, and the spatiotemporal distribution of social interactions. The combination of various emerging urban data together, and with conventional data about cities, has promise as a potential solution to the drawbacks present in individual data streams.

References

Amini, A., Kung, K., Kang, C., Sobolevsky, S., & Ratti, C. (2014). The impact of social segregation on human mobility in developing and industrialized regions. *EPJ Data Science, 3*(1), 6.

Andris, C. (2016). Integrating social network data into GISystems. *International Journal of Geographical Information Science, 30*(10), 2009–2031.

Batty, M., Axhausen, K. W., Giannotti, F., Pozdnoukhov, A., Bazzani, A., Wachowicz, M., Ouzounis, G., & Portugali, Y. (2012). Smart cities of the future. *The European Physical Journal Special Topics, 214*(1), 481–518.

Batty, M., (2013). Urban informatics and Big Data: a report to the ESRC Cities Expert Group.

Blondel, V., Krings, G., & Thomas, I. (2010). Regions and borders of mobile telephony in Belgium and in the Brussels metropolitan zone. *Brussels Studies. La revue scientifique électronique pour les recherches sur Bruxelles/ Het elektronisch wetenschappelijk tijdschrift voor onderzoek over Brussel/ The e-journal for academic research on Brussels.*

Blondel, V. D., Decuyper, A., & Krings, G. (2015). A survey of results on mobile phone datasets analysis. *EPJ data science, 4*(1), 1–55.

Calabrese, F., Smoreda, Z., Blondel, V. D., & Ratti, C. (2011). Interplay between telecommunications and face-to-face interactions: A study using mobile phone data. *PLoS One, 6*(7), e20814.

Dubey, A., Naik, N., Parikh, D., Raskar, R., & Hidalgo, C. A. (2016). Deep learning the city: Quantifying urban perception at a global scale. In *European conference on computer vision*. Springer: Cham, pp. 196–212.

Gao, S., Liu, Y., Wang, Y., & Ma, X. (2013). Discovering spatial interaction communities from mobile phone data. *Transactions in GIS, 17*(3), 463–481.

Gao, S., Janowicz, K., & Couclelis, H. (2017). Extracting urban functional regions from points of interest and human activities on location-based social networks. *Transactions in GIS, 21*(3), 446–467.

Goel, R., Garcia, L. M. T., Goodman, A., Johnson, R., Aldred, R., Murugesan, M., Brage, S., Bhalla, K., & Woodcock, J. (2018). Estimating city-level travel patterns using street imagery: A case study of using Google Street View in Britain. *PLoS One, 13*(5), e0196521.

Gong, V., Yang, J., Daamen, W., Bozzon, A., Hoogendoorn, S., & Houben, G-J. (2018). Using social media for attendees' density estimation in city-scale events. *IEEE Access, 6*, 36325–36340.

Gonzalez, M. C., Hidalgo, C. A., & Barabasi, A-L. (2008). Understanding individual human mobility patterns. *Nature, 453*(7196), 779 –782.

Grauwin, S., Sobolevsky, S., Moritz, S., Gódor, I., & Ratti, C. (2015). Towards a comparative science of cities: Using mobile traffic records in New York, London, and Hong Kong. In *Computational approaches for urban environments*. Springer: Cham, pp. 363–387.

Hristova, D., Williams, M. J., Musolesi, M., Panzarasa, P., & Mascolo, C. (2016). Measuring urban social diversity using interconnected geo-social networks. In *Proceedings of the 25th international conference on World Wide Web*. International World Wide Web Conferences Steering Committee, pp. 21-30.

Janowicz, K., McKenzie, G., Hu, Y., Zhu, R., & Gao, S. (2019). Using semantic signatures for social sensing in urban environments. In *Mobility patterns, big data and transport analytics*. Amsterdam: Elsevier, pp. 31–54.

McKenzie, G., Janowicz, K., Gao, S., & Gong, L. (2015). How where is when? On the regional variability and resolution of geosocial temporal signatures for points of interest. *Computers, Environment and Urban Systems, 54*, 336–346.

Mislove, A., Lehmann, S., Ahn, Y-Y., Onnela, J-P., & Niels Rosenquist, J. (2011). Understanding the demographics of twitter users. In *Fifth international AAAI conference on weblogs and social media*.

Noulas, A., Scellato, S., Lambiotte, R., Pontil, M., & Mascolo, C. (2012). A tale of many cities: Universal patterns in human urban mobility. *PLoS One, 7*(5), e37027.

Olteanu, A., Castillo, C., Diakopoulos, N., & Aberer, K. (2015). Comparing events coverage in online news and social media: The case of climate change. In *Ninth International AAAI Conference on Web and Social Media*.

Psyllidis, A., Bozzon, A., Bocconi, S., & Bolivar, C-T. (2015). A platform for urban analytics and semantic integration in city planning. In G. Celani, D. Moreno Sperling & J. M. S. Franco (eds.) *Computer-aided architectural design futures: New technologies and the future of the built environment: 16th international conference (CAAD Futures 2015) – selected papers*. LNCS, CCIS 527. Springer: Berlin, Heidelberg, pp. 21–36.

Psyllidis, A. (2016). Revisiting urban dynamics through social urban data. *A+ BE: Architecture and the Built Environment 18*, 1–334.

Psyllidis, Achilleas, Jie Yang, and Alessandro Bozzon. 'Regionalization of social interactions and points-of-interest location prediction with geosocial data', *IEEE Access*, 6 (2018), pp. 34334-34353.

Qiu, S., Psyllidis, A., Bozzon, A., & Houben, G-J. (2019). Crowd-mapping urban objects from street-level imagery. In *The World Wide Web Conference*. ACM, pp. 1521-1531.

Ratti, C., Sobolevsky, S., Calabrese, F., Andris, C., Reades, J., Martino, M., Claxton, R., & Strogatz, S. H. (2010). Redrawing the map of Great Britain from a network of human interactions. *PLoS One, 5*(12), e14248.

Sharifi Noorian, S., Psyllidis, A., & Bozzon, A. (2019). ST-Sem: A multimodal method for points-of-interest classification using street-level imagery. In *International Conference on Web Engineering*. Springer: Cham, pp. 32-46.

Sharifi Noorian, S., Qiu, S., Psyllidis, A., Bozzon, A., & Houben, G-J. (2020). Detecting, classifying, and mapping retail storefronts using street-level imagery. In *ACM International Conference on Multimedia Retrieval (ICMR 2020)*. ACM, in press.

Shelton, T., Poorthuis, A., & Zook, M. (2015). Social media and the city: Rethinking urban socio-spatial inequality using user-generated geographic information. *Landscape and Urban Planning, 142*, 198-211.

Silva, T. H., Vaz de Melo, P. O. S., Almeida, J. M., Salles, J., & Loureiro, A. A. F. (2013). A comparison of Foursquare and Instagram to the study of city dynamics and urban social behavior. In *Proceedings of the 2nd ACM SIGKDD International Workshop on Urban Computing*. ACM, p. 4.

Singleton, A. D., Spielman, S., & Folch, D. (2017). *Urban analytics*. London: Sage.

Sobolevsky, S, Bojic, I., Belyi, A., Sitko, I., Hawelka, B., Murillo Arias, J., & Ratti, C. Scaling of city attractiveness for foreign visitors through big data of human economical and social media activity. In *2015 IEEE International Congress on Big Data*. IEEE. pp. 600-607.

Verdone, R., Dardari, D., Mazzini, G., & Conti, A. (2010). *Wireless sensor and actuator networks: Technologies, analysis and design*. London: Academic Press.

Zhu, Y., Deng, X., & Newsam, S. (2019). Fine-grained land use classification at the city scale using ground-level images. *IEEE Transactions on Multimedia, 21*(7), 1825-1838.

5 Interviewing in urban research

Fenne M. Pinkster

Introduction

In urban research, **interviews** are used to provide insight into many different facets of urban life, ranging from the everyday experience of urban places and urban change to the rationalities behind urban policies and the claims of different stakeholders in spatial interventions. Yet while interviewing is one of the most prevalent qualitative research methods, it is also one of the most underestimated. Simply put, doing high-quality interviews is more challenging than many beginning researchers anticipate. Lofland and Lofland (1984, p. 12) describe interviews as 'guided conversations whose goal is to elicit from the interviewee rich, detailed materials that can later be used in qualitative analysis'. There is, however, a fundamental distinction between having an informative conversation and interviewing as a scientific research method. Interviewing requires a rigorous research design, strategic **sampling**, and consistent methodological execution, demanding considerable social, organizational, and analytical skills from the researcher. In this respect, some scholars refer to interviewing as an 'obstacle course' (Hermanns, 2004), full of pitfalls that can reduce the validity of one's research and open up the researcher to the accusations of randomness, triviality and subjectivity.

The purpose of this chapter is therefore to provide starting researchers with a first, basic set of principles for interviewing as a scientific method for gathering data. I first discuss what interviews are 'good for'. This is followed by an introduction on how to design your research, determine your research sample and develop your interview guide. The second half of the chapter focuses on the practice of interviewing: going into the field, how to ask the right questions, and how to process your data during fieldwork.

As a way to illustrate some of the choices to be made in conducting interviews, I will refer to a recent study on the local impacts of urban tourism in the Amsterdam Canal Belt. For this study, we conducted interviews with long term residents to understand how urban tourism changes their sense of place and feelings of belonging (Pinkster & Boterman, 2017).

The purpose of interviewing

The first thing to consider is whether interviewing is a relevant method to address your research question. In general, interviews are useful to study the meaning that people attribute to their social worlds and to understand their social behavior (Bryman, 2012; Boeije, 2010). **Interviews** can provide insight into *why* city residents or urban stakeholders behave in particular ways, thus complementing other methods aimed at studying human behavior, such as **participant observation** (see chapter 3) and the collection of big data or survey data (see chapters 2 and 4) on behavioral patterns. In urban research, interviews are used to provide insight into how urban places, processes and interventions are differentially perceived and experienced by different social groups and stakeholders in the city.

For example, our study in the Canal Belt was originally triggered by expressions of discontent from residents about urban tourism – in angry letters to local newspapers and different forms of anti-tourism protests – at a time when politicians and city administrators still promoted tourism as an important resource for the urban economy. These different ways of talking and thinking about tourism – as resource or burden – contributed to growing frustration amongst residents about how the city was governed.

Urban professionals, residents and other stakeholders may thus attribute very different meanings to the city. These diverging understandings also trigger different responses, forming a potential source of conflict.

Interviewing can thus be used to uncover the motives, attitudes, considerations and experiences that guide people's actions and inform how they relate to and interact with each other. Like other qualitative methods, interviewing is based on a social constructivist paradigm, assuming that people play an active role in constructing and interpreting social reality from their own particular point of view (Flick et al., 2004). Interviews generate verbal accounts of people's thoughts and emotions, opinions, life histories, and experiences, which are captured in audio or video recordings or in written transcripts and can subsequently be analyzed. At the same time, it is important to note some limitations in interviewing. As Jerolmack and Khan (2014) note, there is often a discrepancy between what people say and what they ultimately do. One way of dealing with this is to combine interviews with observations (see chapter 3). Another strategy is to explicitly ask about behavior during the interview itself, either the respondent's own behavior or that of other people.

Developing the methodology: research sample

The next step in designing your research is to determine who you are going to interview. While quantitative research strives for statistical representativeness (requiring a research sample that reflects the composition of an entire population, see chapter 2) respondents for qualitative interviews are selected strategically on the basis of sharing a particular set of characteristics that are deemed relevant to the research question (Boeije, 2010). For example, this may include respondents involved in a particular neighborhood intervention, community-building initiative, or local sustainability project. Or respondents who display particular kinds of behavior that you want to understand, such as using particular modes of transport in the city, sending one's children to a mixed school, or voting for a particular political party. You may also select respondents who share specific background characteristics because you want to study the urban lifeworlds of specific social groups, such as homeless people, middle-class families, racial minorities, or expats.

In short, the researcher formulates specific selection criteria to form a coherent research sample, a process referred to as **purposive sampling**, **nonprobability sampling**, or **theoretical sampling**. Within this particular sample, however, it is important to ensure a certain degree of diversity in background characteristics in order to capture as much variation in experiences, attitudes, or preferences as possible. This is particularly important in exploratory research, when the researcher does not yet know exactly what the range of possible answers might be.

For example, the sample for our study on local impacts of urban tourism consisted of long-term residents in the Amsterdam Canal Belt, who were recruited via door-to-door purposive sampling and selected on the basis of having lived for at least 15 years. Within this sample, we ensured a variation in residents of different tenures (home-ownership and renting, serving as a proxy for different class positions) and residents differentially placed in the neighborhood. This variation helped to capture the different ways in which residents' sense of place may be affected by tourism. While residents living along touristic routes emphasized negative experiences of 'inappropriate' tourist behavior in public space (which they referred to as 'theme park' behavior), residents living in quiet corners were more concerned with the sheer number of tourists who - wandering or cycling along the canals - blocked their daily routes through the neighborhood. Different class positions turned out to be important in the different ways in which resident subsequently coped with negative impacts of tourism. More affluent residents would be able to escape the neighborhood – to summer homes or by traveling themselves – while less affluent residents would retreat from the neighborhood by esconcing themselves in their own homes and retreating to the back of the house.

In terms of sample size, the number of interviews cannot be fully pre-determined. It depends on what information is encountered in the field. When no new information comes up in interviews, your sample is sufficient to stop interviewing (Bryman, 2012). As a rule of thumb, academic researchers usually aim for 15–20 qualitative interviews to reach theoretical saturation. However, when respondents' stories diverge too much, this sample should be expanded. Conversely, if the scope of the project is more modest (i.e. in the case of student projects) or narrow (i.e. focusing on a very specific group of respondents) a smaller sample might be sufficient. In this respect, setting clear selection criteria for your research sample is fundamental: when the original criteria for purposive sampling are defined too narrowly, the researcher may miss the full range of experiences, meanings, or perspectives. If it is defined too broadly, the researcher will end up with an incoherent dataset.

Constructing an interview guide

The next step in developing your methodology is to draw up an interview guide, which serves to structure the conversation. **Interview guides** take different forms. They range from a pre-determined set of questions posed in a fixed sequence – referred to as **structured interviews** (Bryman, 2012) – to **semi-structured** or entirely **open interviews**, whereby the interviewer raises broad, open-ended questions (Legard et al., 2003). Interviews with urban stakeholders, like urban planners, housing professionals, local administrators, community organizers, and resident representatives, often tend to be more structured in nature. Such interviews focus on the interviewee's expertise and in-depth knowledge of, for example, a particular development project, policy or strategic city plan. Such respondents usually have a conscious strategic position in relation to the object of investigation and often they therefore have their own agenda for the interview.

More open interview guides are used when the researcher wants to find out what respondents consider important, letting them prioritize what they want to talk about, or when the respondent is asked to narrate a particular experience or incident from their point of view. This means that the researcher gives the interviewee a leading role in determining the scope and the sequence of topics. Probing questions are then used to expand, steer, or deepen the conversation (a technique which is discussed in more detail below). A distinction can be made between **thematic interviews**, which use an **item list** for follow-up questions on subthemes that are considered relevant to the research, and **narrative interviews**, where the first questions invites the respondent to tell a story and the rest of the interview is organized around asking for clarifications and specifications. In thematic interviews, topics for conversation are derived from the conceptual framework of the research. The core, general concepts are split into more specific subthemes which are operationalized into specific items. Sometimes these are formulated into explicit questions (in the case of a structured interview) or they are used for probing (in the case of a semi-structured or open interview).

Figure 5.1 on page 76 shows the semi-structured interview guide for the interviews with long term residents in the Amsterdam Canal District. An extensive literature study indicated that the core concept of belonging, in the left column, included different dimensions: emotional **belonging**, elective belonging (relating to identification with the neighborhood), and functional belonging (use of neighborhood resources). Each of these was operationalized into specific items, to be explored in the interviews.

One way to think about the interview guide is as a road map that helps the researcher to determine what avenues of conversation are worth following up on. At the same time, the guide should not be used as a blueprint that generates uniform interviews for each respondent. The interviewer may raise topical questions, but the respondent also directs the conversation through his/her answers. For the researcher, interviewing is thus always a balancing act between following and guiding the respondent (Flick et al., 2004, Weiss 1994). An important consideration in this respect is which topics the researcher wants to explicitly bring into the conversation and which topics are only addressed if the respondent introduces them him/herself.

For example, if one wanted to study resident experiences of neighborhood change – which was the focus of our Canal Belt study – different approaches are possible. In a fully open interview, the researcher would ask, 'How has the neighborhood changed?', opening up the conversation for a whole range of answers, ranging from 'Well, it is mostly the same' to 'It is all going down the drain' or 'Well, of course it looks much better, but you know … Those yuppies'. A more semi-structured approach would be to ask 'What aspects of the neighborhood have improved?' and 'What aspects of the neighborhood have declined?' or – even more structured – 'how has the composition of residents changed' or 'to what degree have facilities in the neighborhood changed'? In this last set of questions, the researcher introduces more specific topics that she wants to know about. For our Canal Belt study, we used an open approach, because we wanted to create room for different experiences of urban tourism.

The benefit of a more structured interviewing approach is that the interviewee will discuss all the topics that the researcher is interested in, but the drawback is that the researcher will not know whether the interviewee in fact attaches importance to these. There may also be a risk that the researcher introduces topics that are outside the cognitive scope of the interviewee. With a more open approach, it is likely that respondents will not address all the topics in the guide, simply because they do not think of it. However, rather than a methodological problem, this can be considered a finding, because it provides insight into the personal perspective of respondents. In short, different approaches generate different types of information. Ultimately, the choice for a more open or more structured interview guide is therefore determined by what the object of investigation is and how much knowledge the researcher already has on the topic.

A final aspect of constructing your interview guide is to consider how to precisely formulate questions that invite respondents to share their story. Open questions, starting with 'What', 'How' or 'Could you tell me something about...', are the best way to get your respondent talking and create room for them to explain and elaborate. Closed questions that allow for simple 'Yes' or 'No' answers or questions should be avoided. Questions that generate short factual answers – e.g. How many children do you have? How many years have you worked here? Where are you from? – are best saved for the end of the interview. In formulating your questions, you should also consider the type of respondent. 'Ordinary' residents – with little experience with, or affinity to, academic research – require a different approach than urban professionals with high levels of expertise (and often a strategic, political agenda that frames their answers). In both cases, it is important to phrase questions that fit the interviewee's frame of reference (Boeije, 2010). For non-experts, the aim is to pose short questions in understandable language. In stakeholder interviews, it is important to inform oneself beforehand of the more technical terms associated with the respondent's position or work and try to use their language of expertise. Yet in both cases, it is inadvisable to use academic, conceptual terms from one's theoretical framework. This means that an important step in finalizing your interview guide, before going into the field, is to do trial interviews. This can help to improve the clarity and sequence of questions as well as training the interviewer in working with this particular interview guide.

Figure 5.1: Interview guide, long term residents, Canal District.

	Items for probing	Notes
Introduction	• Explanation research theme • Explanation types of questions • Anonymity and privacy • Informed consent recording	

Residential biography	• Length of residence
	• Reasons for moving
	• Household situation at the time
	• Condition of the house at the time
	• Condition of the neighborhood at the time
	  – Material
	  – Social status
		Could you tell me when and how you came to live here?
		
		What was the neighborhood like at that time?

Belonging	• Emotional, feeling at home
	  – Sense of place
	  – Aesthetics
	  – Insider knowledge
	• Neighborhood as source of identity: being a local
	• Time spent in the neighborhood
	  – Versus time in the city
	  – Versus time away
	• Everyday use
	  – Neighborhood boundaries
	  – Meaningful places
	  – Local activities
	  – Mobility (walking, etc.)
	• Plans to move
	  – Reasons or considerations
	  – Where, alternatives
		How would you like living in the Canal District?
		
		Would you say you feel at home here?

Neighborhood as social space	• Neighbors
	  – Type of interactions
	  – Detailed knowledge
	• Local friends, befrinded residents
	• Familiar strangers, encounters
	• Broader social network
	  – Friends / family
	  – Sense of size
	  – Geographical scope
	• Social changes neighborhood over the years
		What is your relationship with your neighbors like?

▼

Neighborhood change

- Changes
  - Material
  - Resources
  - Rhythm
  - Public space
  - Social
- Sense-making, perceived causes
- Personal experiences
  - Concrete examples
- Evaluation
  - Ambivalences?

How has the neighborhood changed since you moved here?

How do you personally notice these changes?

What do you think of these changes?

Responses

- Coping strategies
  - At home
  - Avoidance in space & time
- Resident protest
  - Participation in collective action
  - Individual contributions
  - Evaluation
- What should be done?
  - Role of local government

How do you deal with these changes?

To what degree have you been involved in forms of protest?

What should be done about these changes/issues?

Background characteristics

- Age
- Gender
- Nationality
- Family living arrangement
- Educational background
  - Type of degree
  - Field of study
- Employment, type of work
- Net household income
- Housing
- Ownership situation
  - Monthly costs
  - Other expenses
- Notes on cultural capital
  - Home decorations

Income ranges
< € 33,000
€ 33,000 – € 43,000
€ 43,000 – € 50,000
€ 50,000 – € 66,000
€ 66,000 – € 100,000
> € 100,000

Ethical considerations and interview protocol

As preparation for entering the field, the next step is to write an interview protocol. This describes how you will communicate with respondents about a number of **ethical** and practical aspects of the research:

1   *The purpose of research*: formulate an introduction to the research topic in simple, everyday language, which is the same for all respondents. Avoid using theoretical concepts and do not include research expectations or your own interpretation about the phenomenon. This guarantees that the researcher does not 'steer' the conversation before the actual start of the interview and that all interviewees start with the same information.

2   *The process of interviewing*: describe how the interview will proceed. This includes explaining that everything that a respondent would like to tell you is appreciated (there are no 'good' or 'bad' answers), that you consider him/her the expert in this respect and that the respondent can at any time redirect the conversation if they do not want to talk about specific topics. This can help put the respondent at ease and shift the power balance from you as researcher to the respondent.

3   *Confidentiality and protection of data*: explain how you will ensure confidentiality and **anonymity** regarding the data storage and reporting. In the case of stakeholders who can easily be identified, anonymity may be difficult. Discuss with them how you will deal with this, for example by letting them approve the **transcripts** after the interview and guaranteeing access to the relevant sections of the research publication before it is made accessible to others. In the case of 'ordinary' respondents, this includes a discussion of how their stories will be used in such a way that they cannot be individually identified.

4   *Permission to record*: in case you want to record the interview, the interviewee should be asked for permission. While recording has become quite easy with current smart phones, making **transcribing** much easier, there may be reasons to decide against it. Not all respondents are comfortable with being recorded. This is particularly the case for video recording, when you are interviewing people online. Recording devices can also contribute to a more formal atmosphere in which respondents are worried about how they say things. Moreover, not all interview settings are conducive to recording, due to background noise, so the interviewer should always be prepared to work without.

5   *Informed consent*: the interviewer should ask the respondent for an explicit confirmation that he/she understands these practical and ethical aspects of the research and agrees to participate and allow you to share the findings. This should be done formally, for example by asking respondents to sign a consent form or by recording their confirmation (with their permission).

Going into the field

When the interview protocol is done, you are ready to approach your respondents. A first necessary step is to draft and distribute a formal text – in the form of a letter or e-mail – explaining who you are, the purpose of the research, and why they are the persons you would like to talk to. This helps to legitimize your position as researcher and to give potential respondents some time to consider whether they want to participate. It also helps to explain where and when interviews might be held (at the convenience of the respondent?) and how much time is needed. In the case of formal stakeholders and professionals, a good strategy is to e-mail first and subsequently follow-up via telephone. 'Ordinary' respondents can be contacted through social media, posters or handing out flyers in specific places, door-to-door sampling, or simply approaching people in public spaces. Of course, for each of these methods, it is important to consider how this might generate a selective sample. For example, reaching out to people through neighborhood institutions will generate a group of respondents who are most likely to be locally oriented in their everyday lives and have a particular view of the neighborhood. If respondents are recruited online, your sample will probably be skewed to social groups who are most active on the internet (younger, higher-educated). A final way to find respondents is to use **snowball-sampling**, by asking your first respondents to refer you to others. An important drawback of this strategy is that it can limit the variation in your sample (and therefore findings), because people tend to refer you to strong ties in their own network, who often most like themselves. This means that you should always use a number of different 'entry points' in snowball sampling.

In the case of face-to-face interviews, another practical consideration is to select the interview setting or location. Here, different considerations come into view. One option is to let the interviewee decide where they would feel most comfortable to do the interview. This can be their own home, but also other locations, ranging from community centers to coffee bars. An interesting option for research with a spatial focus is to conduct walking interviews in public space or site visits, which can generate rich place narratives (Evans & Jones, 2011). In choosing a location, you should consider how different settings might put the respondent at ease and provide enough privacy for the interview, without concerns of being overheard. For you as researcher, safety is an important consideration. In this respect, there are considerable cultural differences between countries and between social groups in whether it is considered appropriate for researchers to do interviews on their own. Moreover, this may also depend on the research population. Some universities do not allow single interviewing by students at all. As a rule, if you intend to do interviews alone, always make sure someone knows where you are and that you 'check in' when you are done. Moreover, always listen to your instincts: if you feel uncomfortable in an interview, you can cut it short. As an alternative, you can work with an interview team, whereby one team member has the role of interviewer and one has the role of taking notes.

The art of interviewing

Finally, it is time for interviewing. As discussed above, generating a rich and reliable data set can be quite challenging. There are different verbal and non-verbal techniques that interviewers can use to open up the conversation and to create room for respondents to tell their story. Beginning interviewers tend to think that interviewing is about asking questions, but in fact listening – perhaps better referred to as active and attentive listening – is an essential skill for interviewers.

The most important tasks for the interviewer is to shift the power balance in the conversation away from themselves to the interviewee. The aim is to make respondents feel at ease and provide them with the opportunity to share their experiences, expertise, and feelings. As Weiss (1994) notes, 'building trust' is fundamental to gain access to a respondent's thoughts and concerns. For this, non-verbal interviewing techniques are perhaps more important than the content of the questions you raise. Sitting with an open posture, making eye-contact, and nodding all serve to show the respondent that you are listening and interested in what they have to tell. While beginning interviewers often feel uncomfortable with silences in the interview and try to fill this with new questions, in fact having a moment of pause can give the respondent time to reflect and step into the silence with new information. A more verbal way in which you can show respondents that you are listening and interested in what they have to say is to summarize their ideas in your own words and adopt their terminology in the questions that you raise. Finally, showing empathy to emotions that sound through people's stories, such as happiness, concern, or fear, is essential to validate a respondent's experience and establish trust.

Non-verbal interviewing techniques	Verbal interviewing techniques
Sitting with open posture	Summarizing
Making eye contact	Adopting respondent vocabulary
Active listening, nodding	Empathizing, acknowledging emotions
Making sounds of confirmation (*hmm*-ing)	Posing questions
Showing empathy	Probing
Moments of silence	Using accessible language

The second task for the interviewer is to guide the conversation by asking questions in the right way. Start the interview with an easy, open question that gets the respondent talking about something that is familiar to them, but that is also relevant to the research.

This helps to set respondents at ease and puts them in the role of 'expert'. The interview guide (see figure 5.1) is then used for probing and introducing new topics. Probing is a technique whereby the interviewer helps the respondent to give a fuller account of their experiences or point of view. There are many different ways the interviewer can probe for more in-depth information (Legard et al., 2003). One way to get beyond a respondent's first general statement is by asking them to particularize (Weiss, 1994), for example by asking for concrete examples of something they experienced. This makes the topic more tangible and personal to the respondent. Probing may also involve raisings questions of clarification ('You mentioned ... can you tell me what you mean by that?' or 'Could you tell me a bit more about that?') or questions about inner feelings ('What do you think about that?' or 'How do you feel about that?'). Another probing technique is simply to repeat the original questions in the interview guide. This means asking questions like 'What are other reasons to ...?'or 'What are other problems you have encountered ...?'. This serves as a check for the interviewer as to whether the full range of experiences or arguments of the respondent have been covered.

There are different 'cues' that can help you identify when you need to probe for further information. Thematically, it is particularly important to pay attention to stories that you have not heard from other respondents. Any new information in an interview can expand the scope of you research and is thus a relevant avenue of conversation. Other cues are comments in which respondents evaluate situations, places, or social encounters as 'nice' or 'ridiculous' or 'uncomfortable', or when they use particular labels or classifications for places or people, such as 'This neighborhood is like a village', or 'Those people are just totally anti-social'. Another thing to look out for is when respondents repeat particular words or ideas. This signals a topic which is important to them and therefore may be worthwhile exploring further. Finally, as interviewer it is important to be responsive to non-verbal emotional responses, such as laughing, hesitation, or frustration, and to take notes during the interview to record such emotions. These will help you to interpret the verbal data during the analysis phase. Note that probing in response to expressed emotions should be done with care as some of these topics might be difficult for the respondent to talk about.

New topics from the interview guide should only be brought into the conversation, when one topic of conversation is exhausted through different forms of probing. Before doing so, however, the interviewer should ensure that he/she has interpreted the information provided by the respondent correctly by briefly summarizing the respondent's narrative. This allows the respondent to either confirm, correct, or expand on their argument. Summarizing can also be used as a form of probing. Of course, the effectiveness of all of these different interviewing techniques depends on the way in which questions and summaries are worded. Formulating coherent, easy and open questions on the spot is not so easy and takes practice. Important pitfalls to look out for are: raising more than one question at the same time, providing suggestions for possible answers, asking too many closed or short factual questions – resulting in a staccato conversation – stepping into the conversation as participant, and providing your own opinions (see Weiss, 1994, for an overview of such pitfalls). Lastly, when you have exhausted most of the topics you had in mind, you can wrap up the interview by asking the respondent whether – in addition to your own questions – there are any additional topics that they would like to discuss.

Finally, it is important to consider the medium through which you are interviewing. Many of the good practices discussed above have been developed in the context of face-to-face, on-site interviews. In the case of interviewing from a distance, for example by phone or online video calls, some of techniques are more difficult to mobilize, like the non-verbal interviewing techniques. It may also be difficult to capture the non-verbal expressions of your respondents. It is therefore even more important that you spend some time at the start of the interview to get acquainted and build trust. In addition, particularly for phone interviews, you want to pay extra attention to posing clear, relatively short, and neutral questions.

Processing your data while in the field

An additional aspect of interviewing is that the researcher should already start processing their interview experiences and data during fieldwork. To improve the reliability of the data, write a short reflection immediately after each interview. This should include a methodological and a substantive component. Methodologically, it is important to describe the setting of the interview, the overall tone of the conversation, emotions displayed by the respondent and your own personal experience of the interview. This information helps to interpret a respondents' comments in the stage of data analysis. Substantively, it is important to record any additional information that came up after the formal interview was finished and reflect on the content of the interview. Identify what seemed particularly important to this respondent and discuss how this particular interview may help you answer your research question and which new information should be followed up on in subsequent interviews. This substantive reflection is crucial to become aware of the variation in experiences and perspectives of respondents and determine when theoretical saturation is reached.

A second aspect of data processing is to transcribe some interviews while still in the field, transforming recordings or fieldwork notes into data that can later be analyzed and used in the research report in the form of quotes. Transcribing while in the field can help you to recognize interviewing pitfalls (do I talk too much? Ask double questions? Use too many difficult words?) and missed opportunities for probing. This can then be corrected in following interviews. Transcribed interviews can also be shared with other researchers to get some feedback to improve one's interviewing skills. Such a dialectical relationship between data collection and data analysis is a fundamental dimension of exploratory research aimed at theory-building.

For example, in our Canal Belt study, several themes – highlighted in yellow in figure 5.1 – were added to the interview guide during the stage of our fieldwork, because these seemed important additions to what was discussed in previous research.

Conclusion

By now you have probably realized that the description of interviews as 'guided conversations' is something of an understatement, making interviewing sound deceptively natural and easy. In fact, interviewing well takes a lot of preparation, practice, feedback, and reflection. The good news, however, is that developing your interviewing skills is something you can practice anywhere. Asking open questions and becoming attentive to cues for probing is valuable in many other work- and social settings outside of formal interview settings. Ultimately, becoming skilled in the art of interviewing can provide unique opportunities to gain an understanding of other people's lifeworlds. Such encounters can leave a lasting impression for you as researcher and, more broadly, contribute to a better understanding of the way in which urban spaces and places are lived, contested and valued.

In our own research, the interviews with residents in the Amsterdam Canal Belt provided insight in the substantial impact that urban tourism can have on the everyday lives of residents, diminishing their sense of home as a result of everyday disturbances by tourists' 'theme park' behavior and creating a sense of powerlessness in the face of fundamental structural changes in neighborhood facilities, housing and community. Their stories, captured in interviews, not only helped to understand current popular discontent with local government, but also provided new insights in individual coping strategies of avoidance, which may – somewhat paradoxically – ultimately further hollow out the city center as a residential neighborhood and transforming it into a tourist enclave.

References

Boeije, H. (2010). *Analysis in qualitative research*. London: Sage.

Bryman, A. (2012). *Social research methods*. 4th edition. Oxford: Oxford University Press.

Evans, J. & Jones, P. (2011). The walking interview: Methodology, mobility and place. *Applied Geography 31*(2), 849–858.

Flick, U., Von Kardorff, E., & Steinke, I. (2004). What is qualitative research? An introduction to the field. In U. Flick et al., *A companion to qualitative research*. London: Sage, pp. 3–11.

Hermanns, H. (2004). Interviewing as an activity. In U. Flick et al., *A companion to qualitative research*. London: Sage, pp. 209–213.

Jerolmack, C., & Khan, S. (2014). Talk Is Cheap: Ethnography and the Attitudinal Fallacy. *Sociological Methods & Research, 43*(2), 178–209.

Legard, R., Keegan, J., & Ward, K. (2003). In-depth interviews. In J. Ritchie & J. Lewis, *Qualitative research practice*. London: Sage, pp. 138–169.

Lofland, J., & Lofland, L. H. (1995). *Analyzing social settings*. 3rd edition. Belmont, CA: Wadsworth.

Pinkster, F.M., & Boterman, W.R. (2017). When the spell is broken: Gentrification, tourism and privileged discontent in the Amsterdam canal district. *Cultural Geographies 24*(3), 457–472.

Weiss, R.S. (1994). *Learning from Strangers: The art and method of qualitative interview studies*. New York: The Free Press.

6 Digging in the crates: Archival research and historical primary sources

Tim Verlaan

Introduction

Historians are particularly interested in the raw materials of the past – that is, the unprocessed and unedited or 'primary' sources produced by contemporaries, which can often only be found in archives. Thus, it should come as no surprise that the archive is the historian's favorite workplace. This is where they find their sources and come to experience what Johan Huizinga labelled the 'historical sensation' after discovering or revealing new facts (Huizinga, 1950, p. 71). Yet what happens to historians and their sources inside the archive usually stays within the archive. By examining the relationship between historians and their work behind the archival scenes, this contribution will reveal the implicit and explicit methodologies of the historian's craft. It will be demonstrated that primary sources hold no value without proper historical examination and contextualization. Gentrification, a popular topic in the field of urban studies, will serve as a case study to examine the advantages and pitfalls of adopting an archive-based approach to researching the city, with a focus on Amsterdam during the post-war period (1950–1990). This chapter aims to bring present-minded scholars and historians hesitant to work on recent topics together, and should be read as a guide to archival research and as a call to social scientists to investigate the 'when' of urban change with the same thoroughness which they employ to examine its 'where' (Suleiman, 2016, pp. 215–219).

When it comes to studying the evolution of cities, urban history has a natural advantage over historical subdisciplines interested in non-urban phenomena. Urban historians are bound together by an interest in space rather than a specific time period, and tend to agree with social scientists that spaces and buildings should be recognized as non-neutral: 'They shape lives, behaviour, perceptions and ultimately policy'. (Rodger & Sweet, 2008) In a recent urban history handbook, Shane Ewen asserts that '[s]ocial identities are constructed and enacted within space, acting upon the design and usage of that space, and involve the actions of property developers, financiers, governments, and residents themselves' (2016, p. 35). Besides a shared interest in the functioning and meaning of space, urban history and urban studies hold in common a belief in the value of comparison and interdisciplinarity: in both fields cities are studied from economic, social, political, and cultural perspectives (Tilly, 1996, p. 702). In addition, both the social and historical sciences have always been interested in the functioning, reproduction, and transformation of social relations (Sewell, 2005, p. 3), for which the city is a primary research area. As this contribution will demonstrate, historicizing urban phenomena such as **gentrification** has the potentional to bring not only time and space but also two disciplines closer together.

What is an archive, and what lurks inside?

Of all their methodologies, **archival research** is still the historian's first and last resort in his or her fact-finding and -checking missions. Archives are virtually always institutions open and free to members of the public, and intentionally or sometimes coincidentally collect traces of the past. Not only is it a physical site of knowledge production and a systematized repository of information (Arnold, 2000, p. 59), but it is also a mechanism for shaping the narratives of history as it decides on which sources are worth saving and sharing (Burton, 2005, p. 2). As traces of the past, **primary sources** come in many shapes and forms, but usually they concern written documents such as memoirs, government records, wills, letters, fiscal accounts, taxation documents, chronicle accounts, and court records. In comparison to other academic disciplines, the historical field is much more accessible to laypeople. It requires little equipment, no laboratories, only a limited number of research protocols and the concepts and terms historians use are relatively easy to understand (Maza, 2017, 118). Pad, pencil, and a laptop seem all a historian needs once he or she has located a relevant archive. Still, doing archive-based history is much more than simply collecting documents and writing stories.

All historians share a fascination with direct evidence, known to them as 'primary' sources. This fetishization of primary source materials – the gold standard of their discipline – came about in the early nineteenth century, when historical consciousness grew and German scholars in particular began advocating a more academic approach to the past. Indeed, the main task of the historian became to 'find out why people acted as they did by stepping into their shoes, by seeing the world through their eyes and as far as possible by judging it by their standards' (Tosh, 2010, p. 8). While the belief that historians can find truth in the archive has come under attack from postmodern scholars, who argue that meaning is put into a text by the reader and that all meanings are equally valid, there is still a consensus among historians that archives are the first place to look for cold hard facts (Evans, 1997, p. 95). Often without explicitly acknowledging this, they are empiricists by believing that true knowledge of the world comes from sense experiences and observations, which should inform hypotheses or theories rather than the other way around. Thus, historical research should ideally be impartial, underpinned by established facts, and guided by an inductive method of reasoning based on archival research (Davies, 2003, p. 4).

Where does the fact-hungry scholar interested in understanding the history of urban change begin? Obviously, the answer to this question depends on his or her research design, spatial focus, and time period. For the Middle Ages, for example, one will probably have to access church records, and this is where the archival researcher is faced with a first obstacle. During medieval times the church wielded as much authority as the state, and in many cases more (Tosh, 2010, p. 71). Contemporary events were usually documented by clerics, who had an interest in presenting their contemporaries as deeply religious. This is why an untrained reader of medieval sources might get the impression that the residents of medieval cities were extremely pious people, overly concerned with spiritual matters (Carr, 1964, p. 14). In a similar way, inhabitants of late nineteenth- and early twentieth-century nation states often seemed obsessed with national pride. Here one needs to put things into perspective as well, as the professionalization of the historical discipline during the nineteenth century was very much biased towards the rising nation state. National archives came into existence and survived because their contents were indispensable to newly-minted states, which needed archival records to collect taxes or set precedents in law-making (see also chapter 2 on quantitative data collected by nation states).

More in general, archives are biased towards lettered individuals and movements who thought of themselves as changing the course of history. This makes colonial archives self-evidently subject to power relations as well. Until recently, such institutions collected sources produced by the oppressors rather than the oppressed and thus left the latter voiceless. Natural or man-made disasters can inflict serious damage to archival materials, as exemplified by the collapse of Cologne's city archives in 2009 and the burning down of the National Museum of Brazil in 2018. Thus, the first questions an unsuspecting visitor to the archives should ask concern their origins, whether they have been subject to regime change, and who decides which documents are to be preserved (Maza, 2017, pp. 149–150). Indeed, archives have dynamic relationships not just with the past and present but also with the fate of regimes, the physical environment, the serendipity of bureaucrats, and the care and neglect of archivists (Burton, 2005, p. 6).

Besides the aforementioned church and national state archives, urban scholars can resort to city archives, newspaper repositories, university libraries, the archives of private firms, and personal archives. Self-evidently, the latter two are most prone to inconsistencies and gaps in the records. During the second half of the twentieth century the growing interest of historians in social and economic themes, which are often urban topics as well, led to the proliferation of city archives. Nowadays every self-respecting city and town has its own municipal archive, although their services are under continuous threat of budget cuts. In some cases, records are confident or have restricted access and require permission from the person or institution who granted the archive their records, which can be a time-consuming effort. An official letter in which the historian explains the indispensability of accessing restricted source materials for the greater good will usually convince the rightholders of a particular archive. Recently the founding of independent and participatory archives, setup by marginalized groups in urban societies who contribute with everyday life experiences and objects, has opened up a new range of research possibilities (Houtekamer, 2015, pp. 28–31). By contrast with 'official' archives, these repositories are often run by volunteers, meaning researchers have to be more understanding and patient when making use of their services. In summary, the first step of historical research consists of locating the archive, establishing its origins and the reasons why it has survived.

Setting foot in murky waters

The second step is getting a grip on the full extent of the sources available. Nowadays this can be done from home, as the vast majority of national and local archives offer online access to their inventories – provided an archivist has taken the trouble of storing and labeling the source materials. Moreover, a rapidly increasing number of written sources is now digitized, granting researchers archival access whenever and wherever they want. As information might get lost in the digitization of written sources and not all transcription software is equally sophisticated, these digital repositories should not be taken at face value. Still, making newspaper databases available online, for example, has drastically cut back the research time of historians working on topics situated in the nineteenth and/or twentieth century. Since late 2013 the Delpher website, launched by the Dutch National Archives, enables researchers to digitally access a vast and expanding collection of historical books, newspapers, magazines, and radio broadcasts (Sanders, 2015, p. 3). However, most historians will urge you to leave your comfortable office chair and actively search and visit specific archives. In addition, for less generic source materials that are not digitally accessible yet, such as the minutes of a city council meeting or a planning memorandum, a physical visit to the archive is required anyway.

Upon the first visit one needs to bring identification and sometimes even a bank statement – archives are rightfully afraid of damage or even thievery. Further essentials are a writing pad and pencil to take notes (pens are usually not allowed), a laptop for transcribing, and a camera in case of time restraint (taking photos of original source materials is virtually always allowed).

Inside the archive, the experienced researcher is time-efficient and inquisitive at the same time. Whereas some historians would still suggest to let the archival findings inform your queries and recommend a 'broad-fronted attack' upon all the relevant material (Green & Troup, 1999, p. 3), today it is common practice to have research questions formulated beforehand. There is a maximum number of items you can simultaneously request, so it is wise to fill in another call slip and politely send the archivist for a new file after returning one. While there seems to be a clear division of labor between archivists and historians, with the first locating the sources and the latter putting them to use, it is advisable to be nice and friendly to the gatekeepers of your raw materials. Here, social skills are as important as the craft of crate digging. Getting local archivists on your side will definitely expedite the research process.

Try not to be overwhelmed by the immense volume of materials available and scan rather than read, take note of the files you will come back to, and be creative in your use of keywords when searching in the archival databases (Steedman, 2013, pp. 25–26). Do not collect your sources all at once, but ensure that your reading is guided and directed by your writing. For example, if you discover that the growing number of students in Amsterdam during the 1960s might have spurred gentrification during later decades, it makes sense to investigate the university archives and take extensive notes on their contents as well. As Edward Carr puts it: 'The more I write, the more I know what I am looking for, the better I understand the significance and relevance of what I find' (1964, p. 28). Thus, research questions and original research objectives should continuously be sharpened by the textual processing of archival findings, and vice versa – a form of inductive reasoning specific to (urban) historians and by extent the humanities.

Historians are often compared to detectives searching for evidence, or journalists weighing sources against each other. The assessment of source materials is just as important as the quest for the places where they are archived. In general, one can opt for consulting all the available sources on any given topic or one can choose to examine sources from a problem-oriented approach in which sideroads are carefully avoided, but 'vital evidence' might be missed. Obviously this is a trade-off between comprehensiveness and quick results. For example, if one limits the timeframe of a study into the history of gentrification from the 1960s until the 1980s, one might miss the first signs of neighborhood change in the 1950s. In the same vein, focusing on just one neighborhood will decrease the study's significance to those scholars unacquainted with local circumstances. A rule of thumb here is that the more sources one can consult, the better, even for those researchers working outside of the historical discipline (Elton, 1967, p. 66).

Having a source in front of you, the third step should be to determine how, when, and why it came into being. Be aware of how representative the source is for the topic you are investigating, the hidden biases of the author, and the possibility of historical gaps. The older the source, the more likely it was produced by a member of the literate elite (Green & Troup, 1999, p. 5). The material should be tested for authenticity and reliability by tracing it back to the original author(s), for example by looking for the same source in different inventories, and by double checking for consistency with known facts, which can be done by consulting secondary sources on the same subject. After this, we need to determine the intentions and prejudices of the author, although bias does not necessarily make the source worthless and can be studied on its own merits (Tosh, 2010, pp. 88–113). Obviously, researchers themselves are also influenced by the present in which they work by using contemporary terms and tools (Carr, 1964, p. 24). Last, but not least, we must establish the historical context in which a source was published by reading secondary sources about the period or topic under research in question, and by collecting additional primary sources that can corroborate preliminary findings (Elton, 1967, p. 66). Only after these three steps have been taken the researcher can sit down and begin compiling his or her findings into a coherent narrative, either as a historical thesis on itself or as the historical background to a broader study.

Case study: The history of gentrification

Urban historians are often present-minded in choosing a research topic. Research questions are usually formulated based on current events, such as the growing importance of **gentrification** for how cities function. As any other urban development, gentrification has a long and multifaceted history. The early stages of gentrification are rarely examined by gentrification scholars, who are usually not steeped in the tradition of archival research and seem only marginally interested in urban affairs predating their own generation, treating these as a mere prelude to contemporary developments. In a best-case scenario, they will agree that history matters because events in the past obviously influence the present. On the other hand, historians seem wary of using the term and might consider the post-war decades too recent for proper historical research, as its contemporaries are still with us today and its primary sources still need to be inventoried (Reick, 2018, pp. 2542-2558; Osman, 2011; Moran, 2007, pp. 101-121). As this final paragraph will demonstrate, researching the history of gentrification can put present-day debates into a historical perspective and makes us better understand the current dynamics of gentrification, as these are often driven by similar politics of cultural authenticity and property mechanisms as those of the recent past.

Step 1: Literature review and finding the relevant archive

The increasing popularity of urban living is one of the most striking phenomena of our time, radically transforming residential, consumption, and investment patterns. Consequently, gentrification has become a key term in academic and popular debates. As in all academic fields, historians kickstart their research by conducting a literature review, usually by 'snowballing' through the footnotes of recent publications on a particular topic. By doing so they will learn that it is only since the last three decades that major Western cities have come to experience substantial demographic growth again. From the end of the Second World War to the mid-1980s, most cities were undergoing an unprecedented loss of both residents and jobs. Simultaneously, throughout most of this period, local governments pursued an agenda of urban redevelopment in which outdated tenement houses and vacant factory buildings would be replaced with modern tower blocks, office complexes and shopping centers (Klemek, 2011). Yet for a rapidly growing city-oriented cohort of artists, students and young professionals, the older structures that had to make way for modernism represented a more authentic and suitable living environment. Their arrival in central districts, which they came to defend against the onslaught of urban redevelopment, set in motion a process we have come to call gentrification, but this is not how historians have told the story so far.

After our literature review, we need to formulate a hypothesis for the scarce historical attention. Based on the secondary sources, we can hypothesize that gentrification was poorly visible in government records because the process was initially not a matter of official policy.

Another hypothesis might be the lack of data on the professions and consumption behavior of local residents, which in the case of Amsterdam is either inaccessible due to privacy issues, or non-existent in the first place due to poor record keeping.

Thus, we are forced to draw on qualitative sources such as municipal surveys and reports, minutes of meetings by government bodies, neighborhood, art and heritage associations, as well as newspaper and lifestyle magazines (compare with the methods of institutional analysis in chapter 8). Examples of useful information we might find here include the alliances between early gentrifiers and media, cultural and political institutions as well as how the latter actors appreciated their arrival. The advantage over quantitative data, which are more often the geographer's weapon of choice (see e.g. chapter 2), is that these sources allow us to explore how contemporaries actually experienced the first stirrings of gentrification – another example of how the humanities are first and foremost interested in how people give meaning to the world surrounding them. By examining a wide array of unexplored primary sources, we supplement the work of our colleagues in the field of urban studies and simultaneously satisfy fact-hungry historians.

Where will we find such sources? From our literature review we might find interesting access points and archival inventories, which in the case of Amsterdam will probably direct us to its comprehensive and easy-to-use city archive. Here we can access minutes of political meetings and community action groups discussing the onset of gentrification. To examine the experiences of early gentrifiers and learn about their lifestyles and consumption behavior, we could resort to Delpher's repository of digital newspapers and magazines.

Second step: Getting grip on the primary sources
Preliminary results from Delpher will demonstrate how the Jordaan, a working-class neighborhood to the west of the urban core, quickly became the epicenter of Amsterdam's bohemian scene. Admiring the influx of aspiring young artists, already in 1970 art critic Hans Redeker spoke of the neighborhood's 'resurrection' as a center for artistic production (*Algemeen Handelsblad*, 9 January 1970). Another newspaper detailed how former manufacturing spaces were converted into residential use or refurbished as ateliers (*De Tijd*, 1973). It was not only affordable housing and cheap working spaces that attracted a younger generation to the Jordaan. According to architecture critic Simon Mari Pruys, here one could be truly free and

experience a social cohesion lost in other parts of Amsterdam (*Algemeen Handelsblad*, 14 March 1970). These reflections, published by contemporary newspapers, demonstrate how during the second half of the 1960s the Jordaan was already becoming a vestige of social and cultural authenticity, thus setting the scene for its gentrification in subsequent decades.

If we want the full picture, avoiding an exclusive focus on early arrivals (the latter often being the case in gentrification studies), we should also investigate the understudied responses of facilitators on the supply-side of urban housing markets, which might concern policy makers, heritage preservation groups, homeowners, and property developers. This part of the research is more challenging, as private institutions are usually not very keen on peeping scholars, but we could start by requesting the minutes of city council meetings at our university library. These are well-documented and since such meetings have always been open to the public, their records are as well. The public minutes and memoranda will reveal where, when, and how gentrification might have originated in Amsterdam by detailing concerns raised by residents and the responses from their representatives.

From here we can trace the activities of private entrepreneurs, who should be approached carefully – preferably with an official request letter in hand from a senior scholar. Underline the historical importance of the company or institution, and make it crystal clear that without their support the pieces of the puzzle will never fall into place. Reassure them by stating that you value their privacy and sensitive materials, and grant company representatives the right to authorize your written work. If these endeavors are unfruitful, you can always fall back on oral history – a relatively young subdiscipline that aims to recreate the past by interviewing contemporaries (Tosh, 2010, pp. 310–338). However, it should be emphasized here that interviewing contemporaries and fact-checking their observations is a notoriously time-consuming line of historical work (see chapter 5 for this method in particular).

Third step: Determining the sources' origins

After collecting the sources, which, as suggested above, should be reciprocal with the writing process, we can assess the value of the materials in front of us. For recent historical events such as the genesis of gentrification, the sources are usually abundant, meaning this final part of the research should be conducted by means of selection and by making deliberate choices (Elton, 1967, p. 61), for example by only focusing on the Jordaan instead of the nineteenth-century districts surrounding the city's canal belt. Edward Carr compares facts to fish swimming about in a vast and sometimes inaccessible ocean of archival materials: 'What the historian catches will depend, partly on chance, but mainly on what part of the ocean he or she chooses to fish in and what tackle he or she chooses to use' (Carr, 1964, p. 23). When we extend this metaphor, researchers should not only inspect the catch of the day, but also wonder about those fishes that passed by or were let off the hook. In other words: be aware of gaps in the records. In a different analogy, Stephen Davies compares historians working in the archives to children in a vast play room, surrounded by piles of plastic bricks which they fit together to form shapes (2003, p. 7). Such metaphors underline the importance of preparatory work, the thoroughness by which we should determine whether our facts fit the historical narrative, and the reproducibility of our quest for the holy historical grail. Historians are known for their abundant use of footnotes, which makes their work falsifiable and reproducible.

Conclusion

While this chapter focuses on a fairly recent urban phenomenon, its findings apply to other case studies of historical urban change as well. By means of briefly discussing the history of gentrification in Amsterdam as a case study, it has become clear which added understandings historical research and archival data can bring to the study of cities. It should be emphasized here that the following conclusions are only preliminary and/or expected outcomes of our research project – it is up to the reader to bring this potential research project into fruition.

Firstly, we might learn that current debates about the growing unaffordability of cities and changing consumption patterns have a long and path-dependent history. Secondly, it might become clear how gentrification occurs in long waves instead of eruptions – something geographers increasingly acknowledge, albeit with scant historical evidence. Thirdly, we might get to know more about how contemporaries actually experienced and interpreted their living environment, which might also offer a sobering perspective on current events. Indeed, Amsterdam's inner-city neighborhoods and central districts in other Western conurbations have seen affluent residents arriving for more than five decades now. By engaging with theories such as gentrification, historians can potentially adjust existing theories and make social scientists aware of the gaps or inconsistencies in their knowledge and how it is produced (Sewell, 2005, p. 5). For the more activistic scholars amongst us, the history of gentrification in Amsterdam might also demonstrate how local residents have successfully protested against the process, and thus can learn from action strategies of the past as well.

More generally, this chapter has shown that the historical discipline has its own distinct but often implicit methods and sources, and that the task of a historian is to deconstruct myths about the past and to recognize similarities and differences. Newly discovered facts and new interpretations of known historical facts can tell us where urban societies come from and might tell us where they are headed. If anything, history tells us that developments are never linear and that they might turn in unforeseen directions, as exemplified in this chapter by the rather unexpected gentrification of the Jordaan amidst the urban crisis of the 1960s and 1970s.

Historical research is not without its limitations. Working in the archives is often a time-consuming endeavor, and you might not always find answers to the research questions you posed beforehand; allow extra time for trial and error. Quantitative data on the recent past is often unavailable due to privacy reasons or poor recordkeeping. And due to its **empirical** nature and the use of unique primary sources, historical research is often difficult to falsify or reproduce by outsiders. Historical research can nevertheless be uniquely rewarding. As historians often proclaim, the past is a foreign country. But like countries and cities, the past can be visited and learned from. One other mantra is that history does not repeat itself, but it often rhymes. Although people never seem to learn from history, we should definitely keep trying, or as Eric Hobsbawm has observed: 'It is the business of historians to try and remove [the blindfolds of history as inspiration and ideology], or at least to lift them slightly or occasionally – and, insofar as they do, they can tell contemporary society some things it might benefit from, even if it is reluctant to learn them' (Hobsbawm, 1997, p. 47).

References

Algemeen Handelsblad. (9 January 1970). Surrealist Podulke en zijn N.V.

Algemeen Handelsblad. (14 March 1970). De Bijziendheid van de Stadsopruimers.

Arnold, J. H. (2000). *History: A Very Short Introduction*. Oxford: Oxford University Press.

Burton, A. (2005). Introduction: *Archive fever, archive stories. In A. Burton (ed.) Archive stories: Facts, fictions, and the writing of history*. Durham: Duke University Press, pp. 1–24.

Carr, E. H. (1964). *What is history?* Harmondsworth: Penguin Books.

Davies, S. (2003). *Empiricism and history*. Basingstoke: Palgrave Macmillan.

De Tijd. (6 June 1973). Amsterdamse Pakhuizen in Britse Greep.

Elton, G. R. (1967). *The practice of history*. London: Methuen.

Evans, R. J. (1997). *In defence of history*. London: Granta Books.

Ewen, S. (2016). *What is urban history?* Cambridge: Cambridge University Press.

Green. A., & Troup, K. (1999). *The houses of history: A critical reader in twentieth-century history and theory*. Manchester: Manchester of University Press.

Hobsbawm, E. (1997). *On history*. London: Weidenfeld and Nicolson.

Houtekamer, M. (2015). Het Performatieve Archief: Participatief Verzamelen in de Bijlmer. *Archievenblad 119*(2), 28–31.

Huizinga, J. (1950). *Geschiedwetenschap en hedendaagsche cultuur. Verzameld werk VII*. Haarlem: Tjeenk Willink.

Klemek, C. (2011). *The transatlantic collapse of urban renewal: Postwar urbanism from New York to Berlin*. Chicago: University of Chicago Press.

Maza, S. (2017). *Thinking about history* (Chicago: University of Chicago Press, 2017)

Moran, J. (2007). Early cultures of gentrification in London, 1955–1980. *Journal of Urban History, 34*(1), 101–121.

Osman, S. (2011). *The invention of brownstone Brooklyn: Gentrification and the search for authenticity in postwar New York*. Oxford: Oxford University Press.

Osman, S. (2016). What time is gentrification? *City & Community, 15*, 215–219.

Reick, P. (2018). Gentrification 1.0: Urban transformations in late-19th-century Berlin. *Urban Studies, 55*(11), 2542–2558.

Rodger, R., & Sweet, R. (2008). The changing nature of urban history. In *History in focus: The city*, at: www.history.ac.uk /ihr/focus/city/articles/sweet.html.

Sewell, W. H. (2005). *Logics of history: Social theory and social transformation*. Chicago: University of Chicago Press.

Sanders, E. (2015). *Digitaal gouddelven bij de KB (Koninklijke Bibliotheek)*. The Hague: Koninklijke Bibliotheek.

Steedman, C. (2013). 'Archival methods', in G. Griffin (ed.) *Research methods for English studies*. Edinburgh: Edinburgh University Press, pp. 18–31.

Tilly, C. (1996). What good is urban history? *Journal of Urban History 22*(6), 702–719.

Tosh, J. (2010). *The pursuit of history: Aims, methods and new directions in the study of modern history*. Harlow: Pearson Longman.

7 Reading spaces: A cultural analysis approach

Daan Wesselman

In the past century of studying the city in the social sciences, it has become a commonplace to observe that the city has important immaterial qualities. To give a classic example, in his book *The Image of the City* (1960), urban planner Kevin Lynch concluded that 'we need an environment which is not simply well organised, but poetic and symbolic as well. It should speak of the individuals and their complex society, of their aspirations and their historical tradition, of the natural setting, and of the complicated functions and movements of the city world' (p. 119). The social sciences have always recognized that the city should be understood as representation, as speaking of something beyond its immediate materiality.

This is where *cultural analysis* can come in: it is an **interdisciplinary** approach within the humanities, developed particularly at the Amsterdam School for Cultural Analysis at the University of Amsterdam, that focuses on reading cultural practices and objects as a way of asking larger socio-cultural and political questions. Cultural analysis can be characterized succinctly as a combination of cultural studies and the practice of **close reading** inherited from literary studies. Two features of cultural studies should be highlighted here. Firstly, it is not limited in what type of object is studied (whereas literary studies focuses on literature, film studies on film, etc.). Cultural studies looks at anything that can be understood as a representation. For example, a perfume ad can convey stereotypes of femininity and sexuality, and a fur coat or a second-hand leather jacket can express class or subcultural affiliation. Secondly, cultural studies approaches have a Marxist critique of power relations in their DNA. The work of Gramsci on hegemony is key, as is Althusser's on ideology, but so are later developments in critical race studies, feminist theory, and postcolonial studies, for example. Cultural studies does not analyze objects and practices merely to disinterestedly 'understand' them, but because there is something at *stake* in meaning, representation, and culture, something that matters politically, especially when focusing on people who are pushed to the margins by dominant power relations.[1]

To the socio-cultural and political concerns and diversity of objects from cultural studies, cultural analysis notably adds the importance of close reading. This is a method drawn from literary studies, of which the basic premise is that the meaning of a text – and by extension any representational object of study – is never obvious, so reading requires close attention. For example, reading a fourteen-line sonnet takes more time than reading a fourteen-line newspaper report. A poem's meanings may not be apparent upon first reading, and its resonances and ambiguities require further interpretation. The same applies when analyzing urban spaces and objects as representations. You 'read' a space in order to get beyond its surface, which takes time and close attention, and is *interpretative* in nature. A classic connection here is ethnographer Clifford Geertz's *The Interpretation of Cultures* (1973), for whom the meaning of cultural practices and phenomena is brought out through 'thick description' – as opposed to 'thin', merely factual, description – which explores all layers of associations and implication. Like **thick description** (see chapter 3), close reading emphasizes the scholar's active role: you *construct* a reading. Your interpretative activity, therefore, is not receptive but productive; it is an act of writing.

In this chapter, I present two tools from the cultural analysis methodology – semiotics and discourse analysis – for analysing representations in and of an urban space. The space of De Hallen serves as my case study and the **aesthetics** of **gentrification** are my main concern. **Semiotics** allows me to decode the 'messages' conveyed by a selection of elements from within the space of De Hallen; **discourse analysis** enables a broader overview of the rhetorical shaping of the space. Together these analyses make it possible to critically unpack the political dimension of the aesthetics of gentrification.

Object, concerns, and research questions

De Hallen is a former tram depot that has been converted into a 'vibrant center for fashion, art, culture, f & b [food and beverages] and craft' (De Hallen, n.d.), which includes a food court, a cinema, restaurants, shops, events, and a library. Following lengthy renovations after the complex ceased to function as a tram depot in 1996, De Hallen opened in 2014 and has become, at the time of writing in 2019, a successful fixture in Amsterdam's landscape of culture, food, and shopping.

[1] For further reading: a key book on the methods of cultural analysis is Bal (2002), one of the founders of the Amsterdam School for Cultural Analysis; for an introduction to the concerns of cultural studies, see Hall (2019) and Williams (2005).

This description might sound familiar as a textbook case of a site of gentrification. Gentrification is a profoundly political matter, quite literally a question of who owns the city - in terms of real estate, for example (see the chapter 9) - but also in terms of everyday life and ordinary practices: who is included or excluded in a place like De Hallen, who is it *for*? Analyzing a site like De Hallen is important with a view to understanding gentrification's exclusionary dynamics.

Figure 7.1: De Hallen, Hannie Dankbaarpassage (main hallway) (photo by author)

The politics of gentrification are usually not overtly stated or policed. For example, there is no security guard or ticket vendor at the entrance to De Hallen who determines who has access, but such places communicate, through their aesthetic appearance, who has a place there. They usually adopt a recognizable aesthetic that is 'legible' for users through a socially and culturally maintained system of codes. My aim in analyzing De Hallen is to inquire into these codes, because they appear simple on the surface - a certain fashionable 'look' - but they are exclusionary in much more understated and inapparent ways, signalling *who does not have a place* in De Hallen. The critique of gentrification can thus be supported through analysis of these codes. This conceptualization of gentrification in terms of inclusionary/exclusionary codes underpins my choice for De Hallen as object of analysis, since it foregrounds aesthetics and thereby the codes of gentrification so clearly, in line with the literature.

One should also recognize that the aesthetics of gentrification - like its practices and politics - are rarely total. Exclusion is not the only thing taking place in a site like De Hallen. For example, there is a public library, activities for children and freely accessible events, which all cater to people who need not be gentrifiers. Likewise, not all signs in De Hallen communicate the exclusionary dynamics of gentrification. Nonetheless, on the basis of familiarity with the literature, I argue that gentrification and its exclusionary dynamics are the *dominant* feature of De Hallen – it is what characterizes the space the most. So while exclusionary dynamics are overtly the stakes for my approach, my analysis does not purport to reduce De Hallen entirely to that; there are always other stories to be told as well. In sum, for my case study of De Hallen, my overarching cluster of related research questions is therefore: *What aesthetics can be seen to be at work in De Hallen? What do these aesthetics represent?* and *How can visual and discursive processes of signification contribute to the politics of gentrification in De Hallen?*

Object selection, research questions, and analytical toolkit

As with all qualitative research, the cultural analysis approach hinges on how convincing your reading is. Two factors are crucial: selection of your object, and identifying details within your object that speak to your object as a whole. These matters are best explained in relation to a case.

I take De Hallen in Amsterdam as an example of a site of gentrification (see chapter 6). De Hallen follows a formula familiar from global trends in gentrification: redevelopment of a disused site, foregrounding culture and (upmarket) consumption (see Cameron & Coaffee, 2005; Zukin & Braslow, 2011; Chang, 2016). While some scholars view gentrification positively (for critical reviews, see Slater, 2006; Lees, 2008; Chaskin & Joseph, 2013), the literature makes abundantly clear that gentrification processes lead to increasing rents and real estate prices, advancement of the middle classes, and thereby to the displacement of the urban poor and increasing inequality.

Gentrification is also a matter of representation and meaning. In addition to economic factors – like the price of a sandwich – gentrification crucially involves *aesthetics*, for instance in the type of activities that are foregrounded (for analyses of the aesthetics of gentrification, focusing on consumption and a middle-class aesthetic disposition based on the work of Bourdieu, see Bridge, 2001; Ley, 2003; Lees, Slater & Wyly, 2008). But this aesthetic dimension also crucially involves the 'look' of a place itself.

But how can I assess whether a specific research site, place or object like the Hallen is a *good* example of a space of gentrification? Here, one must recognize what cultural analysis can, cannot, and wants to do. Analyzing the aesthetics of a site, place, or object is not predicated on 'proving' anything. The logic of cultural analysis is predicated on *argumentation* more than on proof, so the testing ground is whether analysis is convincing. A crucial factor here is the selection of objects and details that you analyze. Apart from addressing your broader concerns (for me: De Hallen as site of gentrification), the details from that space should be distinctive for your object and representative for it as a whole. This provides you with freedom – and responsibility – in selecting objects, but you cannot cherry pick your objects simply to suit your argument. The quality and plausibility of your reading rests on your judgement of the representativeness of your object selection.

Selection of objects

For the analysis of a space like De Hallen, it is important to identify representative details that you would not find elsewhere in the same configuration. For me that was the tram tracks in the floor, but you might start with something else - though starting with the designer hamburgers in the Foodhallen, for example, would be less productive: while certainly a sign of gentrification, they are not particularly distinctive for De Hallen.

Given my concern with the aesthetics of gentrification, I was primed to look for elements that produce a distinctiveness for De Hallen - its 'look', its 'story' - in such a way that they ignore or distort certain relations (e.g. the ignoring of the local, the slippage in the relation to the market outside). Yet what you incorporate in your analysis also depends on the 'story' you want to tell. To illustrate possibilities, I selected a material object (the tracks), a representation (the website) and an instance in the discourse on the Foodhallen.

Lastly, understanding gentrification as aesthetically coded also calls for specific analytical tools. In this chapter, I will briefly illustrate two: semiotics and discourse analysis. In a nutshell, semiotics is the study of signs, which tries to break down a representation – be it a text, an image, or a space – into distinct elements and trace what these elements mean.[2] Semiotic analysis is built on the idea that a sign has a surface appearance and a straightforward ('denotative') meaning, but also appeals to codes operating less overtly through associated meanings ('connotation'). Semiotics can thus be understood as a way to 'access' the codes of culture, moving from the surface appearance of individual signs to their underlying system of meanings.

Semiotics can be complemented with discourse analysis, which can be thought of as analyzing patterns in a broader domain of texts – in a sense, this is not unlike archival research (see chapter 6). In brief, discourse analysis looks at a range of actual expressions – e.g. in newspapers and on blogs, as I have done – in order to get at the broader practices that structure and govern how certain topics are spoken

---

2   For semiotic analysis, the work of Roland Barthes is indispensable – e.g. his classic *Mythologies* (1972 [1957]). A specialized field of 'urban semiotics' never really took off, but a worthwhile example is still Gottdiener and Lagopoulos (1986).

about, for example, what is colloquially understood as 'public debate' on an issue.[3] In practice, it involves assembling a 'corpus' of materials which you analyze for recurring patterns. Taken together, semiotics and discourse analysis can be thought of as combining micro- and macro-levels of analyzing meanings that are at work in a space.

Denotation and connotation

For example, a bicycle with a price tag outside a shop (see figure 7.2) obviously denotes a bicycle shop, but other less 'functional' elements – e.g. the leather on the handlebars or the retro color of the frame – clearly align with a style or code associated with upmarket aesthetics (again, in line with the literature on aesthetics and gentrification).

Figure 7.2: De Hallen, Hannie Dankbaarpassage (main hallway) (photo by author).

Analyzing aesthetics and discourse

So where does one begin analyzing the aesthetics? Simple: you go there, spend time in the space, and observe (without the aim to participate, as discussed in chapter 3). You will likely find that there are many things that speak to you, or speak of what goes on in the space. Spaces do not have a clear 'starting point' for analysis (what would you do with a space like De Hallen, which has multiple entrances?), so bring a notepad and a camera if possible, make sure you slow down, look closely, and let yourself be receptive to details that you might not otherwise notice. Importantly,

---

3   Discourse analysis in this vein is heavily indebted to the work of Michel Foucault (2002). For a general introduction, see Mills (1997).

cultural analysis is not done in broad strokes; you need to ground yourself in the details of your object. Moreover, it is impossible to deal with all facets or details of any space – nobody would expect you to – so the key is to select representative details that speak to your object as a whole. After all, interpreting details serves to make an argument about the whole, not about the details themselves.

But once you have identified distinct and representative details for a space, what do you base your further selection on? In this chapter, even though I can only briefly address a few objects, my choices are guided by what I want to argue, motivated by my critical perspective on the exclusionary nature of gentrification. Exclusion tends not to work through signs that literally say 'We are not looking to attract lower-middle-class people', but more subtly or insidiously. This is why semiotics and discourse analysis are apt tools for my questions: they are micro- and macro-level tools for getting beyond surface meanings, at codes that govern perceptions and power relations. But this is only one of many possible analyses, of course. You might want to make a different argument, for instance based on a person's experience (e.g. a more phenomenological approach), or focus more on the architecture and materiality than I did in the case of De Hallen, which steers you towards different objects (De Hallen is densely packed with signs). The crucial thing, therefore, is to align your argumentative goals and your objects of analysis.

While semiotics hinges on the interpretation of detail, the more 'macro-level' analysis of the discourse about a space requires a broader approach. You compile a larger representative set of 'utterances', which can be texts like newspaper articles and blogs, but also tweets or social media posts, or visual materials like photographs or ads. Once you ensure that you are not analyzing an isolated utterance but a broader pattern (of rhetoric, metaphor, linguistic structure, etc.), the next step is to also look beyond the surface: what is *not* being said, what assumptions underlie the recurring discourse? Patterns in discourse produce norms, often through unsaid or understated means, for example by leaving out groups of people (e.g. women, minorities, or the poor) from what is being said. An important added value of discourse analysis lies in exploring how power relations – such as the exclusionary politics of gentrification – are reproduced in discourse through repetition of normalizing patterns.

Analysis of a material object as sign

For a reused space like De Hallen, the reuse itself is what draws my attention particularly. Inside you can clearly see that De Hallen is a former tram depot: there are tram tracks everywhere. On either side of the concrete floor, old rails are still in place (see figure 7.1). But are they really remnants left in place? I would argue that there is something odd or contradictory about them – and they are also examples of material objects that seem merely functional but should be seen (or so I argue) as signs.

The tracks are clearly not in use, since there are no machines to run on them. They run the length of the main hallway, with tracks leading into each shop on either side (see figure 7.3). These last tracks are notably short and perpendicular to the tracks in the hallway, so no machine *could* meaningfully run on those short bits of track. In other words, they are useless as tracks. They appear to have been selectively repositioned as visual guides to lead you through the hall and into each shop. When these tracks were put back after renovating the building's foundation, this was therefore not a matter of 'restoring' a monument – for example, there are fewer tracks than there used to be – but a matter of a new design for the space.

The tracks therefore function primarily as *signs* that gesture towards the past of this space. They *construct* – rather than faithfully *reconstruct* – an 'authentic' history of the space, so historical accuracy is seemingly not at issue. Instead, these formerly functional objects have been reused as visual *ornaments*, foregrounding the aesthetics of the space itself. A similar point could be made about the exposed pipes near the ceiling, for example: leaving them exposed adds to the *look* of post-industrial reuse.

Figure 7.3: De Hallen, entrance to one of the stores in the main hallway (photo by author).

The oddness of these tracks as signs stems, in my view, from the contrast between how, as 'real' tracks, they point towards the past, but have no real existence as (functional) tracks in the present. This point even extends to the grooves remaining intact (see figure 7.2): they really are intact rails. Yet defunct tracks in the city streets are usually filled with asphalt to prevent things getting stuck in them, like leaves or the wheels of your bicycle. This contrast with real defunct tracks becomes even more problematic once you recognize that apparently wheelchair users are simply expected to avoid getting stuck in the tracks in De Hallen.

The next step in the close reading is to interpret the effect of these signs: on the surface, the tracks seem to point towards the history of the space, but that upon closer scrutiny they speak more of what the space is in the *present*. De Hallen is not a monument that recalls a former world of old trams, but a contemporary environment for fashion, art, culture, and food, which has an aesthetically foregrounded past in which functional objects are converted to decorative ornaments that foreground the *look* rather than the *history* of the place. I would argue that the past is aesthetically mobilized as 'branding' for the type of food-art-culture consumption of contemporary gentrifiers.

Figure 7.4: De Hallen website (n.d.). https://dehallen-amsterdam.nl/. Retrieved March 5, 2020 (screenshot by author).

Analysis of a representation

A further simple example, more familiar as 'sign', that is telling in how De Hallen ignores the local is De Hallen's website. The design features lines that connect different bits of text, e.g. in the outline of De Hallen's history, or in schedule of activities (see figure 7.4). These lines are reminiscent of a public transport map, with nodes of information indicated with a circle as though they were stops on the line. This seems to appeal to the tram depot's history. However, the design is very recognizable: it recalls specifically the iconic map for the London Underground originally designed by Harry Beck in 1931. The website therefore connotes public transport, but *not Amsterdam's* public transport – a gesture again ignoring the specificity of the local. The connotation is 'iconic-international' rather than 'Amsterdam', so I would argue that even the locals planning to go to the cinema are addressed as though they were tourists.

Analysis of discourse on the Foodhallen

As an example of discourse analysis in relation to an urban space, I would like focus the rhetoric with which the De Hallen sells itself. One of the main draws in de Hallen is the Foodhallen, a food court with a variety of food, from Vietnamese street food to designer hot dogs. From the beginning, the

Foodhallen was pitched as 'inspired by the indoor food markets of other big cities like Madrid, Copenhagen, and London' (De Hallen, n.d., translation by the author). This description seems to have been shared by a great deal of publicity surrounding De Hallen. To give a small selection of examples: well-known food blog *Your Little Black Book* described it as 'our own Chelsea Market meets Borough Market' (De Buck, 2014); a critical review in Dutch national newspaper *De Volkskrant* compared the Foodhallen, unfavorably, to the Mercado de San Miguel in Madrid and La Boqueria in Barcelona (Van Dinther, 2014); a later culinary review in *Het Parool* drew the comparison to La Boqueria in Barcelona and the Torvehallerne in Copenhagen (Versprille, 2015).

Figure 7.5: Foodhallen (photo by author).

While there is no room here to do a full analysis of the discourse surrounding De Hallen (which could also include policy documents, media reports, interviews, etc.), the quick handful of media descriptions above already confirm a pattern of comparisons to international food markets. But as the critical reviews mention, the Foodhallen is not actually like its international 'counterparts' at all.

The question is then: what is the effect of the recurrent comparison? I would argue that the international comparison makes De Hallen recognizable for visitors, both local and international, who have traveled to these popular destinations. The comparison puts De Hallen on the map, so to speak, for a particular kind of tourism. The comparison to London's Borough Market is illustrative here, because that has also become a prime example of gentrification. The discourse on the Foodhallen, therefore, 'pro-actively' pitches it as belonging to an international trend in gentrification. The recurring discourse therefore shapes a visitor's interpretation of the aesthetics of De Hallen even before an actual visit.

Yet the difference with London's Borough Market is also illustrative for how the discourse on the Foodhallen – and by extension De Hallen as a whole – is exclusionary. Borough Market is a market where you can buy produce, as well as prepared food for eating immediately. There has been a market on that spot in London for centuries, and the current building dates from the nineteenth century. In contrast, the Foodhallen only serves prepared food, which is why it is closer to a food court. But there is an actual food market right outside on the Ten Katestraat, which has been there for a century and has little to do with De Hallen. It is a typical Dutch street market, with stalls that are removed every day, where you can buy produce cheaply. Hence, the market caters to people with less disposable income, quite unlike the Foodhallen.

The comparison between the Foodhallen and international food markets, then, creates a certain slippage between meanings and associations. The comparison to other markets seems to associate 'market' with the Foodhallen, facilitated by the market outside on the street. The quality of affordability and accessibility that cling to 'market' – a public space, accessible to all, and particularly to lower income groups – are thereby transferred to the Foodhallen. So the image of a market is projected in the comparison, while the actual market, and its clientele with typically less disposable income, are ignored. The comparison, therefore, can be understood as a rhetorical strategy to make De Hallen appear less exclusionary than it actually is.

Reflection

This cultural analysis approach makes certain investigations possible, but also has limitations of course. As with all qualitative work, there is always the risk of bias in interpretation, especially given the argumentative nature of the approach. In a cultural analysis approach the political perspective is overt, but objects should not become 'alibis' for a political argument. Likewise, you should remain open to the bigger picture, to avoid circularity: my critical stance towards gentrification guides me to objects that call for critique, but the result of analysis should not just be self-affirmative. Analysis must be thoroughly underpinned and you should always remain open to what the specificity of an object can tell you. Otherwise your analysis cannot be convincing, which is of course the ultimate test. (You could do that as a methodological exercise: from your disciplinary background, do you agree or disagree with the brief readings in this chapter? Would you argue otherwise, and with what type of approach?) On this point, it is also vital to **triangulate** with other approaches and forms of knowledge (hence my turn to the literature on gentrification within geography). The case of gentrification is illustrative: gentrification is not a matter of *either* aesthetics *or* real estate prices *or* of changing populations – which is why a cultural analysis approach has a place in the broader study of urban spaces and culture.

Conclusion on De Hallen as case

My analysis of De Hallen has focused on what meanings are communicated, and who and what are being represented. To recap: the tracks look like remnants but are actually deliberately put in place to ornamentally suggest a generic past quality; the website tells a local history of public transport by appealing to another city's iconic tube map; the Foodhallen is presented as a market but it is actually an expensive food court. In sum, the aesthetics of De Hallen are oriented towards the *surface* of signification, while upon closer reading they tell a different story. It is a *spectacle* of history and of consumption, in line with a gentrification aesthetic that caters to the tastes of a global middle class.

The gentrification aesthetic also makes clear who the place is *not* for, precisely through what it downplays or ignores. In De Hallen, chief among these omissions is the *local*, which can also be read as not representing the local people. Specifically, the area surrounding De Hallen used to consist mainly of dense, small social housing, with a population with little disposable income – precisely the people for whom the Ten Kate market was established. By shifting away from specific local history, the aesthetics of De Hallen make clear that it is not a place for this particular group of people. In fact, in seeking a connection to international 'counterparts', the discourse on De Hallen is even ignoring the specificity of Amsterdam, and its people, as a whole. Instead, as with all spectacles, De Hallen is geared towards attracting new people: new residents in a rapidly gentrifying neighborhood, but also a particular kind of middle-class tourist for whom De Hallen is a destination itself.

General conclusion

Within a cultural analysis approach, semiotics and discourse analysis provide tools for getting at the meanings at work in the aesthetics of a micro level of individual elements in (or related to) the space and a macro level of broad descriptions circulating in the media and online. Together they allow me to investigate how a certain site, space or object can aesthetically communicate its politics. By way of conclusion, I should re-emphasize that cultural analysis geared towards cultural objects and practices, matters of meaning and ideas. It does not ask questions with discrete answers like 'Is the neighborhood of De Hallen gentrifying?' or 'Who actually uses De Hallen?', which require different methodologies (on the basis of quantitative data) and have different aims. Yet many socio-political questions about the city – like one of the guiding questions for this book, 'Who owns the city?' – look as though as though they have discrete answers, but the politics of such issues crucially also involve representation: who is spoken and thought about, who is addressed, who is left out. A cultural analysis approach offers tools for engaging precisely such questions.

References

Bal. M. (2002). *Travelling concepts in the humanities: A rough guide*. Toronto: University of Toronto Press.

Barthes, R. (1972 [1957]). *Mythologies*. Trans. A. Lavers. New York: Noonday Press.

Bridge, G. (2001). Bourdieu, rational action and the time-space strategy of gentrification. *Transactions of the Institute of British Geographers, 26*(2), 205–216.

Cameron, S., & Coaffee, J. (2005). Art, gentrification and regeneration–from artist as pioneer to public arts. *European Journal of Housing Policy, 5*(1), 39–58.

Chang, T. C. (2016). 'New uses need old buildings': Gentrification aesthetics and the arts in Singapore. *Urban Studies, 53*(3), 524–539.

Chaskin, R., & Joseph, M. (2013). '"Positive" gentrification, social control and the "right to the city" in mixed-income communities: uses and Expectations of space and place'. International Journal of Urban and Regional Research, 37(2), 480–502.

De Buck, Anne. (2014). Paradijs voor foodies bij de Foodhallen in Amsterdam [Paradise for foodies at the Foodhallen in Amsterdam]. October 13, 2014. Retreived from https://www.yourlittleblackbook.me/nl/de-foodhallen-in-amsterdam-west-is-open/.

De Hallen (n.d.). De Hallen Amsterdam. Retrieved from https://dehallen-amsterdam.nl/.

Fairclough, N. (2003). *Analysing discourse: textual analysis for social research*. Abingdon: Routledge.

Foucault, M. (2002). *The archaeology of knowledge*. 1969. Trans. A.M. Sheridan Smith. Abingdon: Routledge.

Geertz, C. (1973). *The interpretation of cultures*. New York: Basic Books.

Gottdiener, M. and A. Lagopoulos (eds.) (1986). *The city and the sign: An introduction to urban semiotics*. New York: Columbia UP.

Hall, S. (2019). 'Cultural Studies: two paradigms'. 1980. *Essential Essays, vol. 1*. Ed. D. Morley. Durham, NC: Duke University Press, pp. 47–70.

Lees, L. (2008). Gentrification and social mixing: towards an inclusive urban renaissance?. *Urban Studies, 45*(12), 2449–2470.

Lees, L., Slater, T. & Wyly, E. (2008). *Gentrification*. Abingdon: Routledge.

Ley, D. (2003). Artists, aestheticisation and the field of gentrification. *Urban Studies, 40*(12), 2527–2544.

Lynch, K. (1960). *The image of the city*. Cambridge, MA: MIT Press.

Mills. S. (1997). *Discourse*. London: Routledge.

Slater, T. (2006). The eviction of critical perspectives from gentrification research. *International Journal of Urban and Regional Research, 30*(4), 737–757.

Versprille, H. (2015). Walhalla? *Het Parool*, February 28, 2015.

Van Dinther, Mac (2014). Struinen en proeven ineen [Strolling and tasting at once]. *De Volkskrant*, November 27, 2014.

Williams, R. (2005). *Culture and materialism*. London: Verso.

Zukin, S., & Braslow, L. (2011). The life cycle of New York's creative districts: Reflections on the unanticipated consequences of unplanned cultural zones. *City, Culture and Society, 2*(3), 131–140.

8 The practice of institutional analysis in urban contexts

Federico Savini

Objectives and motives of institutional analysis

Institutional analysis in urban studies can explain why urban spaces are used and transformed in the way they are. It can explain the underlying power structures that have shaped those spaces and the social relations that those spaces represent. As such, the study of the change of institutions is crucial for urban studies, especially in fields that are prone to action-oriented research and to engaged scholarship. Institutions regulate power and power determines how to address particular social and urban problems. By explaining how and why institutions change or last, it is possible to understand how to tackle existing systems of authority in order to address existing socio-ecological problems.

Institutions are concretized patterns of social norms, and they are historically contingent and always evolving (March & Olsen, 2010). All institutions change in history, often through slow and conflicting processes. They are not set in stone. The institutions that change more slowly in history are those that have strong moral roots, namely those engrained in long-term cultural values and ideologies (Habermas, 1996).

Social norms are therefore the bricks through which institutions are built; they are the rules that orient people's behavior in their daily life. As binding structures, they establish what people consider appropriate, legal, allowed, and conversely what is not. As such, they give certainty about the behavior of individuals and their organization, and allow coordination of complex and messy social life. These norms are visible in formally written texts such as legal frameworks that forbid or oblige to do something in a particular place. They are also tacit, because they are internalized in people's worldviews and minds (Helmke & Levitsky, 2006).

Urban spaces are the historical product of the changing of these social norms (Giddens, 1981). Institutions are the materialization of these layers of norms. For instance, the institution of private property – the system of norms that establish the capacity of a specific subject (collective or individual) to own and dispose of something exclusively – is far from a 'natural' state of humans, but is historically constructed from practices of appropriation and dispossession that were undertaken since the mid-seventeenth century. Other examples of institutions that change in history include nation states, regional or municipal authorities, or the European Union.

An institutionalist approach to the study of urban problems starts from a fundamental distinction between means and ends, between structures and aspirations, in the way social reality unfolds (Khalil, 1995, p. 447). The difference between ends and means is an analytical construct that the social scientist should utilize to obtain significant results of research. Yet the social scientist should also be aware that this is the first bias of her research. In the social world, it is not self-evident to what extent means determine the ends, and vice versa. The actual co-existence of means and ends is a core philosophical problem of (neo) institutionalism.[1] Yet the artificial exercise that the methodologist does when separating the two is a necessary (yet reductive) step towards understanding a particular phenomenon. Any methodology has this problem/advantage and there is no methodology that cannot avoid reducing reality. It is just a matter of choosing one particular form of reductionism or another.

In order to distinguish between means and ends, institutional analysis relies on mapping and categorizing sets of norms and resources, and describing how they are used in practice. However, the most important challenge for institutional analysis is to explain how social norms are reproduced in the practices of living in cities. As Nee puts it, an institutionalist approach in sociology must 'explain the connection between the sub-institutional domain of social action and concrete relationships, and the meso- and macro-institutional domains of custom, conventions, law, organizations, ideology, and the state' (Nee, 1998, p. 3). There are therefore two general questions for institutional analysis. First, how do particular social norms influence behavior? And second, how do social norms change in history? Depending on the particular epistemology of institutional analysis, studies can focus on one or the other, or on both (Hall & Taylor, 1996).

---

[1] The approach explained in this chapter belongs to the stream of institutionalist analysis defined as 'neo-institutionalism'. The shift from older forms to a new wave of institutionalism occurred in the early 1980s to stress the importance to look at the enactment of norms in social context. Today, it makes little sense to study institutions without studying the social enactment of norms and it is hardly possible to find research that appeals to a pure form of old institutionalism (at least in academic scholarship). The word 'neo' will therefore be omitted.

In what follows, I will explain three main steps of institutional analysis and show examples in the context of a particular case study developed by the author in Amsterdam between 2010 and 2015. The overall research was published in Savini (2013); Savini and Dembski (2016). These steps are iterative. They trigger each other as **empirical research** is always complex and requires a feedback loop between researcher's expectations and the empirical investigation.

> The aim of the research was to understand the political power shifts in Amsterdam, through the institutional analysis of the redevelopment of Amsterdam North IJ-Banks, the waterfront of the city. One of the case study areas of the research was the NDSM-warf, a 40-hectare area in the northwest of Amsterdam. Historically the location for the large-scale shipping industry of the city, today it has become one of the most appealing spots of Amsterdam for urban redevelopment. NDSM is an interesting case for institutional analysis because different socio-political groups with different views, ambitions and resources challenge its development. The area is a symbol of the industrial past of the city but also a valuable land site to realize real-estate development. Different visions of place therefore are confronted with each other there. The study was part of a broader research that answered the question: 'How do the changing of regimes of power impact on the spatial development of urban peripheries?

Distinguishing and connecting levels of analysis departing from institutional tensions

Institutional research searches for tensions and collision between actors' goals and norms. It is through this tension that the norms become visible in practice. A particular social order (specific in space and time) is identified by the particular set of sanctions and incentives that exist in order to maintain existing social norms in place. It is through the deviation from a particular norm (or sets of norms) that the institutional architecture of social action is open for change. This deviation manifests through processes of contestation, tensions, and/or conflict (Giddens, 1984). These conflicts are everywhere in society because actions can shift rapidly, in unpredictable and creative ways. In addition, norms can be in conflict with each other, and social norms are not a coherent and stable whole but a nexus, organized in multiple layers.[2] In short, it can be argued that norms that create no conflict are

---

2   The state of conflict between actions and norms has been defined in different ways depending on the specific schools of thoughts. It can be referred as a 'void', 'mismatch', 'rupture', 'window of opportunity', 'stretching', 'vacuums', and many more. It is typical of institutionalist scholars to define these moments in original ways. It is beyond the scope of the chapter to present a review of these terms.

either obsolete (e.g. old laws that are today useless) or unnecessary (e.g. in the case of laws that are never used). Social norms are enacted through actors' interactions. They can be studied only by a careful **observation** of their infringement and enforcement and the only way possible is to study how actors (e.g. individuals or organizations) interact with each other. The infringement of norms is visible through the mobilization of sanctions, which can have different forms, from a simple administrative fine to a verbal argument.

For institutional analysis to happen, researchers need to define the *units of analysis* and the *units of observation*. In the study of regimes of institutions the unit of analysis is a particular process of development that can be identified historically and spatially (such as a changing urban waterfront). The unit of observation are instead the specific agents that are looked at in order to reveal how norms are enacted. These can be the social groups and organizations operating in the space.

The first step of research was to identify the existing tensions in the area and build on those tensions to define which particular agents could become the unit of observation of the study. To do so, it was important to do some preliminary analysis of the place and eventually add a pilot **interview** round with experts in the area. The most evident tension in the area was the management of the hangars , so the hangars were selected as a unit of analysis in the study (as part of the broader area). The units of observation – the source of data – were instead the different social groups and organizations that intervened in the transformation of that space. The analysis revealed that in 2000 a group of squatters occupied one of the vacant large hangars used to store ships. The occupation generated a controversy around the use of the area and a response by the city, which started to talk about the area, to define masterplans and to formalize the squatters by using an urban policy framework called 'broedplaats' ('breeding grounds') to settle the controversy. In 2005, more conflicts emerged when the city decided to contract out the development task in the area to a private company, giving it the formal authority to manage the space. The formalization through contract created dissent with both the early squatters and the local residents. The squatters started a campaign to protect the culture of the place. The inhabitants also started to vote against the local government, to sanction the decision to redevelop the area with a plan that did not match the identity of the place.

The units of observation, the source of information on the sanctions, are usually the social groups and individuals that perform in the space. However, these actions take place within institutional contexts that are the analytical target of the research. The notion of 'regime' is for example used to refer to the set of regulations and power that are being analyzed. Through the experiences of the agents, their stories and their strategies, researchers can appreciate the enactment of social norms. Looking at the enactment in practice allows explaining how particular social practices are embedded in broader institutional frameworks. The focus on enactment is therefore not a mere description of the specific practice at hand but it is a way to reach a broader analytical level.

In order to look at the enactment of norms, researchers focus on *episodes*, time and place specific circumstances of interaction between agents where norms are reproduced (see also Giddens, 1984). These episodes themselves do not explain alone how institutions change. They provide with the **empirically observable** situation of how institutions works. In rigorous empirical analysis, it is therefore very important to combine more observations of episodic practices, confronting different places and times, so to grasp their differences and reach a stronger explanation of how norms work and why they exist.

Observations in institutional analysis provide **thick descriptions** of how one particular norm influences a particular episode of action. These descriptions focus on particular situations and provide detailed accounts of how each actor relates to a particular norm, its perceptions and strategies. However, institutional analysis also shifts to a larger perspective both in space and time, looking at the way norms work throughout long periods of history or larger spatial scales (such as the EU or globally). By relating the scale of practices to that of structures, it has the advantage to map how norms change and how norms relate to others norms. It can appreciate macro systems of norms (e.g. national authority in infrastructural policy) and can explain how these norms are institutionalized in different countries.

What is generally defined as regime analysis is a useful methodology to explain the relation between the everyday practices of norms enactment and the changing broader institutional context. While it may be challenging in terms of research time and resources, it is always desirable to combine elements of the first and the second: to take broad regulatory frameworks and observe how they are produced and enacted *on the ground*. In this way, the researcher can validate evidences obtained from the study of agents' preferences within the context of macro-processes.

To proceed with a step towards the macro scale of institutional regimes, it is useful to focus on the specific episodes of institutional change identified before. In this case, it was thus possible to identify the establishment of a particular development agency, called Noordwaarts, as one of the episodes of institutional change triggered by the local conflicts on development. The agency was instituted after a first masterplan by the city provoked large dissent in the area. Citizens argued that the plan was not representing the industrial history of the place. Through the eyes of the planners involved in this agency, it was possible to understand the political rationale of this institution. Noorwaarts was a compromise between the development ambitions of the city officials pushing for real-estate development and for a post-industrial transition towards creative industries, the different plans of the local district council, and the increasing dissent from the inhabitants in the area. By focusing on the story of the agency, it became clear how an emerging coalition of governments and businesses actively promoted the post-industrial redevelopment of the city. The municipality enacted the policies for creative industries development (reuse and incubators), and were also backed up by rising funds from national governments in promoting these industries. The government was indicating these industries as the future economic engine of the country, through programmatic documents promoted by coalitions of high-tech, knowledge, media industries, and liberal parties searching for the creation of new jobs in the changing industrial areas. The commercial redevelopment of the area was also justified by the motivation of the liberals of the city of Amsterdam to please the industrial groups still active in the Amsterdam harbor.

Setting operational grids to set up the analysis

As explained, an institutional analysis's unit of observation is the agents and their behavior in particular episodes. The selection of episodes is crucial to start the research because it provides with the spatial and temporal boundaries of action. Yet why should a researcher choose one particular episode rather than another? The choice of both the unit of analysis – the area of focus – the unit of observation – the individuals or groups – depends on the actual aim of the research. The aim could be the study of environmental justice, social justice, identity, multi-scalar governance, social innovation, and many others. In this chapter, we take the phenomenom of 'ownership' as particular target.

To approach the complexity of norms that determine and influence ownership is a task that requires strong degrees of selectiveness. Firstly, the researcher may argue to study a particular case, a bounded zone where ownership can be empirically observed. In urban studies, case studies often refer, more or less explicitly, to particular zones (e.g. a square, a neighborhood, or a municipality), particular sectors of cities (e.g. housing, transportation, energy infrastructures, green areas) or processes (e.g. a particular participatory process, a strategic policy, or investment strategy). Scholars may take one or more of these objects of analysis, keeping in mind that the more of them there are, the less detailed the analysis of enactment (if time and resources available to the researcher remain the same). All of these follow (rather than precede) the selection of the specific phenomenom of analysis.

In NDSM, the study of ownership was based on the assumption that ownership structures would determine the particular redevelopment of the area and that this redevelopment would represent the emerging urban politics in Amsterdam region. Institutions represent political power structures. The researcher focused on specific places in the area to see how ownership unfolds in practice. The west side of the area, the monumental side, was identified as a sub-area of focus. The hangar occupied by the squatters was in this sector, as well as other buildings representing the industrial archeology of the place. This area was also formally registered as 'non-development' by the NDSM-Houthavens Covenant, signed in 2006 by the city of Amsterdam, the province of North-Holland, the company Cargill, the Amsterdam Harbour and the North and West city districts. The contract was an interesting norm to study because it was the product of a long debate about the challenges of development in the area and showed the conflicting views between different actors claiming their 'ownership' of place.

Within a particular selected case, the researcher will have to both focus on particular practices and develop an operational grid of analysis for the type of enactment. The **operationalization** of a complex notion like ownership will of course be reductive and it depends on the particular objective of the research. Moreover, while it is necessary to have a first list of possible dimensions/indicators of ownership to be observed, this list should not be too detailed. Reality will surprise the researcher with unexpected insights and it is very common to discover evidences of unexpected social norms in practice. Yet a basic grid of analysis is important to concentrate the focus on particular types of data sources and to be sure that the research appreciate the diversity of social norms and agents and in order to be able to structure interviews, **surveys**, or other techniques of data gathering to be used (compare chapter 3, on **participant observation**, chapter 5 on **interviewing**, and chapter 6 on **archival research**).

Building on the literature, ownership could, for example, be operationalized distinguishing between legal, performed, or perceived dimensions of ownership. This is a common way to define phenomena, based on a triad that is often used in philosophy (such as Lefebvre's ontology of space: Lefebvre, 1974). By establishing this basic distinction, the researcher can be more attentive to the diversity of norms that enact ownership. The operational grid to analyze the complex phenomenon of ownership allows establishing which data to collect and how to collect them in order to understand how ownership is instituted. This operationalization is not set in stone but works as a guideline framework that allows the researcher to focus on different practices and episodes and to appreciate the relation between the three dimensions of ownership. Moreover, this operationalization must be built upon a rigorous and extensive review of the literature on ownership in the urban context. The literature review should be carried out at the beginning of the research to conceptualize the phenomenom at hand.

In NDMS West, the researcher pre-identified three dimensions of ownership, building on a literature review and an analytical grid. *Legal ownership* is enacted though the enforcement of property rights titles. The land in NDMS was legally owned by the city of Amsterdam, which, however, contracted out the redevelopment task to a particular private development firm. *Performed ownership* works on a different level and it is enacted through norms that determine how people use the space. In NDSM, the performing owners of place are the social groups settling in the vacant properties, as well as the early companies that have brought their activities there (such as MTV Europe or Greenpeace) and the inhabitants of the surrounding areas. Finally, *perceived ownership* can be observed through the subjective perspectives of individuals, their stories, expectations, plans, and vision for a particular space. In NDSM, the city government officials started to propose alternative visions of place, built on the idea that NDSM was in fact a central part of the city of Amsterdam. Yet, this view clashed with the local inhabitants views that saw the place as the unique heritage of Amsterdam industrial and productive past

If necessary according to the research question, the researcher could also focus on one particular dimension of ownership, leaving the others aside, but always trying to keep the awareness of the weaknesses of this focus. This would mean that the research question could be better profiled, by asking, for instance, 'How is private land ownership impacting urban development in Amsterdam?' or 'In what way do public space users appropriate publicly owned space?' or 'How does private property rights impact the affordability of housing?' As said before, to opt for a very precise definition of ownership allows for in-depth analysis but it reduces the possibility to understand how particular norms change. Institutional change is a process that invests multiple factors such as the change of cultural imaginaries of place, technological advancements, and political conflicts. By limiting the definition of ownership to, for example, the legal field of coded property rights, would make it hard to explain the influence of political shifts on legislation.

Gathering and analyzing data in a targeted way

Taking the example of a three-dimensional analysis of ownership mentioned above, it is clear that any institutional analysis may gain from a combination of different techniques of data gathering. As mentioned before, norms become visible when they are enforced and used, through sanctions or systems of monitoring. The gathering of data should therefore be targeted towards those episodes where these sanctions can be visible. Figure 8.1 represents visually the empirical targets of data gathering. Each of these conflicts are substantiated through the analysis of the data.

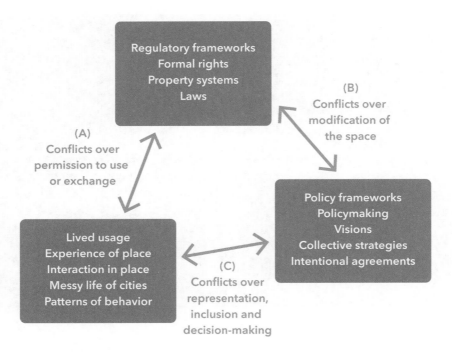

Figure 8.1: An example of operationalization of the notion of ownership to identify possible conflicts.

Conflicts of type (A) involve conflicts over permissions, accessibility, and usage of a particular space. These conflicts include practices of infringement of excludability from space, unauthorized access, or unauthorized appropriation. Empirically, the conflict can be studied observing formal legal procedures of enforcement (e.g. a lawsuit to remove squatters from a building) or ethnographically observing how security systems are used to keep individuals out of the private property (e.g. cameras, house rules, or many others). These are examples of the enactment of regulations that allow studying how property norms actually work.

In NDSM, the researcher identified different cases of conflicts between actions and rules. Firstly, there were the squatters occupying the hangar, which was a publicly owned property but given in concession to a development corporation for its redevelopment. Other conflicts of this type emerged in the negotiations that led to the signature of the NDSM-Houthavens Covenant in 2006. In the negotiations the plans to redevelop the area were infringing the 'environmental zoning' rights of the existing companies of the harbor to use their noise and safety space till 2030 for their production activities. The later conflict between the noise of festival and public events in the area and the right to silence (regulated by maximum dB levels) of the new inhabitants became also an example of this particular ownership conflict. These conflicts emerge from the tension between the everyday life in the area, and the macro regulatory structures for planning, that include environmental zones to protect livability as well as the partial centralization of these regulations at national (and even EU level) to homogenize land use rights.

Conflicts of the type (B) can be instead observed by looking at the way formal ownership is enacted against the right to modify and transform a particular area. This is often the case in planning processes oriented to redevelop particular urban areas that address particular environmental problems. In these cases, issues of competence rise when public plans (the visions enacted by public authorities) clash with the right of owners to decide how to change and manage their properties. Data can in this case be all kinds of transaction deeds, transfers, as well as processes of negotiation between public and private actors. In these cases, it can be also useful to include archival historical research on the past conflicts over development of the private property. The **close reading** of public tenders and procurements document can permit to understand under which conditions a particular good (land, space, or infrastructure) is given in concession. These processes explain the formalized agreement beyond the specific aims of the actors.

In NDSM this tension was visible in the early stalemates between the municipality's plans and the obstructionism of the local districts and inhabitants. The institution of the office Noordwaarts, a city office co-directed by the local district was a compromise to manage the conflict between the political right of the local community to define the future of the place and the formal responsibility of the city council to redevelop the area. The project was at that time a responsibility contested between different levels of scale.

To limit the study of ownership on the legal aspect has the risk to make the explanation too formalist. The study of the conflicts between performed and perceived ownership (i.e. how people use a space and how that space is transformed and managed) can enlarge the explanatory power of the research by explaining how less formal norms such as democracy and citizenship are enacted as forms of ownership. This type of conflict (C) is visible through the encounters between what users desire, wish and want of a particular space, and the way that particular space is managed and transformed by other actors. Such conflicts occur in all kinds of processes in which users are involved in the self-management of space or in the decision making process for its transformation.

To study these conflicts, it is useful to observe how individuals use the space and how these individuals organize their claims in the management of the space. For the former, the researcher could collect data that are visual, such as photographs, as well as textual, such as written accounts referring to the experiences and strategies of the users themselves. **Narrative interviews** are useful in this case, as are extensive surveys when larger samples are available. **Semi-structured interviews** organized around normative issues identified through preliminary analysis can provide a more effective focus.

In NDSM these types of conflicts include conflicts between different social groups, their imaginaries of place, and the different plans of the city and the development company. Early settlers in 2000 see the place as the symbol of the workers culture of the city of Amsterdam. They claim it is important to preserve this symbol. The study of the redevelopment of the NDSM-Warf revealed that the development company had particular ambitions of dense real-estate development, to maximize land value and to increase the housing stock. The city of Amsterdam was split between a vision that privileges dense development and one that privileges livability and creativity in place making. The local communities in the North feared **gentrification** and instituted committees to supervise these processes.

In our particular case at hand, interview questions could include: 'So, do you perceive this space to be accessible?', 'How do you deal with the fact that property is privately managed?', or 'Do you feel welcome, and what type of usages do you perceive as allowed here or not?'. In the study of national policy making processes, questions to a policy maker might include: 'How did you manage the formal process of decision making?', 'Which conflicts did you experience and why do you perceive them as conflicts?', or 'How did you change your own strategies to deal with existing protocols?'. The answers to these questions tell us something about how agents organize themselves to deal with structures and resources, as well as how structures and resources impact on choices of agents.

Similar data can be collected through documents that regulate the use of space, its management and its coordination. These might include the content of statutes but also episodes of public hearings, which are formal moments in which inhabitants are involved in discussing and designing the space. These data could be analyzed through open-coding techniques that search for 'patterns' in the way actors negotiate, contest, or defend particular house-rules of the place. Participant observation is also a very common tool used to actually see how the space is used.

To organize the complexity of information collected on the use and perception of the particular space, scholars may also chose to execute an institutional mapping of the episode at hand (see for example Aligica, 2006). Institutional mapping is a technique that allows schematizing the network of actors involved in the process. These maps will show the interests and statements that have been produced around a particular area, allowing the researcher to establish a preliminary list of the individuals to interview and approach.

The challenges of institutional analysis

Institutional analysis is suited for the study of how urban phenomena such as ownership, citizenship, sustainability, and many others are institutionalized in society and represented in spatial practices. It allows researchers to identify the particular social norms at stake in a particular context. As such, it is suited for a **critical analysis** of the political economy and political ecology of urban processes. It can be used for macro studies of state restructuring and global governance as well as for micro-studies of spatial appropriation, spatial conflicts, and social cooperation. As with any methodology, it is based on assumptions that direct but inevitably also limit the study. The basic assumption of institutional analysis is the analytical distinction between a social norm and its performer, and the recognition that a norm influences the performer and vice versa.

Institutional analysis also brings challenges. First, it is important yet difficult to include different levels of analysis in any institutional study. For instance, to study the phenomenom of ownership in cities it is very important to alternate 'zoom-in' and 'zoom-out' observations. This means starting from concrete episodes (e.g. a project, a space, a decision) and then locate these episodes within the macro structures that influence it (e.g. the national legal frameworks, regional authorities or long-term policy making processes, long-term investment regulations, etc.). This level shifting can often be messy and labor-intensive but it is indeed necessary to explain how structures of power and social norms shape cities.

Secondly, institutional analysis could still be accused of being rather anthropocentric, by putting at its center a notion of goals that may not be suitable for studying the role of non-human subjects in social reality.

Thirdly, empirical institutional analyses can reach two forms of distortions. First, it could *subjectivize* institutions and norms by explaining them exclusively through the views of the single unit of observation (a subject or a document). Just because one interviewee mentions a conflict with existing regulations does not justify the conclusion that there is, for example, an unjust situation. The second distortion is methodological *reification*. This consists in making institutions into objects that exist independently from the individuals that enact them. Without studying the reality of social agency, researchers may end up providing static descriptions of formal institutional structures.

To deal with these three challenges, the institutionalist researcher could consider doing the following:

1 never limiting their research to a singular dimension of the social phenomenon at hand, but always adding more than one, depending on time and resources available (which also allows them to achieve mixed-method research designs);
2 increasing the sensitivity of the research proposal to physical and material conditions influencing the social phenomenon at hand, including ecological factors that impact on social action (e.g. water shortage, biodiversity, waste, materials resources, etc.);
3 maintaining constant iteration between the gathering of data, the observations, and the analysis in order to counter-validate the arguments of interviewees and confront them with written texts and visual evidences.

In sum, this methodology is geared towards studying how macro phenomena such as culture, ideology, nation states, and legal systems interact in space and overlap in time. This potential, however, should not obscure the ability of institutional analysis to observe norms in their enactment, in practice and in action. The challenge of institutional analysis is to connect the scales of practices and that of institutions by combining observation at both levels of scale. In this manner, researchers can better appreciate the complexity of the normative infrastructures of society, from the lived processes of social interaction to the structured dimension of formal judicial systems.

References

Aligica, P. D. (2006). Institutional and stakeholder mapping: Frameworks for policy analysis and institutional change. *Public Organization Review, 6*(1), 79–90. http://doi.org/10.1007/s11115-006-6833-0

Giddens, A. (1981). *A contemporary critique of historical materialism* (Vol. 1). Berkeley, CA: University of California Press.

Giddens, A. (1984). *The constitution of society: Outline of the theory of structuration*. Oxford: John Wiley & Sons.

Habermas, J. (1996). *Between facts and norms: Contributions to a discourse theory of law and democracy*. Cambridge, MA: MIT Press.

Hall, P. A., & Taylor, R. C. R. (1996). Political science and the three new institutionalisms. *Political Studies, 44*(5), 936–957.

Helmke, G., & Levitsky, S. (2006). *Informal institutions and democracy: Lessons from Latin America*. Baltimore: Johns Hopkins University Press.

Khalil, E. L. (1995). Organizations versus institutions. *Journal of Institutional and Theoretical Economics (JITE) / Zeitschrift Für Die Gesamte Staatswissenschaft, 151*(3), 445–466.

Lefebvre, H. (1974). *The production of space*. Blackwell: Oxford

March, J. G., & Olsen, J. P. (2010). *Rediscovering institutions*. New York: Simon and Schuster.

Nee, V. (1998) Sources of the new institutionalism. In M. Brinton & V. Nee (eds.) *New institutionalism in sociology*. London: Sage.

Savini, F. (2013). Political dilemmas in peripheral development: Investment, regulation, and interventions in metropolitan Amsterdam. *Planning Theory & Practice, 14*(3), 333–348.

Savini, F., & Dembski, S. (2016). Manufacturing the creative city: Symbols and politics of Amsterdam North. *Cities: The International Journal of Urban Policy and Planning, 55*, 139–147.

9 Household preferences and hedonic pricing[1]

Hans R.A. Koster and Jan Rouwendal

Introduction

When economists consider choices people make, they usually assume that the behavior of people can be modeled as the outcome of the maximization of a *utility function*. When applied to the housing market this concept seems to make sense: when a household considers their choice of location within, say, Amsterdam, it considers a wide range of characteristics of the available houses and their location, such as floor space, the number of rooms, the access to urban amenities, the crime level, access to open space, etc. Eventually the household will choose the property that makes the happiest and so maximizes its **utility**, *given* its available budget. Hence, households' location choices and the amount of money they pay for a property provide useful information on the preferences of households for locations.

In this chapter we outline one of the most popular ways in the field of urban economics to measure those preferences and quantify the so-called **marginal willingness to pay (MWTP)** for location and housing characteristics. This method is referred to as *hedonic pricing analysis* and requires information on many location choices, the prices of properties, as well as location and housing characteristics. Given the surge in the availability of **big data**, this information is often readily available. The biggest advantage of estimating the MTWP of households for location and housing characteristics is that benefits can be calculated for public goods provided in cities, which is otherwise nearly impossible. For example, the costs of investing in urban renewal, open space, infrastructure, and historic amenities are usually pretty straightforward to calculate. The benefits, however, are much harder to estimate. The hedonic price approach provides a useful method with which to do this by estimating the MTWP of households for these public goods.

---

[1] We thank Luca Bertolini, Jos van Ommeren, Erik Verhoef, and Nanke Verloo for useful comments on previous versions of this chapter.

So what is a hedonic price function precisely?[2]

> A hedonic price function is a description of the **equilibrium** prices of varieties of a **heterogeneous** good, which are influenced by supply and demand.

An immediate implication of the above definition is that if preferences, quantities, or qualities of the heterogeneous goods on offer change, the hedonic price is also likely to change.

Pioneering work on hedonic price functions dates back to Court (1939), who was the first to model the prices of automobiles as a function of their characteristics. However, hedonic pricing was popularised by Griliches (1961) who showed how hedonic price functions could be used to develop a quality-adjusted price index for cars. In 1974, Rosen formalized the method by clarifying the relationship with conventional supply and demand analysis, thereby providing the link with standard micro-economic theory. In particular, he showed that the marginal price of a characteristic implied by the hedonic price function – that is, the first derivative of the hedonic price function with respect to that characteristic – could be interpreted as the marginal willingness to pay. The hedonic price method has been widely used since then to measure, among other things, the costs and benefits of good air quality, hazardous waste sites, historic amenities, school quality, open space, proximity to wind turbines, power plants, and the effectiveness of place-based policies. In all these studies the heterogeneous commodity studied is housing.

As these examples suggest, the hedonic price method is often used for research relevant to policy making. The underlying reason is that it provides a way to investigate the welfare consequences of external effects and public goods for which no markets exist. The powerful characteristic of hedonic price techniques is that house prices provide information on the marginal willingness to pay – the equivalent of the price of market goods – of people for public goods and location characteristics, for which it is otherwise hard to measure the benefits.

---

2   While the current chapter focuses on the housing market, the hedonic price approach can be also applied to other markets, such as the labor market and the market for automobiles.

Historic amenities and house prices (1)

In the Netherlands governments devote con-siderable amounts of money to investing in preservation of historic buildings and neighborhoods. The idea is that historic amenities may attract shops, restaurants and other modern urban amenities, and thereby contribute to a higher quality of life in cities (Brueckner, Thisse & Zenou, 1999; Glaeser, Kolko & Saiz, 2001). Historic amenities will most likely imply positive *external effects*; benefits are not only enjoyed by, say, the inhabitants of a historic building, but also by visiting tourists and residents living close to a historic building (Koster & Rouwendal, 2017). By looking at housing prices, we may come up with an estimate of the *external* benefits of historic amenities and compare those to the costs of investing in cultural heritage. This implies that we can undertake a social cost benefit analysis using changes in house prices.

As an application of the hedonic price method in this chapter we discuss the study by Koster & Rouwendal (2017) who investigate the impact of investments in cultural heritage in the Netherlands. We use data on about 650 thousand housing transactions between 1985 and 2011. Most of these transactions (96%) took place in urban areas (i.e. in areas with a population density exceeding 1000 people per km²). Moreover, we obtain data on almost 12 thousand investment projects in cultural heritage since the 1980s. The total investments are about €3 billion of which about €1 billion is a subsidy. We focus on smaller scale projects that are in the vicinity of residential properties. In total we analyse the effects of €1.63 billion worth of investments in historic buildings.

Hence, we aim to identify the MTWP of homeowners for historic amenities, and thus employ a hedonic price approach. The idea is then to compare price changes of otherwise identical properties, located on sites that differ in the amount of investment they received. From the spatio-temporal differences in prices between the properties one may then infer the marginal willingness to pay for historic amenities.

When estimating a hedonic price function one relies on standard **regression** techniques such as **ordinary least squares**, by regressing the total price of a property on its characteristics.[3] However, although this may seem straightforward, there are at least two issues when estimating a hedonic price function:

---

3   For a review of standard regressions techniques we refer to standard textbooks such as Cameron and Trivedi (2005), Angrist and Pischke (2008), Stock and Watson (2011) or Wooldridge (2015).

1 When the hedonic price regression is linear in the characteristics, the marginal prices are constants.[4] Hence one implicitly assumes that homebuyers all have the same marginal willingness to pay, while people are likely heterogeneous in their preferences and hence have different MWTPs. When assuming a linear hedonic price function (or alike), the hedonic price function will therefore probably be misspecified.

2 There is also the issue of **omitted variable bias**. That is, the estimated marginal willingness to pay for a certain characteristic may depend on characteristics that are omitted in the regression.

In this chapter we will discuss how existing studies have dealt with both issues.

Historic amenities and house prices (2)

When aiming to measure the **MWTP** for historic amenities, we may suffer from omitted variable bias and misspecification, which may imply that the estimated impact of historic amenities on house prices will be wrong.

Let's consider the simple example where you compare two properties with differences in the presence and quality of nearby historic amenities. The question is, however, if those two properties are really identical. It is for example likely that historic amenities are disproportionately clustered in city centres, where prices are higher for other reasons. If the properties that are compared are not really the same except for access to historic amenities, our estimates suffer from an omitted variable bias, and hence our estimate of the MTWP will be incorrect.

The second issue implies that people in the two properties considered may have a different preferences for historic amenities. For example, houses in the city centre are more often occupied by richer people who may like historic amenities more than families with lower incomes who live more often in the suburbs (Koster et al., 2016). Hence, even if you compare two identical properties, a hedonic price function may not identify the marginal willingness to pay of either of these households, but some kind of average.

This chapter is structured as follows. First, we will provide the economic foundations for hedonic pricing theory, by relying on standard micro-economic theory. Then, we discuss the main empirical issues when bringing hedonic price techniques to the data, followed by a summary in Section 4.

---

4 Recall that these are the first derivatives with respect to the characteristics.

Micro-economic foundations

The marginal willingness to pay

A standard assumption in textbook microeconomics is that commodities are available at a given quality. In reality we see a lot of heterogeneity in almost every commodity purchased by households. For example, a large home means that the house has a higher quality. Let us consider the case where people derive utility from a **composite good** q (think of food, healthcare, etc.) and housing, denoted by k. Hence, k denotes the quality of housing. In what follows we usually treat k as a **scalar**, but it could also be a **vector** (so that houses have multiple characteristics). We now specify the utility function as:

$$u = u(q,k) \tag{1}$$

The price of the heterogeneous commodity is a function of the quality chosen. We therefore write the **budget constraint** as:

$$q + p(k) = y \tag{2}$$

This formulation assumes that the unit price of the composite good equals 1, while $p(k)$ is the house price or housing expenditures. This model was used by Rosen (1974) in his analysis of heterogeneous goods markets.

If we maximise utility (1) using a Lagrangian subject to the budget constraint (2) by choosing q and k, the first-order conditions are:

$$\frac{\partial u}{\partial a} = \lambda \tag{3}$$

$$\frac{\partial u}{\partial k} = \lambda \frac{\partial p(k)}{\partial k} \tag{4}$$

as well as the budget constraint (2). Note that λ is the Lagrange multiplier and represents that marginal utility of income.

We can combine equations (2.3) and (2.4) to get:

$$\frac{\partial u / \partial k}{\partial u / \partial q} = \frac{\partial p(k)}{\partial k} \tag{5}$$

This equation tells us that the marginal willingness to pay for housing quality k is equal to the partial derivative of the price specified as a function of quality. Or in other words, the derivative of the hedonic price function with respect to housing quality is equal to the marginal rate of substitution of housing quality with respect to a composite good.[5] This relationship plays a key role in hedonic price studies.

---

5   The marginal rate of substitution is the rate at which someone gives up some amount of one good in exchange for another good while maintaining the same level of utility.

To illustrate this with a simple example, let's consider the following hedonic price function:

$$p_i = \alpha_0 + \alpha_1 z_i + \xi_i \qquad (6)$$

where p_i is the house price of property i, and z_i denotes the presence and quality of historic amenities. In Koster and Rouwendal (2017) we proxy this by past cumulative investments in cultural heritage in the neighborhood. Further, α_0 and α_1 are the parameters to be estimated and ξ_i is a residual. Given this linear hedonic price function, the marginal willingness to pay for a one unit increase in historic amenities is given by $p^i / z^i = \alpha_1$ (see equation (5)). Because homeowners are expected to value historic positively, we expext $\alpha_1 > 0$. Since this specification implies that the **marginal willingness to pay** is identical for all households, it may not considered to be very useful for empirical work, as noted earlier.

The value function

To analyse the equilibrium in a market for a heterogeneous good, Rosen (1974) introduced the concept of a value function. It gives the willingness to pay of the consumer for a variety of the good with a particular quality, that is, the maximum amount of money the consumer is able to pay for that variety, while still being able to reach a particular utility level. The value function is related to the bid rent function that plays an important role in other urban economic models, such as the **monocentric city model** (see e.g. Alonso, 1964; Mills, 1967; Muth, 1969). It gives combinations of price and quality that provide the consumer a given level of utility and can therefore be considered as a kind of **indifference curve**.

To define the value function, let P denote the willingness to pay for the heterogeneous commodity. We substitute housing expenditures in (2), and use the resulting equation to rewrite the utility function (1) as:

$$u = u(y - P, k) \qquad (7)$$

We now ask the question: what is the price the consumer is willing to pay for quality k if her utility must be equal to a predetermined value, say u^*? To answer this question, we write this condition as:

$$u(y - P, k) = u^* \qquad (8)$$

and invert the utility function with respect to $y - P$. After rewriting the resulting equation, we find:

$$P = y - u^{-1}(u^*,k) \qquad (9)$$

The above equation gives us a relationship between the price the consumer is willing to pay and the quality of the heterogeneous commodity for given income y and utility level u^*. In other words, it gives the value a consumer attaches to quality k of the heterogeneous commodity at the given utility and income levels.

It is useful to consider the relationship between P and the variables on the right-hand side of the equation. Starting from (9), we can verify the following relationships:[6]

$$\frac{dP}{dy} = 1 \qquad (10)$$

$$\frac{dP}{dk} = \frac{\partial u / \partial k}{\partial u / \partial q} \qquad (11)$$

$$\frac{dP}{du^*} = -\frac{1}{\partial u / \partial q} < 0 \qquad (12)$$

Equation (10) states that changes in income are completely translated into changes in the willingness to pay for quality. The reason is that consumer's utility is constant on each value function. Equation (11) says that the value attached to the heterogeneous good is increasing in its quality. Note further that the denominator of (11) is the marginal utility of income; a lower value at a higher income means a higher MWTP.

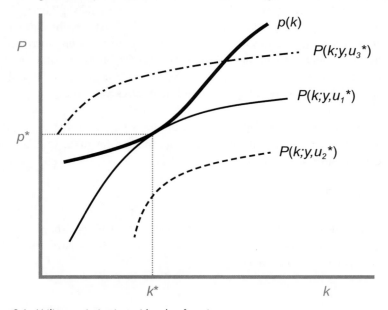

Figure 9.1   Utility maximization with value functions.

---

6   To do so you could apply the concept of the total differential to (8).

The right-hand side of this equation is indeed again the marginal willingness to pay for housing quality (which is identical to (5)). Equation (12) shows that the willingness to pay for the heterogeneous good decreases if the consumer has to reach a higher level of utility at a fixed income level.

The solid line in figure 9.1 shows the willingness to pay P as a function of quality k for a given utility level u_1. The function is increasing and we know from (11) that its slope equals the marginal willingness to pay for quality. The marginal willingness to pay for quality is equal to minus the slope of the indifference curve for quality and the composite good that corresponds to the same utility level. The indifference curve is **convex**, which implies that the marginal willingness to pay for quality is decreasing in quality. For this reason, the value function P is **concave** in quality.

The two dashed lines in figure 9.1 show the value functions of the same consumer for a higher utility level u_2 and a lower one u_3. That the value function corresponding to a *higher* utility level lies below the one corresponding to a *lower* level can be understood as follows: if a consumer chooses quality k of the heterogeneous good and the price P to be paid for it goes down, then (8) shows that (all else equal) more will be spend on other consumption goods and utility goes up. Equation (9) shows that when income increases, the value function shifts upwards parallel to itself. The shift in the value function is equal to the shift in income. The reason is that with given utility, consumption of the composite good should remain unchanged, which is only possible when total change in income is spent on the composite good.

The value function must be distinguished from the hedonic price function. The latter gives the market price for the heterogeneous good as a function of its quality. The value function gives the willingness to pay for the heterogeneous good of a *single* consumer as a function of her income and a given utility level. However, it will not come as a surprise that there is a relationship between the hedonic price function and the value function.

The bold line in figure 9.1 shows the hedonic price function and three value functions. We can analyze consumer behavior with respect to the heterogeneous product in a similar way as is done in the standard textbook treatments of utility maximizing behavior if we consider the value function as a kind of indifference curve. Each value function gives the combinations of quality and price that allow the consumer to reach a particular level of utility. The hedonic price function shows the combinations of quality and price that are available to the consumer. Just as the consumer in the textbook case attempts to reach the highest possible indifference curve, the consumer in figure 9.1 attempts to reach the *lowest* possible value function. In the situation shown in the figure, this is the value function corresponding to utility level u_1. The optimal combination of price and quality is found at the point where this value function is tangent to the hedonic price function. Hence the utility maximizing consumer pays a price p^* for her optimal quality k^*.

Consumers differ in tastes and incomes and therefore in the curvature of their value functions.[7] The situation as shown in figure 9.1 would then refer to one combination of prefer- ences and incomes, and show the relevant price/quality combination for this type of consumers. Other consumers, with different value functions, would have optimal price/quality combinations that are located on different points of the hedonic price function.

A final important aspect of figure 9.1 is that the value function and the hedonic price function are tangent to each other: they have only one point in common. At that point, the marginal willingness to pay for quality of the consumer equals the slope of the hedonic price function. Other points of the hedonic price function coincide with the marginal willingness to pay of other consumers. The implication is that it is in general not appropriate to compare different points of hedonic price function and to interpret the difference in price as the willingness to pay for the difference in quality. This is a clear limitation of hedonic price analysis. Formally, its restricts its application to small changes in characteristics. In practice the results of hedonic price analysis are often also applied to evaluate larger changes in air pollution, traffic noise, etc. Although this is not justified by the theory, the hope of pragmatic policy analysts is that the results are still a reasonable approximation to the actual willingness to pay of consumers for the actual changes.

Demand functions for quality characteristics

We have seen that the hedonic price function reveals the marginal willingness to pay for quality characteristics of heterogeneous goods (see equation (5)). This marginal willingness to pay is important for the purpose of economic welfare analysis. To see its role, return to equation (1) and derive the marginal rate of substitution between quality and the composite good. Start by writing down the **total differential**:

$$du = \frac{\partial u}{\partial q} \, dq + \frac{\partial u}{\partial k} \, dk \qquad (13)$$

Then let's find the change in the amount of the composite good that compensates exactly for a change in the quality. We impose $du = 0$ and rearrange:

---

7   If all consumers had the same preferences and incomes, they would all have the same value functions. This would imply that, with the given hedonic price function, only one variety of the heterogeneous good would be traded. Such a situation is not completely impossible. For instance, if the heterogeneous good is produced in a competitive industry, the market price of all varieties would be determined completely by production costs (the hedonic price function simply reflects the production costs) and it could be the case that only one possible price/quality combination is available on the market. However, in such a case we would not observe a hedonic price function. Instead we would see a homogeneous commodity. It may also be noted that even with identical tastes and incomes a continuum of price/quality combinations can be available on the market if the hedonic price function tracks (a part of) the value function. Clearly, this would be a very special situation.

$$-\frac{dq}{dk} = \frac{\partial u / \partial k}{\partial u / \partial q} = \frac{\partial p(k)}{\partial k} \qquad (14)$$

The second equality sign in this expression uses the first order condition (5). In fact, this just repeats our earlier conclusion that the first derivative of the hedonic price function can be interpreted as the marginal willingness to pay of a utility maximizing consumer. This result is of great importance for applied welfare **economic analysis**. Its significance becomes even clearer if we realise, from the budget constraint, that $q = y - p(k)$. Using this, we can rearrange the first and third parts of (14) as:

$$dy = \frac{\partial p}{\partial k} \, dk \qquad (15)$$

The left-hand side of this equation gives the change in income that is necessary to compen- sate the consumer for a small change in quality. However, it should be realised that (15) holds only for small changes in quality because the value function and the hedonic price function coincide only in one point.[8]

In fact an analysis of the compensating changes in income that are necessary with finite, but not necessarily small, changes in quality was the main purpose of Rosen (1974). He attempted to interpret the characteristic k as a commodity whose demand function could be found from observations of consumer behaviour. However, this is not a trivial task because demand functions are defined for commodities traded at a given price per unit, whereas this is not the case for the characteristics of heterogeneous good. To see how this idea could nevertheless work, consider figure 9.2. This figure shows an indifference curve, derived from utility function (1), and the budget restriction (2), which has been rewritten as:

$$q = y - p(k) \qquad (16)$$

In drawing the budget line, it has been assumed that the hedonic price function is convex, which implies that the marginal price $\partial p/\partial k$ is increasing in k: additional quality becomes more costly when the quality level is already high. It follows than that the amount of money left for consumption of the composite good is a concave function of quality: for each additional unit of quality more consumption of the composite good has to be given up. As figure 9.2 indicates, there is no constant unit price of quality – the budget line does not have a constant slope – and therefore the concept of the demand function cannot immediately be used.

With some elaboration, we can nevertheless describe the consumer's demand for quality using the concept of a demand function. The trick is that we have to linearize the budget constraint. Figure 9.2 shows that the optimal amount of quality

---

8 Equation (15) is in fact always an approximation if dk is finite, but the implied error is negligible for small changes. The discussion at the end of the previous section is also relevant here.

consumed is k^*. The marginal price of quality at this point is $\pi(k^*) = \partial p(k^*)/\partial k$. We can draw the straight line with slope $\pi(k^*)$ that passes through the consumer's optimal combination of quality and the composite good. This is the bold straight line in figure 9.2. The consumer's choice behavior with the actual, non-linear budget constraint is clearly identical to what it would have been with this counterfactual linear budget constraint. This observation allows us to describe the behavior of the consumer using an ordinary demand curve.

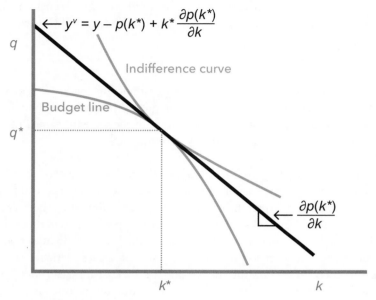

Figure 9.2 Linearising the budget constraint.

We have already determined the slope $\pi(k^*)$ of the linearized budget constraint, which is equal to that of the actual non-linear budget constraint in the consumer's optimum. The intercept of the linearized budget constraint differs from that of the actual budget constraint (for which it is equal to $y - p(0)$). The intercept of the linearized budget constrained is often referred to as virtual income, denoted as y^v, and can be computed as

$$y^v(k^*) = y - p(k^*) + k^* \frac{\partial p(k^*)}{\partial k} \qquad (17)$$

Using a linearization of the budget line, we can describe quality choice behavior of the consumer on the basis of a demand function:

$$k = k(\pi, y^v) \qquad (18)$$

Using this function, we could compute the exact welfare measures that we need for the analysis of non-marginal changes in quality characteristics.

To implement this idea, Rosen (1974) suggested a two-step analysis. In the first stage the hedonic price function $p(k)$ is estimated, while in the second step the researcher estimates the demand function (18). The basic idea is straightforward: if income and quality choice of consumers and the hedonic price function are known, it is possible to compute the marginal price π and the virtual income y^v that are relevant for each consumer. Using this, we can fit a regression line in the usual way and consider the result as the demand function.

However, some complications arise. In the conventional situation, where the unit price is a constant, the equivalents of marginal price (the constant unit price) and virtual income (the consumption budget) can be regarded as given for the consumer. But here the situation is different: marginal price and virtual income both depend on the chosen quality, as is apparent from the notation we used above.

The problem is that a consumer may choose a higher than average level of quality k^h for unknown idiosyncratic reasons, for instance because she has a particularly strong taste for quality. With a convex hedonic price function (as we used in figure 9.2) this would imply that she pays a particularly high marginal price $\pi(k^h)$. Another consumer, with a particularly low taste for quality would have a much smaller k^l and pay a lower marginal price $\pi(k^l)$. This is illustrated in figure 9.3. If we would use these observations in an attempt to estimate the demand function (18), we could easily come to the conclusion that the demand function is upward sloping: a low marginal price is associated with a low demand for quality, and a high marginal price with a high demand, which is unrealistic.

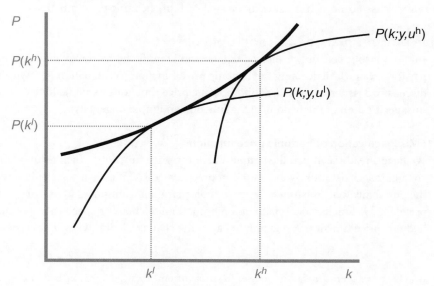

Figure 9.3 Choices of consumers with different tastes for quality.

In other words, a major problem is that that unobserved heterogeneity among consumers is important, which causes differences in choice behavior that are difficult to disentangle from price and income effects.[9]

Rosen (1974) realised this problem to some extent and suggested the use of instrumental variables. However, the difficulty of finding good instruments only became fully apparent in later years with analyses by Epple (1987), Bartik (1987) and others. The basic problem is that consumers with identical tastes and incomes will choose the same point on the hedonic price function. It follows that different combinations of marginal prices and quantities correspond in principle all to different demand curves. Of each demand curve only a single point is observed and this severely limits the possibilities to estimate price or income elasticities.

More recent studies by Ekeland, Heckman, and Nesheim (2002; 2004), Bajari and Benkard (2005), Bajari and Kahn (2005), and Heckman, Matzkin, and Nesheim (2010) show that **non-parametric methods** can be used to identify individual (inverse) demand functions, even if there is only one observation per individual. One may also use repeated observations of individuals (as in Bishop & Timmins, 2018), but then one has to make the strong assumption that people's preferences do not change between the different decisions. The latter seems unrealistic in the housing market where people mostly move when preferences have changed (e.g. because of changes in family situation, job, etc.). Because methods to estimate non-parametric regressions are not easy to apply, in this chapter we will not further pursue the issues associated with estimating demand functions for characteristics. In what follows, we will discuss econometric issues associated with the hedonic price function.

Econometric estimation of hedonic price functions

In the previous section we showed that we can identify the marginal willingness to pay for a characteristic using the hedonic price function (see equation (5)). We aim to discuss two issues when estimating hedonic price functions using real-life data: (i) **misspecification** of the hedonic price function and (ii) **endogeneity**.

Issue 1: Misspecification of hedonic price functions

We have already seen that the simplest hedonic price function, which is linear in characteristics, is unlikely to be valid in practice because it does not take into account the possibility that consumers differ in their marginal willingness to pay, or implicit price, for a characteristic. It is therefore important to choose a specification of the hedonic price function that is non-linear in the characteristics. We will now consider

---

9   Of course, there are also differences in virtual income induced by choice behavior, and this complicatesthe story a bit further. It is, for instance, not difficult to check that the virtual income of the consumer with a weak taste for quality is lower than that of the consumer with the strong taste for quality when the actual incomes of both consumers are identical. This means that income effects are also hard to estimate.

how this can be done without making the function non-linear in the parameters to be estimated, which would complicate the econometrics.

Often, the first step to allow for heterogeneity is to estimate a simple **log-linear** hedonic price function of the following form:

$$\log p_i = \alpha_0 + \alpha k_i + \xi_i \qquad (19)$$

Note that one may also take the logarithm of k_i if it is a continuous variable. There are two reasons why in practice one almost always estimates **log-linear** hedonic price functions:

1   House price data are often strongly skewed with a few observations having very high prices. This means that these outliers may disproportionately impact the estimated coefficients.
2   The coefficients are intuitive and easy to interpret as (semi-)elasticities.

Historic amenities and house prices (4)

Let us now investigate the impact of invest- ments in historic amenities on house prices in the Netherlands in order to identify the marginal willingness to pay of households for nearby historic amenities. Our analysis is based upon a house transactions dataset from the **NVM** (i.e. the Dutch Association of Real Estate Agents). It contains about 75% of all transactions between 1985 and 2011. For 657, 574 transactions, we know the sales price, the exact location, and a wide range of housing attributes such as size (in m²), house type, and construction year. We further gather data on investments in cultural heritage from the Department of Cultural Heritage. Because we are interested in the investments on surrounding properties, we exclude investments to the interior of buildings (about 7% of the projects).

We illustrate the issue of skewness of house prices in figure 9.4 where we plot the distribution of house prices. What we see in figure 9.4a is that prices are right-skewed. However, when we take logs in figure 9.4b we find that log house prices are (more or less) normally distributed, so that the issue of outliers is mitigated.

Note that with log prices, one can derive the marginal willingness to pay $\partial p_i / \partial k_i$ for each observation. We can write (19) as $p_i = e^{\alpha_0 + \alpha k_i + \xi_i}$. Now we calculate the derivative using the chain rule of differentiation and use equation (5):

$$\frac{\partial u_i / \partial k_i}{\partial u_i / \partial q_i} = \frac{\partial p_i}{\partial k_i} = e^{\alpha_0 + \alpha_1 k_i + \xi_i} \alpha_1 = \alpha_1 p_i \qquad (20)$$

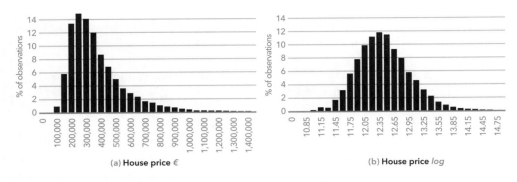

Figure 9.4 *Histograms based on NVM data from Amsterdam and surroundings.*

The above formula implies the marginal willingness to pay for one unit increase in k_i is heterogeneous and dependent on p_i. Note that this formula implies that the marginal willingness to pay is higher for households living in more expensive housing, as seems likely. However, note also that we cannot be sure that this specific type of heterogeneity is really present in the data, because it is entirely implied by the (arbitrary) assumption of a log-linear hedonic price function.

Historic amenities and house prices (5)

Let's say you estimate the following linear regression using ordinary least squares:

$$\log p_{int} = a_0 + a_1 z_{nt} + \theta_t + \xi_{int} \qquad (21)$$

where p_{int} is the house price of property i in neighborhood n in year t and z_{nt} denotes the cumulative investments in cultural heritage per km² in neighborhood n in year t, and θ_t are year dummies to control for general price trends.

In Table 9.1 we report regression results. The coefficient a_1 in column (1) implies that when investments per km² increase by €1 million (about 3 standard deviations), prices rise by about 4%. You then may use equation (20) as well as observations on prices and the value of investments z_{nt} to calculate the marginal willingness to pay for each property. However, we already anticipate that this effect may be overstated, because we do not include any control variables yet.

It may therefore be preferred to allow for more flexible heterogeneity in $\partial p_i / \partial k_i$ by letting the data tell how housing characteristics are related to prices. As already indicated, Ekeland, Heckman, and Nesheim (2002; 2004), Bajari and Benkard

(2005), Bajari and Kahn (2005), and Heckman, Matzkin, and Nesheim (2010) propose strategies to estimate so-called 'non-parametric' hedonic price functions.

Table 9.1   Regression results

	(1)	+ Controls (2)	+ House f.e. (3)
Investments in historic buildings (in million € per km²)	0.0389** (0.0160)	0.0411*** (0.0142)	0.0151*** (0.00514)
Housing control variables (17)	No	Yes	Yes
Year fixed effects	No	Yes	Yes
Property fixed effects	No	No	Yes
Observations	657,574	657,574	657,574
R²	0.400l	0.763	0.982

Notes: The dependent variable is the log of the house price. Standard errors are clustered at the neighborhood level and in parentheses.
*** p < 0.01, ** p < 0.05, * p < 0.10.

Issue 2: Endogeneity

So far we have considered houses with only one characteristic k, which is unrealistic. Let's say you aim to estimate a multivariate linear hedonic price function:

$$p_i = \alpha_0 + \sum_{c=1}^{C} \alpha_c k_{ic} + \xi_i \qquad (22)$$

where p_i is the price of property i, k_{ic} are housing characteristics, where $c = 1, ...,C$ and ξ_i is a housing characteristic that is unobserved by the econometrician.

An important issue in estimating the preferences for housing and location is the issue of endogeneity: the researcher is unlikely to observe all characteristics that are relevant to buyers, and these omitted variables may lead to biased estimates of the marginal willingness to pay. For example, the economist may observe the size of the house, the number of rooms and the average age of buildings in the neighborhood. However, she is unlikely to observe the quality of the trees and facades of buildings, and may for example also fail to get data on the crime rate. *If these omitted characteristics are correlated to the observed characteristic of interest*, this implies a bias (Bajari, Fruewirth & Timmins, 2012).[10]

---

10   Note that if there is no correlation between unobservable characteristics and the characteristic of interest, the marginal willingness to pay is unbiased.

There are typically three possible solutions.

1 One may try to find instrumental variables. The instrument should then be sufficiently strongly correlated to the characteristic of interest, but not directly to unobserved housing or location characteristics. In practice this is not so easy, but some examples are given in Koster, Van Ommeren, and Rietveld (2014) and Koster and Rouwendal (2017).

2 Another solution is to include **fixed effects** at a low level of spatial aggregation and use temporal variation in the characteristic of interest to identify the effect of interest. Although this controls for all time-invariant characteristics of the house, price trends related to unobservable characteristics of the house may still be correlated to the characteristic of interest.

3 An increasingly popular solution to the problem of omitted variable bias is the use of quasi-experimental methods. Using random variation in the determination of the treatment status to a policy one can identify the causal effect of that policy (Gibbons & Overman, 2012). However, quasi-experimental settings are often not available and also have their disadvantages. For example, one only can identify the average treatment effect based on the assumption that the treatment effect is similar across the population. Furthermore, quasi-experimental settings may not be comparable to situations that occur in everyday life.

Of course, no 'one-size-fits-all' solution is available to endogeneity issues, but every study applying hedonic price techniques should carefully think about and discuss the necessary identifying assumptions under which one can identify causal effects of housing characteristics on prices.

Historic amenities and house prices (6)

Let's go back to Table 9.1. In column (2) we first include 17 housing **control variables**, such as house size, number of rooms, maintenance quality, etc. The impact of the listings rate is similar to the previous specification without control variables.

In column (3) we include property fixed effects, which means that we identify the ef- fect of the listings rate and housing prices based on variation over time. Recall that if a variable does not change over time, it will be controlled for by the property fixed effects. Hence, property fixed effects control for difficult-to-observe characteristics of houses and locations that are time-invariant. We see that this matters for the results: a one million euro increase in investments in historic amenities increases house prices by 1.5% instead of about 4%.

One may still be worried that this effect is not a causal effect of investments, because, for example, investments mainly take place in areas with many historic buildings. Those areas may have different price trends, e.g. due to gentrification. In Koster and Rouwendal (2017) we therefore take a couple of additional steps to further address omitted variable bias.

Summary

A hedonic price function is a description of the equilibrium prices of varieties of a heterogeneous good, which is influenced by supply and demand. In this chapter we explained how *hedonic pricing* techniques can be used in order to identify preferences of people for houses and locations. This is important for policy evaluation as the benefits of public investments in say clean air, improved infrastructure, open space, neighborhoods and historic amenities, among others, can be investigated, which is something that is very hard to do otherwise.

We first discussed the micro-economic foundations of hedonic pricing techniques and showed that the marginal rate of substitution of a housing characteristic with respect to a composite good is equal to the willingness to pay for such a characteristic. Hence, by taking the derivative of the hedonic price function with respect to a characteristic, we can identify the willingness to pay for a housing or location characteristic.

Lastly, we turned our attention to two main issues when estimating hedonic pricing techniques: omitted variable bias and arbitrary functional form assumptions. We argued that one should carefully think of an identification strategy to deal with omitted variable bias. We further showed that semi- or non-parametric estimation techniques can be used to allow for flexible data-driven relationships between housing characteristics and the price.

Historic amenities and house prices (7)

Are the total benefits of investments in historic amenities – measured by the willingness to pay – on surrounding houses larger than the costs? In Koster & Rouwendal (2017) we calculate that the total external benefits of investments in cultural heritage are €1.85 billion. This is more than the €1.63 billion of investments in cultural heritage. More specifically, the results suggest that the benefits are about 14% higher than the costs. If we take the upper bound estimated price effect, the benefits-to-costs ratio is considerably higher. These calculations provide suggestive evidence that investments in cultural heritage generate substantial positive benefits for homeowners.

References

Ahlfeldt, G. & Maennig, W. (2010). Substitutability and complementarity of urban amenities: External effects of built heritage in Berlin. *Real Estate Economics* 38(2), 285– 323.

Ahlfeldt, G., Maennig, W., & Richter, F. (2017). Urban renewal after the Berlin Wall: A place-based policy evaluation. *Journal of Economic Geography 17*(1), 129–156.

Alonso, W. (1964). *Location and land use. Toward a general theory of land rent.* Cambridge, MA: Harvard University Press.

Anderson, S. & West, S. (2006). Open space, residential property values, and spatial context. *Regional Science and Urban Economics 36*(6), 773-789.

Angrist, J. & Pischke, J. (2008). *Mostly harmless econometrics: An empiricist's companion.* Princeton: Princeton University Press.

Bajari, P. & Benkard, C. (2005). Demand estimation with heterogeneous consumers and unobserved product characteristics: A Hedonic Approach. *Journal of Political Economy 113*(6), 1239-1276.

Bajari, P. & Kahn, M. (2005). Estimating housing demand with an application to explaining racial segregation in cities. *Journal of Business and Economic Statistics 23*(1), 20-33.

Bajari, P., Fruewirth, J.C. & Timmins, C.. (2012). A rational expectations approach to hedonic price regressions with time-varying unobserved product attributes: The price of pollution. *American Economic Review 102*(5), 1898-1926.

Bartik, T. (1987). The estimation of demand parameters in hedonic price models. *Journal of Political Economy 95*(1), 81-88.

Bayer, P., Ferreira, F. & McMillan, R. (2007). A unified framework for measuring preferences for schools and neighborhoods. *Journal of Political Economy 115*(4), 588- 638.

Bishop, K. & Timmins, C. (2018). Using panel data to easily estimate hedonic demand functions. *Journal of the Association of Environmental and Resource Economists 5*(3), 517-543.

Black, S. (1999). Do better schools matter? Parental valuation of elementary education. *Quarterly Journal of Economics 114*(2), 577-599.

Boes, S. & Nüesch, S. (2011). Quasi-experimental evidence on the effect of aircraft noise on apartment rents. *Journal of Urban Economics 69*(2), 196-204.

Brueckner, J., Thisse, J. & Zenou, Y. (1999). Why is central paris rich and downtown Detroit poor? An amenity-based theory. *European Economic Review 43*(1), 91- 107.

Cameron, A. & Trivedi. P. (2005). Microeconometrics: *Methods and application.* New York: Cambridge University Press.

Chay, K. & Greenstone, M. (2005). Does Air Quality Matter ? Evidence from the housing market. *Journal of Political Economy 113*(2), 376-424.

Court, A. (1939). Hedonic price indexes with automotive examples. In: *The dynamics of automobile demand.* New York: General Motors, pp. 98-119.

Davis, L. (2011). The effect of power plants on local housing values and rents. *Review of Economics and Statistics 93*(4), 1391-1402.

Dröes, M., & Koster, H. R. A. (2016). Renewable energy and negative externalities: The effects of wind turbines on house prices. *Journal of Urban Economics 96*, 121-141.

Ekeland, I., Heckman, J., & Nesheim, L. (2002). Identifying hedonic models. *American Economic Review 92*(2), 304-309.

Ekeland, I., Heckman, J., & Nesheim, L. (2004). Identification and estimation of hedonic models. *Journal of Political Economy 112*(S1), S60-S109.

Epple, D. (1987). Hedonic prices and implicit markets: estimating demand and supply functions for differentiated products. *Journal of Political Economy 95*(1), 59–80.

Gibbons, S. (2015). Gone with the Wind: Valuing the local impacts of wind turbines through house prices. *Journal of Environmental Economics and Management 72*, 177–196.

Gibbons, S., Machin, S., & Silva, O. (2013). Valuing school quality using boundary discon- tinuities. *Journal of Urban Economics 75*(1), 15–28.

Gibbons, S., & Overman, H. (2012). Mostly pointless spatial econometrics? *Journal of Regional Science 52*(2), 172–191.

Glaeser, E., Kolko, J., & Saiz, A. (2001). Consumer city. *Journal of Economic Geography 1*(1), 27–50.

Greenstone, M., & Gallagher, J. (2008). Does hazardous waste matter ? Evidence from the housing market and the superfund program. *The Quarterly Journal of Economics 123*(3), 951–1004.

Griliches, Z. (1961). *Hedonic price indexes for automobiles: An econometric of quality change.* NBER, pp. 173–196.

Heckman, J., Matzkin, R., & Nesheim, L. (2010). Nonparametric identification and esti- mation of nonadditive hedonic models. *Econometrica 78*(5), 1569–1591.

Hurvich, C., Simonoff, J. & Tsai, C. (1998). Smoothing parameter selection in nonpara- metric regression using an improved akaike information criterion. *Journal of the Royal Statistical Society B 60*(2), 271–293.

Imbens, G., & Lemieux T. (2008). Regression discontinuity designs: A guide to practice. *Journal of Econometrics 142*(2), 615–635.

Irwin, E. (2002). The effects of open space on residential property values. *Land Economics 78*(4), 465–480.

Koster, H. R. A., & Rouwendal, J. (2017). Historic amenities and housing externalities: Evidence from the Netherlands. *Economic Journal 127*, F396–F420.

Koster, H. R. A., & Van Ommeren, J. N. (2019). Place-based policies and the housing market. *Review of Economics and Statistics 101*(3), 1–15.

Koster, H. R. A., Van Ommeren, J. N. & Rietveld, P. (2014). Agglomeration economies and productivity: A structural estimation approach using commercial rents. *Economica 81*(321), 63–85.

Koster, H. R. A., Van Ommeren, J. N. & Rietveld, P. (2016). Historic amenities, income and sorting of households. *Journal of Economic Geography 16*(1), 203–236.

Mills, E. (1967). An aggregative model of resource allocation in a metropolitan area. *American Economic Review 57*(2), 197–210.

Muth, R. (1969). *Cities and housing: The spatial pattern of urban residential land use.* Chicago: University of Chicago Press.

Rosen, S. (1974). Hedonic prices and implicit markets: Product differentiation in pure competition. *Journal of Political Economy 82*(1), 34–55.

Silverman, B. (1986). *Density estimation for statistics and data analysis.* New York: Chapman and Hall.

Stock, J. & Watson, M. (2011). *Introduction to econometrics*. 3rd edition.
Cambridge, MA: Pearson.

Wooldridge, J. (2015). *Introductory econometrics: A modern approach*.
Scarborough ON: Nelson Education.

10 Urban research in another dimension: methods for modelling historical cities

Claartje Rasterhoff

Introduction

Did you know that Google offers the option of time travel? Satellite images in Google Earth will transport you back in time some ten years, sometimes even in 3D. Take the city of Amsterdam, for example. When we zoom in on one of the main streets in the city centre, the Rokin, we see a busy street with metro stops and a flurry of parasols. Five years ago: a building site with cranes and holes in the ground. Another five years back, and we see lots of traffic and bustle. Those who are familiar with trends in urban development know these observations testify to significant changes in Amsterdam, such as the construction of the new north–south metro line, and the increasing importance of leisure and touristic venues in the city centre.

The images come with structured information, also known as data. On the map you will see little icons for, for instance, museums, music venues, restaurants, hotels, and even the university buildings. When we click on the little coffee cup at the corner of Rokin and Nieuwe Doelenstraat, we find café *Katoen*, characterized in Google maps as 'Charming little café at central corner', with the unsolicited note that, by car, this is 19 minutes to my house.[1] The application also provides me with images of its interior, an address, opening hours, a website address, and a score (not bad: 4.2 out of 5, based on over 350 reviews). Surely this offers a convenient service for those who are looking for a place to eat and drink in Amsterdam, but, and this is perhaps less obvious, it is also an interesting example of the prototype interface that urban scholars are increasingly using for research purposes.

A 2018 article in WIRED referred to maps as the new search boxes, as they are increasingly becoming the front door to an ocean of online digital information (Hempel, 2018). Digital maps, or spatial representations with layers of data, can help structure and present expanding and increasingly complex webs of digital

---

1   *Charmant cafeetje op centrale hoek.* Google Maps. Last accessed 28 October 2019.

information in ways that we – humans – can more easily access and understand. Notably, municipalities like Amsterdam dedicate sections of their websites to interactive maps, and scholars are also increasingly using mapping to organise their data and present their results.[2] Admittedly, all of this is not time travel of the type portrayed in popular movies or graphic novels, but as more and more data is visualized in 3D and made accessible through webpages, as well as Augmented or Virtual Reality applications, it comes pretty close. For most historians who research how people's lives have interacted with their urban surroundings across different time periods, the twenty-first century is, however, a bit too close to home. For us historians, the question of whether it would it be possible to apply new mapping approaches to view, or perhaps even experience, long-term patterns of urban change and continuity, is particularly intriguing.

Mapping and modeling methods

We can use the virtual reconstruction of cities to better understand how the cities that we now live in came into being. This is important for two reasons, one practical and one more abstract. First all, urban planning models build on social and spatial infrastructures that have developed over the course of centuries. In recent years, for instance, repairing and maintaining the many bridges and quays in the city has become an urgent issue for the municipality. While it may seem mundane, these efforts are vital to maintaining urban public infrastructure and they are strongly related to important topics such as accessibility, sustainability, and governance. Historical data on the existing civic infrastructures is crucial to properly inform urban planning models and simulations. Secondly, and this less readily apparent, studying the urban pasts can bring awareness of unintended consequences of planning decisions, and provide us with alternatives to dominant modes of thinking and planning. Especially in this period of heated debates about expansive and expensive urban renewal and the construction of new neighborhoods, the development of visual representations and simulations of historical cities can stimulate us to imagine and discuss alternative paths of development.

There is little doubt that many such virtual reconstructions of historical cities will be on offer in the near future. In fact, computer scientists and tech companies are working hard on creating so-called 'mirror worlds': virtual places that overlay actual places (Gelernter 1993; Kelly 2019). Gaming companies create entire past cities, which are mostly fictional but also based on historical information: think of the action-adventure game series Assassins Creed and their reconstructions of 1789 Paris or ancient Egypt.[3] Urban historians, for their part, have slowly but surely been embracing digital technologies by setting up their own historical mapping projects, with examples ranging from historians playing around with the video game

2 https://maps.amsterdam.nl/. Last accessed 23 November 2019.
3 Paris: Assassins Creed Unity: https://www.ubisoft.com/en-us/game/assassins-creed-unity. Egypt: https://assassinscreed.ubisoft.com/origins/en-us/home/. Last accessed April 28, 2020.

SimCity in their spare time to academic involvement in large and costly complex infrastructure projects.[4] Online resources and projects such as Venice Time Machine, Visualising Venice, Layers of London, Locating London's Past, Digital Harlem, and Amsterdam Time Machine, however varied in scope and background, share forms and goals.[5]

In this chapter I argue that collectively these initiatives are more than accessible and entertaining visualisations, and that they help shape new methodologies for urban (historical) research. Historical modeling and simulation can be seen as action-based methods that make our assumptions and their implications computationally and visually explicit and that invite experimentation to further test and refine hypotheses. The textboxes throughout this chapter illustrate steps in the process of virtually reconstructing the city of Amsterdam:

1 making data;
2 sharing data;
3 mapping data;
4 analysing data.

Although I mainly focus on urban history and the case of Amsterdam, these developments (as well as their affordances and limitations) are part and parcel of the larger trends of **digitization** and **digitalization** in society and academia.

Linking up with my own research, I will mainly use examples from the study of urban cultural life, focusing on spatial methods such as **digital mapping** and 3D modeling. Surprisingly, the socio-spatial organisation of historical nightlife venues and its effect on the production and consumption of urban cultural life has received little systematic analysis beyond cases studies on individual venues – especially in the Dutch context. Venues such as cinemas, theaters, clubs, restaurants, and bars can, however, also be viewed as socio-cultural spaces through which expressions, identities, and social relations are negotiated and shaped, possibly through conflict and sometimes with great emancipatory effects (i.e. Chatterton & Hollands, 2003; Schlör, 1998; Erenberg, 1981). This research engages with the broader question of who owns and governs the city by viewing constellations of nightlife venues as a form of (semi-)closed public space.

---

4   Sim City: https://www.ea.com/nl-nl/games/simcity/simcity.
5   Venice Time Machine: https://www.epfl.ch/research/domains/venice-time-machine/;
    http://www.visualizingvenice.org/visu/; https://www.layersoflondon.org/; https://www.
    locatinglondon.org/; http://digitalharlem.org; https://amsterdamtimemachine.nl/. Many
    of such local platforms are being developed with the large program Time Machine. https://
    www.timemachine.eu. Last accessed April 28, 2020.

From dusty old archives to fuzzy new data

Mirror worlds are virtual places that overlay actual places. While virtual worlds can be completely fictional or partly based on reality, mirror worlds need to be connected to the 'real world'. Or in other words: to reconstruct historical cities, we need data on places, people, events, and artifacts. While companies such as Google, but also entities such as the municipality of Amsterdam, have ample access to information that was already created in digital form, historians have to add a very time-consuming step to the process: they first have to digitize their sources and then turn them into data.[6] In order to really understand the added value of mapping and modeling methods, it is necessary to quickly summarize this process.

For a long time, historical researchers have been collecting information by putting in hours of hard labor in the archives. While they often stored their findings in paper notebooks or basic word documents, many historians, inspired by the Annales School and aided by programs such as Excel or Access, also transformed old records into structured (tabular) data. The uptake of new technologies (in particular the Internet) in society and in academia has further shaped the historian's engagement with data and sources. Memory institutions and companies specializing in digitization are collaborating in making high-quality images of historical material and publishing them on the web.[7] Some are freely available – take the well-known examples of Delpher, a broad selection of Dutch historical newspapers, or the high-quality images that can be freely downloaded from the website of the Rijksmuseum – whereas others are paywalled by publishers.[8]

It should be noted, though, that many transcriptions and data still sit idly on personal hard drives and in some cases, fittingly, on historical artifacts such as floppy disks. Last year, for instance, my colleagues in the *CREATE* research program at the University of Amsterdam had to demolish a laptop from the 1980s when they tried to recover data on Amsterdam theater history from its hard disk (a strategy that failed and for which the experts from the computer museum had to come to the rescue). This means that we have access to a range of selected **primary sources** from behind our computers, but that this selection is notably incomplete and biased. When historians engage in analyses of digital sources, then, they should apply their trademark source criticism skills (as discussed in chapter 6 on archival research) as much to these sources or datasets as they would to their physical counterparts.

---

6   With the exception of those historians who study internet societies. Born digital data as found websites is partly archived by Libraries such as Royal Library, and by the Internet Archive, accessible via Wayback Machine https://archive.org/web/. Last accessed 23 November 2019.

7   See for instance the work by the company Picturae: https://picturae.com/nl. Last accessed 23 November 2019.

8   For instance paywalled digitized by Brill: https://primarysources.brillonline.com. Delpher: https://www.delpher.nl; Rijksmuseum: https://www.rijksmuseum.nl/nl/rijksstudio. Last accessed 23 November 2019.

New technologies facilitate automatic data extraction from these sources. However convenient, digital scans of old documents need to be further processed before they are machine-readable and we can search them or automatically extract information such as names from them. The older the sources, the trickier this step is, as the fonts and types used in printed text vary greatly and handwritten texts are particularly difficult to read without training. These older sources are therefore often manually annotated for specific types of content by scholars or **citizen scientists**. Automatic transcriptions generated by handwriting recognition software, which uses machine learning techniques to recognize and read complex handwriting, are still checked and corrected by humans.[9] This also means that for some sources all words from an original document are digitally available, whereas for others the information is curated and only includes selected information, such as persons, dates, locations, or events. New technologies help to create and unlock the ingredients for our historical urban reconstructions, but the historical data is, like the sources themselves, the result of a series of selection choices, and this greatly affects their scope and depth (Cordell, 2017).

1 Making data: automatic extraction

In order to model nineteenth- and early twentieth- century **spatial patterns** in urban culture and leisure, we use different sources. While information on the location of established Amsterdam institutions, such as museums, theaters, cinemas, and music halls, is by now relatively easy to come by, the composition of the many small businesses in the hospitality and nightlife industries is not yet systematically mapped. To redress this, my colleagues at CREATE analyzed, for instance, historical address books, the 'Yellow Pages' of their time. These books, which list most of the businesses, their locations, and proprietors' names, have been digitized and are available for download on the website of the City Archives.

The information in the books is not available as neat tabular data, but it contains clear organizational properties that are fairly structured and consistent over time, which means that it can be processed by computers relatively easily. This made it possible to automatically extract information rather than transcribing everything by hand. We extracted all persons whose occupations were in the food and drink service industries, such as 'koffijhuishouders' [coffee shop holders] and 'tappers' [tavern keepers], but also theaters, cinemas, and music venues. Once digitized, an automated comparison of these books significantly reduced the need for manual correction of OCR errors, spelling variation, and other errors. Other sources, such as the Amsterdam Citizen Registry, could then be used to validate names, occupations, and locations in the automatic extraction from the address books.

---

9   Well-known Dutch crowdsourcing platforms are *Vele Handen* https://velehanden.nl/ and *Het Volk* https://hetvolk.org. Last accessed 23 November.

Read more: https://amsterdamtimemachine.nl;
https://archief.amsterdam/inventarissen/details/30274.

Before we delve deeper into the modeling of cultural life in historical cities, there are two more crucial steps in the data-pipeline: linking and publishing. Even when you have the information digitally at your fingertips, it is hardly ever neatly combined in one dataset and ready for use. To integrate data that is located in different collections at various institutions in different kinds of formats we can use web-based technologies. For computer programs to be able to communicate well and share data between them (interoperability), the historical information needs to be, to some extent, standardized. Correcting, for example, spelling variation makes it possible to identify individuals, objects, places, or events between sources, and to search across source sets. Not all collections and datasets have aligned their terminologies and standards, and while we are not even quite there yet when it comes to agreeing on standards, it is clear that such agreements and technologies will make sharing data and reusing it for varying purposes, such as the reconstruction of historical urban life, considerably easier.[10]

2 Sharing data: Wikidata style

One of the main sites in the data we uncovered from the address books was, not surprisingly, one of Amsterdam's most famous nightlife sites: the Rembrandtplein. To share and publish data for analysis and presentation, we need to make sure datasets can 'talk' with each other. Changes in names over time, as well as many spelling and data modeling variations, make this more difficult. Rembrandtplein, for instance, has also been known as Boter Markt, Botermarct, Osse marct and Rembrandtsplein. Even the famous Rembrandt himself suffers from spelling variations. Many databases of researchers, museums, and archives, have entries for *Rembrandt*, *Rembrandt van Rijn*, and *Rembrant* – as if they were three different persons. While we know the names refer to one and the same person, the computer does not automatically know this. To help solve such coordination issues within their own collections and to share information between them, many knowledge and heritage institutions

---

10 See for Amsterdam: Adamlink: https://adamlink.nl/ last accessed 23 November 2019. On a national scale, Stichting Nationaal Digital Erfgoed is developing a terminology network that will greatly facilitate interoperability between heritage collections across institutions. For academia, similar work on humanities and social sciences data is being done with the CLARIAH (Common Lab Research Infrastructure for the Humanities). https://www.netwerkdigitaalerfgoed.nl/ and https://www.clariah.nl/en. Last accessed 23 November 2019.

such as universities, libraries, museums, and archives are collaborating in aligning and publishing their data. Amsterdam heritage institutions have begun to connect descriptions of places and other units of analysis in their collection to shared, unique, and persistent identifiers that are comparable with an address, very much in the same as Wikidata does. Rembrandtplein/ Boter Markt/Osse marct, then, becomes https://adamlink.nl/geo/street/ rembrandtplein/3785, and everyone can add this reference to their own metadata or datasets. The set of practices for publishing and linking across datasets is known as Linked Data.

Read more: https://adamlink.nl; Oldman, Doerr and Gradman (2016); for a more hands-on explanation of Linked Data see https://programminghistorian. org/en/lessons/intro-to-linked-data.

Urban mapping and models

Let us assume that we have access to the right sources, that we can extract data from the sources, and that we can connect this extracted dataset to other online historical data. How do we then analyze and make sense of what we find? Fortunately, in the digital world, the presentation of information and knowledge is (or can be) visual and hypertextual, more so than in the historian's traditional medium: the written word (cf. the idea of Hypercities in Presner, Shepard & Kawano, 2014).[11] There are many different ways to process and present data (just consider the popularity of data science and data visualization), but for the purpose of this chapter we will zoom in on spatial tools such as digital mapping and 3D modeling. The go-to technology for studying the 'where', and this is of course not new, is spatial analysis (Guldi 2010; Gunn 2001).

While interest in space, place, and spatiality is in itself not new to the historical discipline, new information technologies greatly contribute to the growing popularity of using digital maps and geographic information technologies (see also chapter 11) to visualize and analyze our data. In a quest for more nuance and flexibility, 'deep mapping' has emerged as a central approach to visualizing the biography of a place (Bodenhamer, Corrigan & Harris, 2015). The term **deep map** refers to a digital map that goes beyond two-dimensional images of places, names, and topography, by adding additional layers of information. While this could be any type of information, deep maps are often used to support subjective descriptions and spatial narratives, and combine structured data with, for example, egodocuments, visual or audio sources.

---

11   See also *HyperCities*, an early Digital Humanities 2.0 project that aims to enable users to navigate and collaboratively create the histories of city spaces across the world: https:// www.hypercities.com. Last accessed April 28, 2020.

Most historians do not use many satellite images, like Google, but we do have historical maps of cities. For Amsterdam alone, thousands of maps were created across the centuries. While they are engaging, informative and sometimes simply beautiful artifacts, in general maps are not factual representations, and should therefore often be read as sources revealing how contemporaries viewed their cities rather than sources for extracting the exact dimensions of the streets, buildings, and waterways (arguably this also applies to some extent to maps drawn in our own time; see also chapter 11). To build a grid of urban structures over time, we also need less visually attractive information: the exact location of streets, lists of street names, addresses, and neighborhoods of buildings, both lost and extant. Ideally, we also have geometries and coordinates that can be read by computers, so that we can use GIS systems such as freeware QGIS and licensed ArchGIS for the analysis and visualization of **spatial data** on the level of, for instance, plots or parcels (see chapter 11).

When combined, all this locational data is the backbone of digital mapping, as we can connect textual and visual information on people, places, events, concepts, or artifacts to it. Such digital representations, however rich, are still flat. How can we move them into the third dimension? What if we, for instance, want to understand patterns in, for instance, mobility or feelings of safety in relation to the spatial dimensions of a city?[12] Historians can probe the archives for specific information on the height of buildings, the width of streets, or the depth of a house, but in most archival sources this type of information is few and far between. Another option can be to derive information from images such as photographs and pictures (photogrammetry). Archaeologists and building historians, for instance, use scanners and drones to take present-day pictures of historical sites. The information on these images can then be used to make digital models of the sites; the current reconstruction of Notre Dame in Paris, for instance, relies heavily on such models.

Of course, much has changed over the course of the centuries and many buildings and streets have not survived.[13] In these cases, historians fall back on digitized historical image archives, from which they estimate spatial dimensions. These pictures, drawings, or paintings, once produced for artistic or documentary purposes, now represent a large collection of data records. New computer vision technologies allow us to query them for use in statistical analyses or to directly generate historical 3D models (Bruschke et al., 2017). Take, for instance, the work being done by *HistStadt4D* on Dresden, whose city centre was flattened during World War II.[14] This project investigates and develops access to image repositories by identifying the spatio-temporal locations of historical photographs and maps, and places them within a 3D model of the city centre. Using algorithmic learning, they estimate image orientation, identify objects, and calculate the geometry of buildings. On the basis of this, they develop 3D models for different moments in time (so-called 4D models, where time features as the fourth dimension) and using contemporary 3D city models also display the images online in their current spatial context.

In a different way, the interdisciplinary research project *ArchiMedial Enriching and linking historical architectural and urban image collection* also bridges data science and research on contemporary and historical built environments.[15] By developing state of the art algorithms this project enables place recognition for historic images for which **geolocation** tags are unavailable. The project uses, amongst other case studies, the case of historical Amsterdam. Combining deep learning techniques with practices of crowdsourcing for 360,000+ historical images from the Image Library (*Beeldbank*) at the City Archive, they identify locations. This approach, in turn, can also help us to identify spatial dimensions of historical sites and buildings.

---

12 Consider for instance the use of historical 3D models in the current research project *Freedom of the Streets*, led by Danielle van den Heuvel, which focuses on gendered mobility patterns in early modern Amsterdam and Edo. https://www.freedomofthestreets.org/. Last accessed 23 November 2019.

13 See this online resource for lost buildings. http://verdwenengebouwen.nl/. Last accessed 23 November 2019.

14 HistStadt4D. https://www.urbanhistory4d.org/wordpress. Last accessed 28 April 2020.

15 Archimedial. http://archimedial.net/. Last accessed 28 April 2020.

4 Modeling data

As part of our research on the socio-spatial organisation of cultural life in Amsterdam, we used 3D modeling to reconstruct of one of the earliest cinemas in Amsterdam, the Cinema Parisien at Nieuwendijk. This type of research can help reconstruct the history of cinema-going and emphasizes the social implications of the spatial properties of cinemas. It thereby contributes a unique dimension to the historical study of the actual use and appropriation of urban cultural spaces. While there is data on **ownership**, locations, and programming, cinema-going practices remain more elusive. For instance, a simple question like 'Did people stand or sit while watching movies in Cinema Parisien?' was not yet conclusively answered. An anecdote from the owner's granddaughter suggested that people were not seated, but later cinema researchers questioned this. The virtual reconstruction of the cinema prompted researchers to actively search for sources on seating and they were able to show that by the time the cinema opened, chairs had been ordered and delivered. Moreover, to increase transparency about the type and quality of historical evidence, they also developed color schemes to annotate levels of certainty. Researchers at the University of Amsterdam are also using 3D modeling in an archaeological/historical investigation into material life, ethnicity, and diet in the district of Vlooienburg in Amsterdam in the seventeenth and eighteenth centuries, and in the research project *Freedom of the Streets: Gender and Urban Space in Eurasia 1600-1850*. In the latter project, researchers use spatial analysis and modeling to challenge assumptions about gendered mobility patterns in Amsterdam and Edo (present-day Tokyo).

Read more: Noordegraaf et al. 2016; https://amsterdamtimemachine.nl/cinema-parisien-3d-2/; https://diasporaarcheologyamsterdam.nl/; https://www.freedomofthestreets.org/.

In addition to these computational projects, historians and archaeologists also develop fine-grained 3D models of individual buildings and neighborhoods based on extensive archival research.[16] Trying to get as close as possible to historical reality is a process that is very time consuming and sometimes frustrating, as there are many unknowns. For historians, 2/3/4D modeling can be used a research tool, and

---

16 Examples of the reconstruction of individual buildings include the houses of the sixteenth-century banker Pompeius Occo or painter Dirck Barentsz by Madelon Simons and Loes Opgenhaffen (University of Amsterdam): https://amsterdamtimemachine.nl/category/data/3d-models/. Other interesting models include De Beurs, de Synagoge and the French Theater, by Timothy de Paepe: https://3dtheater.wordpress.com; and even non-academic enthusiasts make fascinating visual reconstructions of notable sites, such as the Haarlemmerpoort, by Todd van Hulzen. https://www.vanhulzen.com/nl/2019/03/15/animatie-van-de-oude-haarlemmerpoort. Last accessed 28 April 2020.

it is perhaps more about the process than the outcome. They are fully aware that it is impossible to make 100 percent historically accurate and complete 3D models of the city, but using mapping technologies reveals unknowns, challenges assumptions, and helps raise new questions about space and how it was used. This also makes it an interesting teaching tool, as for instance in the Urban History MA course *De Digitale Stad* (The Digital City) at the University of Amsterdam, where students make detailed reconstructions with GIS and 3D software.

Using mapping as an exploratory tool enables researchers to, for instance, combine very different datasets as well as different levels of analysis. In a project on the reconstruction of early Amsterdam cinema culture, for instance, colleagues plotted cinema locations on a digital map (Baptist, Kisjes & Noordegraaf, Van Oort, 2019). When looking for possible explanations for their spatial distribution, the team stumbled upon an early twentieth-century map that depicted public transport routes in the city. After comparing the two maps, it became evident that cinemas were, almost without exception, located along the routes of the trams. This finding, in turn, stimulated new questions and hypotheses.

The value of digital mapping also lies in its ability to facilitate analyses at different scales. In the project *Virtual Interiors as Interfaces for Big Historical Data*, for instance, an interdisciplinary group of researchers use mapping to analyze patterns of cultural consumption in seventeenth-century Amsterdam. On the one hand, they trace patterns in household possession across the city and compare these with socio-economic indicators such as rent levels and taxes. On the other hand, they try to assess how cultural objects such as paintings, books, and porcelain functioned in the homes and lives of inhabitants by reconstructing the interiors of several houses in 3D. This zooming in and out on different spatial levels, but also between structured data unstructured data, or even economic and cultural data, has been described as a macroscope-like process that allows the user to integrate practices of close and distant reading, and to navigate different perspectives (Graham, Milligan & Weingart, 2015).

This points us to a final dimension (and growing subfield) of this type of research: **historical simulation**. In simulation, scholars have computer models of social life create a simulated world based on rules and then subject that world to analysis (Gavin, 2014). In urban research, such techniques are often used to develop planning scenarios, especially in this age of **smart city** policy and **big data**.[17] In a similar way, we can use historical data to construct various versions of the same historical city, or, for instance, calculate different growth scenarios, walking routes, or reconstructions of important events. In the case of ancient Rome, for instance, simulation techniques

---

17 See for instance Urban Strategy, a calculation model for interactive planning by TNO, that has been used for the city of Amsterdam. In Amsterdam you can also find the City Simulation Lab at Amsterdam Institute for Advanced Metropolitan Solutions (AMS).

were used to calculate how long it would have take for Colosseum visitors to take their seats (Gutierrez et al., 2007).[18]

To some historians, such simulations might feel too much like gaming or natural science research, but it is essentially not so different from historians generalizing on the basis of limited archival sources (chapter 6). We should therefore view simulation as one of the means we can use to represent a framework of interpretation used to categorize real phenomena, include a 3D representation, a replica, or even a case study (Gavin 2014). In this way, we can use them as means to better understand how our cities came into being and help us plan for the future.

Discussion

Results from a recent interdisciplinary project demonstrate how these different steps in digital mapping

1 making data
2 sharing data
3 mapping data
4 analyzing data

contribute to a better understanding of historical urban life. The research brought together data and insights from different humanities disciplines (media studies, socio- economic history, and linguistics) to study the emergence of cinema as a new form of entertainment at the turn of the twentieth century against the background of the existing forms of entertainment and the socio-economic composition of the neighborhoods in which this entertainment was located (Noordegraaf et al., 2020). Combining data on Amsterdam dialects, occupational status, and leisure venues and visualising them in the new GIS infrastructure discussed above allowed us to test the platform's capacity for interdisciplinary research on twentieth-century urban life in the capital.

The researchers compared two sample years: 1884, when the city had been expanded by a new nineteenth-century belt, and 1915, when the first permanent cinemas had been established in the city. In 1884, all theaters were located in areas with a relatively high elite density. They found no theaters in comparatively poorer areas of the cities, nor in the 'golden bend', the most affluent area of the canal ring. When compared with the 1915 patterns, very little overlap between the location of theaters and cinemas was found. This suggests that the new form of entertainment found a place in other, less affluent areas of the city (as measured by 'elite density' and dialects). These

18 The Colosseum was formerly believed to be a very efficient 'people-mover', but the models reveal some possible bottlenecks.

initial findings might be explained by the fact that most of the 1915 theaters had already been established in the period 1880-1890, but can also suggest that the new form of entertainment was seen as less respectable and geared towards the lower income groups. The project also demonstrated that, with some modifications, the mapping infrastructure worked well in connecting different types of data and in visually exploring possible (cor)relations. In order to further explain the socio-spatial patterns who 'who owned cultural life in the city' however, additional data is required, such as information from business archives, play bills, ticket sales information, but also mentions of shows in letters and diaries that could provide additional insights here. The digital mapping infrastructure allows these and other data layers to be added to the grid of urban cultural life and shared for exploration in future studies.

Conclusion

Like many urban historians, I view the city as a research lab, or as Charles Tilly put it, 'as a privileged site for study of the interaction between large social processes and routines of local life' (Tilly, 1996, p. 704). Novel technologies such as the ones discussed in this chapter allow us to build a digital version of such a research lab, as they make it easier to integrate many small and **heterogeneous** observations on the routines of local life and compare them to patterns of, and narratives on, social change. Digital mapping projects help to integrate heterogeneous sources and data types for both quantitative and qualitative analyses, and they allow researchers to play around with the level of these analyses, as one can zoom in or zoom out, depending on one's research questions. As historians are increasingly developing their own versions of mirror worlds, we can start to see how these can be employed as research tools for scalable and mixed method analyses.

Current mapping projects, many of which were initiated by universities or research collectives in the first decade of the twenty-first century, also demonstrate that while the idea seems simple enough, the practice of creating and applying such tools and resources for both research and public purposes is challenging. For example, online visualisations are often insufficiently transparent to enable meaningful application in research; specialist researchers critique their user interface and missing or erroneous data; and non-experts, in their turn, find them too academic and not intuitive or easy to use. On the back-end too, the road to historical modeling of cities is anything but straightforward. Many technologies are in the process of being built, only a fraction of the sources have been digitized, and the choices for source selection have been influenced by political and commercial motives. Another limitation, and perhaps an ethical concern, is that there is a systemic bias towards sources that are often used and currently most popular or relevant (Zaagsma, 2020).

With this chapter I hope to have demonstrated that it is exactly this complexity that makes (historical) urban mapping an exciting and valuable methodology for research and education. The value of such platforms for urban research is not so much in a final product, but in defining a shared goal and in trying to get there. This process is broadening our views on what sources are, how we integrate and organize them, how we analyze and how we present them to our colleagues and interested audiences. It makes visible that which we do not know, which we have not yet uncovered, and it pushes and enables us to collaborate with people from different disciplines such as urban studies, computer science, and heritage studies, and with people in the public and commercial domains, such as municipalities and designers (chapters 15 and 16). For students (and ourselves), we can also consider mapping and modeling as didactical tools that stimulate a more playful approach, in which research is less about the end product, and more about learning and trying new things.

Using new and poorly understood technologies is not or should not be antithetical to historical practices, because using these technologies is about the fundamental aspects of what historians have historically been trained to critically reflect on: ambiguity, context, alternative scenarios, and narrative thinking (see chapter 6). At a time when (urban) contemporary life is increasingly expressed in data and virtual representations of reality, as per the smart cities hype, historical scholars are well positioned to question the affordances and risks of such technologies and the socio-technical imaginaries that underpin them – not by standing on the sidelines, but by engaging with and critically participating in their development. This helps to place history in society, and the past in the present – and if we happen to build a time machine along the way, well, that's a nice bonus.

References

Baptist, V., Kisjes, I., Noordegraaf, J., & van Oort, T. (2019). Amsterdam Cinema Audiences: A Geospatial Analysis of Film Exhibition and Consumption in Early 20th Century Amsterdam. Paper presented at *EBHA Congress*, Erasmus University, Rotterdam, 29-31 August, 2019.

Bodenhamer, D. J., Corrigan, J., & Harris, T. M. (eds.) (2015). *Deep maps and spatial narratives*. Bloomington: Indiana University Press.

Bruschke, J., Niebling, F., Maiwald, F., Friedrichs, K., Wacker, M., & Latoschik, M. E. (2017). Towards browsing repositories of spatially oriented historic photographic images in 3D web environments. In *Proceedings of the 22nd International Conference on 3D Web Technology*. Web3D 2017, 18:1–18:6. ACM, New York. https://doi.org/10.1145/3055624.3075947.

Chatterton, P., & Hollands, R. (eds.) (2003). *Urban nightscapes: Youth cultures, pleasure spaces and corporate power*. New York: Routledge.

Cordell, R. (2017). 'Q i-Jtb the Raven': Taking dirty OCR seriously. *Book History* 20(1), 188–225. https://doi.org/10.1353/bh.2017.0006.

Erenberg, L. A. (1981). *Steppin' out: New York nightlife and the transformation of american culture, 1890–1930*. Chicago: University of Chicago Press.

Gavin, M. (2014). Agent-based modeling and historical simulation. *DHQ: Digital Humanities Quarterly* 8(4), 1-1.

Gelernter, D. (1993). *Mirror worlds, or: The day software puts the universe in a shoebox... How it will happen and what it will mean*. Oxford: Oxford University Press.

Graham, S., Milligan, I., & Weingart, S. (2016). *Exploring Big Historical Data: The Historian's Macroscope*. London: Imperial College Press and at http://www.themacroscope.org/2.0/. Last accessed April 29, 2020.

Guldi, J. (2010), *What is the Spatial Turn?* Charlottesville: University of Virginia Scholars Lab. http://spatial.scholarslab.org/spatial-turn/what-is-the-spatial-turn/. Last accessed April 29, 2020.

Gunn, S. (2001). The Spatial Turn: Changing Histories of Space and Place. In S. Gunn and R. J. Morris (Eds.), *Identities in Space: Contested territories in the Western City since 1850*. Aldershot: Ashgate, pp. 1-14.

Gutierrez, D., Frischer, B., Cerezo, E., Gomez, A., & Seron, F. (2007). AI and virtual crowds: Populating the Colosseum. *Journal of Cultural Heritage 8*(2), 176-185. https://doi.org/10.1016/j.culher.2007.01.007.

Hempel, J. (2018). How maps became the new searchboxes. *Wired*, June 13, 2018. https://www.wired.com/story/how-maps-became-the-new-search-box/. Last accessed November 23, 2019.

Kelly, K. (2019). AR will spark the next big tech platform–Call it Mirrorworld. *Wired*, February 12, 2019. https://www.wired.com/story/mirrorworld-ar-next-big-tech-platform. Last accessed April 29, 2020.

Noordegraaf, J., Opgenhaffen, L., & Bakker, N. (2016). Cinema Parisien 3D: 3D Visualisation as a Tool for the History of Cinemagoing. *Alphaville 11*, 45-61.

Noordegraaf, J., van Erp, M., Zijdeman, R., Raat, M., van Oort, T., Zandhuis, I., Vermaut, T., Mol, H., van der Sijs, N., Doreleijers, K., Baptist, V., Vrielink, C., Assendelft, B., Rasterhoff, C., & Kisjes, I. (2019). Semantic deep mapping in the amsterdam time machine: Viewing late 19th- and early 20th-century theatre and cinema culture through the lens of language use and socio-economic status. Paper presented at *Conference on Research and Education in Urban History in the Age of Digital Libraries & Digital Encounters with Cultural Heritage*. UHDL: Dresden, October 10-11, 2019. Berlin: forthcoming.

Oldman, D., Doerr, M., & Gradmann, S. (2016). Zen and the art of linked data: New strategies for a semantic web of humanist knowledge. In S. Schreibman, Siemens, R, Unsworth, J. (Eds.). A New Companion to Digital Humanities, Wileys Blackwells: pp. 251-273.

Schlör, J. (1998). *Nights in the big city: Paris, Berlin, London 1840-1930*. London: Longman.

Schreibman, S, Siemens, R, Unsworth, J. (Eds.). *A New Companion to Digital Humanities*, Wileys Blackwells.

Tilly, C. (1996). What good is urban history? *Journal of Urban History 22*(6), 702-719, 704. https://doi.org/10.1177/009614429602200603.

Zaagsma, G. (2020). The digital archive and the politics of digitisation. Paper presented at *Digital Past 2020 - New Technologies in Heritage, Interpretation & Outreach*. Aberystwyth, Royal Commission on the Ancient and Historical Monuments of Wales, 12-02-2020 to 13-02-2020.

11 Mapping the city: Geographic Information Systems and science in urban research

Rowan Arundel

Introduction: space matters

Longley et al. (2015, p. 1) begin their classic volume on **Geographic Information Science and Systems** with the seemingly mundane claim that 'Almost everything that happens, happens somewhere. Knowing where something happens can be critically important'. Such a statement could be paired with the similarly unassuming truism reflected in Tobler's 'First Law of Geography' that 'everything is related to everything else, but near things are more related than distant things' (Tobler, 1970). Whether we choose to focus on the spatial dimension or not, space plays a role in everything we do, as the medium of interactions between us, and in our interactions with the world around us. Simply put, *space matters*. But if space matters more generally, nowhere is this perhaps truer than in urban settings, where by their very nature, an abundance of phenomena, activities, people, physical, and social environments collide across a particularly confined and complex spatial landscape.

As a geographer, I am likely predisposed to be drawn to the *where* questions. But, of course, these are not simply questions of geographic location, but of how the 'where' plays a part in shaping or mediating the 'what' and the 'why' of the world around us. In other words, 'knowing where something happens can help us to understand what happened, when it happened, how it happened, and why it happened' (Campbell & Shin, 2012). The argument is by no means that all research requires a spatial understanding. Indeed, many curiosities about the world around us may be largely non-spatial in nature. Nonetheless, there is great value and much to be learned in considering the spatial dimension of an object of research. This chapter presents the potential of Geographic Information Science and Systems[1] and their application in uncovering the spatial dynamics that characterize the urban context.

---

[1] As discussed in this chapter, the abbreviation of GIS itself has evolved from a focus on GI systems to include a wider GI science. Here, I discuss both but choose to spell out 'systems' versus 'science, when the distinction is important.

Over the years that I have worked with GIS, I'm often faced with explaining to those without experience in the field what it is that I do. Invariably, their initial reaction usually follows along the lines of 'Ah, so maps on computers, then.' This is not, on the surface, wrong. GI systems are at their root an information technology made possible with the advances of computing and the proliferation of different forms of **digitalized spatial data** (see also chapters 4 and 10). Simply speaking, **GIS** researchers and practitioners spend a lot of time working with 'maps on computers,' or in other words, with digital representations of the world. However, this shorthand in no way captures either the scope or capabilities of GI science and systems.

On the applied side, when we think of the technological tool of GI systems, we do refer to a particular type of computer program. On the one hand, GIS thus represents a special category of software having the capacity to store, retrieve, organize, process, analyze and visualize **spatial data** and its attributes. A simple deconstruction of the term reveals its key components: 'G' for *geographic* emphasizes that it is concerned with data that can be linked to a location on the globe, 'I' points to its purpose of understanding and generating new *information* through the application of its functions, and 'S' underscores its central role in linking together multiple components in a *system*, whether layers of data or a package of analysis and visualization functionalities.

Beyond the technological definition of GIS, there has been a recognition of its entanglement in a broader geographic information science (Goodchild, 1992). GI science is strongly embedded in geography, as well as linked to, the disciplines of urban planning, urban studies, and computer sciences, among others. The science of GIS engages with both the developments of new methods of spatial analysis and modeling and with the broader questions of how geographic information and its interpretation provide a method for discovering new knowledge. GI science is thus 'concerned with the concepts, principles, and methods that are put into practice using the tools and techniques of GI systems' (Longley et al., 2015, p. 11). In other words, confronting the essential questions about what can be asked and answered through GIS, its engagement with and potential contributions to scientific theory, its associated limitations, as well as its societal consequences.

This demands a critical approach to reflecting on how data can produce knowledge. Not least, this involves grappling with the inherent reductionism of quantitative representations of the world around us. As reflected in Monmonier's seminal book *How to Lie with Maps*, cartographic visualizations can deceive. The author contends that 'not only is it easy to lie with maps, it's essential' (Monmonier, 2018, p. 1). The very act of attempting an interpretable depiction of the real world involves a necessary abstraction or distortion – viz. Korzybski's (1931) axiom that the 'map is not the territory'. However, it is above all key to acknowledge that maps lie to different extents and for different purposes: from the benign, necessary, and useful to, in some cases, the malevolently misleading. Most of us are very familiar with the transit maps of major cities, where colored metro lines criss-cross each other in simple geometric angles. Clearly such representations of a transport network are, in fact, 'lies' insofar as the actual geography of transit routes has been simplified and distorted in multiple ways. While this represents an intentional distortion, we are generally aware that it has been done for benign reasons and, indeed, helps make the network much more easily legible. On the other hand, visualization of data may be more subtly adjusted through careful selection of data breaks or colors to misleadingly overemphasize certain outcomes over others. Relatedly, the expert knowledge associated with carrying out GIS analyses raises concerns with the potential of GIS as a 'black-box' where complex and opaque methods can assert undue confidence in what should be a more nuanced understanding. This is further linked to critiques in terms of power imbalances between those who create and consume GIS outputs (see Harley, 1989).

GIS researchers, as well as map readers, therefore need to remain critical both of the use (and power) of GIS applications and in the interpretation of its outputs. This involves questioning how data is manipulated (in the neutral sense of the word), with what aim, and how the communication of information – particularly but not exclusively through maps – may emphasize, distort, or obscure information. More broadly, a welcome critical turn in GIS has underscored the need to more strongly embed GIS in a critical scientific framework. This has encouraged an engagement with social theory and post-positivist epistemological questions on how geographic knowledge is produced and communicated (Sheppard, 2005; O'Sullivan, 2006). One related development has been a growing field of public participation GIS which aims at a democratization of spatial data and a collaborative approach to information generation (Craig, Harris & Weiner, 2002; Ghose, 2017). An additional engagement with theories on gender and feminist geography in GI science (see Kwan, 2002; Schuurman & Pratt, 2002; Elwood & Leszczynski, 2018) have brought valuable critiques in how these fields 'intersect in their concerns with the grounded contexts of everyday life and in dealing, either implicitly or explicitly, with conceptions of power and empowerment' (McLafferty, 2002, p. 265 in O'Sullivan, 2006).

While GIS retains a strong basis in quantitative research approaches, developments in critical GIS have also been associated with a burgeoning field of qualitative GIS. Qualitative turns have sought to emphasize more strongly how geographic knowledge and meanings are 'produced and negotiated' and have further argued for the possibilities of including traditionally non-cartographic spatial information (Cope & Elwood, 2009). Examples of qualitative GIS have been mapping and visualizations of individual activity spaces of respondents (Mennis et al., 2013), processing and interpreting 'mental maps' of neighborhood space through a GIS (van Gent, Boterman & van Grondelle, 2016), or mapping emotions, such as interpretations of fear and safety in respondents' trajectories through the city (Kwan, 2008; Gargiulo et al., 2020).

This does not only make for interesting cartographic processing and representations of qualitative data, but also calls for fruitful mixed method approaches. As testified by this volume, urban studies presents an ideal field of research where understanding what constitutes the 'city' can be tackled through a multitude of approaches. There are great opportunities for GIS in mixed methods research wherein it can incorporate different forms of quantitative and qualitative knowledge (Cope & Elwood, 2009). Gargiulo et al. (2020) offer a valuable research example looking at safety perceptions in urban stream corridors in Barcelona. Recent technological advances beyond the static printed map provide further opportunities through online mediums that can link interactive maps with a multitude of data forms from narrative text, photos, recordings and videos, to diverse qualitative and quantitative visualizations (as discussed in chapter 4 and also applied in chapter 10). One interesting example is ESRI's StoryMaps platform that allows GIS users to publish online narrative interactive maps (see ESRI, 2019a). Examples include a countermapping project on the conflict between indigenous livelihoods and oil concessions in Ecuador (ACT, 2019) or on urban experiences of commuting in Washington DC (ESRI, 2019b).

The argument is in no way that qualitative approaches may replace more quantitative GIS. Of course, much GIS research undertaken in the field remains focused on questions that are (partly) quantitative in nature and are best answered through such an approach. The value lies in recognizing the many opportunities to enrich understanding of a subject through opening up research to complementary qualitative methods, or vice versa, complimenting qualitative research with a quantitative and spatial understanding.

Who owns the city? An example GIS approach

In this chapter, I will present an example GIS approach in order to illustrate the process of GIS research (provided in these adjoining textboxes). Here the question 'Who owns the city?' is tackled. In this textbox, I begin by looking at the question through a spatial lens and presenting a specific GIS research angle for this topic. Subsequently, I will introduce the analysis approach and data needed to address this investigation, followed by an outlining of the applied methods I undertook to answer the question, making use of the GIS toolbox. Finally, I present the results of the GIS analyses and their implications.

Who owns the city? is of fundamental interest to urban studies scholars as well as being broad and flexible enough that it could be approached in a multitude of ways. What would a GIS researcher think of when faced with this question? While one could expect much variety among GIS researchers, they will invariably be drawn to questions of space and spatial relationships. A simple primary interest is in thinking broadly of how space in the city is divided and classified according to **ownership**. Of course, 'ownership' could be thought of in numerous ways, from official legal titles to informal claims. Ideas of ownership can also vary greatly across socio-cultural and institutional contexts reflecting different degrees of informality and regulation (e.g. Saharan, 2018). Even when considering official divisions of ownership in the city, one could limit understandings to land ownership or one could consider how official decrees set out differentiated *use* of space. For example, the fact that a municipal works storage and a public park are both on land 'owned' by the local government may matter less for most residents than the fact that one is (generally) open to everyone while the other is mostly off-limits. Of course, this is not to say that legal land ownership does not matter, given its substantial influence on the scope of control over land, as well as economic implications in the division of assets.

Here, the question of *who owns the city* has piqued a specific interest of mine: one arising from my daily experience in the city where I live and the spatial lens with which I look at the urban space around me. I spend much of my time walking or biking through Amsterdam. While almost all of my travels occur on land which is ostensibly 'public space,' it is nonetheless partitioned in very specific ways and proscribed to different users. Especially in a dense city such as Amsterdam, almost all public space has been legally divided in precise ways and allocated different primary functions, whether roads, sidewalks, parking areas, patios, playgrounds, parks, canals, etc. At the same time, Amsterdam, more than almost any city is associated with a particular activity in its public realm: bicycling. In 2016, 48% of commuting trips were made by bike, while car trips made up only 21% (Harms & Kansen, 2018); when including all trips these shares were 35% and 19% respectively (Amsterdam Gemeente, 2019a). Amsterdam has often been seen as exemplary of what is possible in an arrangement of urban form that encourages sustainable modes of travel and discourages car use (Feddes, 2019; Frame, Ardila-Gomez & Chen, 2017). While the vast majority of Amsterdammers travel by bike, on foot, or by transit, I often still marvel at how much of the limited public space appears reserved for cars. These musings lead to my particular take on the question of *who owns the city* and the following more specific research question:

What share of Amsterdam's streetscape is assigned to automobile use and how does this compare to space primarily assigned for bicycle use or for pedestrians?

Applying a GIS approach to research

In the paragraphs above, I have argued for the value of GIS as well as the need to be a critical and reflective scientist in understanding its role within social science research and theory. Here we delve further into the *practice* of GIS research. I engage with the following key issues: What type of questions do GIS researchers ask?

What are the considerations in terms of the data needed? And what is the toolset of the GIS researcher? In the accompanying textboxes, these issues are additionally presented more concretely through an example GIS research approach towards answering the book's thematic question on 'Who owns the city?'

GIS research questions

It goes without saying that your research question is central to the research endeavor. As discussed in the introduction of this volume, what starts with a broader area of interest needs to be specified into a clearly formulated question that guides you towards a more precise focus. A research question also implies a certain relevant methodological approach. GIS methods are logical for research questions that have a spatial angle. The type of questions GIS researchers tackle involve, either explicitly or implicitly, matters of 'where' and tend to look at issues of *spatial*: distributions, patterns, relationships, interactions, concentrations, clustering, or siting. Many common concepts in urban studies inherently involve spatial dimensions – i.e. segregation, accessibility, or neighborhood effects – providing numerous fruitful opportunities for GIS investigations. Other common concerns of urban studies may not directly be spatial but have myriad spatial dimensions and consequences that pique the interest of the GIS researcher, such as inequality, gentrification, sustainability, (environmental) justice, social cohesion and conflict, the provision and access to public space, etc. In the first textbox, I provide an example of how I define my research question on addressing the theme of 'who owns the city'. For further examples, van Maarseveen, Martinez and Flacke (2019) present a nice compendium of urban GIS research centred on issues of sustainability, inclusivity, and resilience.

Who owns the city? Data and operationalization

Having established my research question (see first textbox), I will need to define, or **operationalize**, my key concepts. These include what I consider the 'streetscape', as well as how I will define 'space assigned to automobile use' versus 'space primarily assigned to bicycle use' or 'to pedestrians'. I present here a limited example GIS investigation; however, for a related and extensive application of streetscape land-use assessment in Amsterdam, see Nello-Deakin (2019).

Since in my case I am interested in formal proscriptions for the use of space, I turned to official data on the division of land-uses in Amsterdam. I make use here of the Large-scale Topographical Register of the Netherlands – in Dutch: *Basisregistratie Grootschalige Topografie* (BGT). The BGT represents a legal register by the Dutch government and provides, according to its documentation, the most detailed 'unambiguous' assessment of land-use across the country (Rijksoverheid, 2019). The spatial dataset provides an accuracy down to 20 cm covering precise divisions of physical space in terms of buildings, infrastructure, roadways, water, greenspace, etc. The BGT is also available through an open data portal (see PDOK, 2019). For my focus on streetscapes, I use the subset on the *wegdeel* – often translated as 'roadways', but more correctly representing all types of 'routes' in public infrastructure space – available as polygon data. For this example research, I use this as the base of my initial operationalization of Amsterdam's 'streetscape'.

My further operationalization of assigned land-use divisions of the streetscape is derived from predefined classifications within the BGT dataset. There is some leeway for different operationalization choices and these decisions are clearly of central importance in the research process. As this remains an example **GIS** approach, I do not go over specific operationalization choices in more detail, but it is essential that in a full study, this process is carefully considered, explained and justified. In the table below, I present my example operationalization based on the BGT classifications. Further details on the variables can be found in the dataset's official documentation (see Amsterdam Gemeente, 2019b).

Table 11.1: Operationalization of streetscape land-uses

Concept	Sub-category	BGT wegdeel classifications included
Space assigned to **automobile** use	Automobile travel	Local car lane (*rijbaan locale weg*) / major road car lane (*rijbaan autoweg*) / regional road car lane (*rijbaan regionale weg*) / highway car land (*rijbaan autosnelweg*) / onramp (*inrit*) / overpass (*overweg*)
	Automobile parking	Parking space (*parkeervlak*)
	Automobile mixed	'Living street'(*woonerf*) / 'automobile travel' plus any other use / 'automobile parking' plus any other use
Space primarily assigned to **bicycle** use		Bicycle path (*fietspad*)
Space primarily assigned to **pedestrians**		Pedestrian area (*voetgangersgebied*) / Sidewalk (*voetpad*) / Sidewalk on stairs (*voetpad op trap*)
Space assigned to **transit**		Transit lane (*OV-baan*) / Transit lane (*OV-baan*) plus either bicycle and/or pedestrian
Excluded from my definition of streetscape		Airport runway (*baan voor vliegverkeer*) / horse-riding path (*ruiterpad*) / train tracks (*spoorbaan*) / unknown space in transition (*transitie*)

Spatial data

No research can be undertaken without data. Data is essential to all types of research and all types of data exist. The prerequisite of GIS research is that this data needs to also include spatial information. More precisely, in GI science, we work with data which can be related to a location on the globe (expressed through coordinates) and provides information about this location (the associated attribute data).

We live in a time when huge volumes of data are continuously generated (see also the discussion in chapter 2). New sources of data are produced through our increasing engagement with digital technologies (Arribas-Bel, 2014). To the advantage of GIS research, an increasing amount of information we generate is also spatial. This 'data deluge,' however, brings additional concerns. The hype around '**Big Data**' has been tempered by an important realization of its limitations. This necessitates a critical approach of GIS researchers in questioning the quality of (spatial) data. There is, however, nothing new here and considerations of data quality always need to be taken into consideration (see chapter 2 on quantitative data). Nonetheless, new data sources often necessitate a renewed vigor of critical assessment, insofar as they are much more likely to be messy, unstructured, biased in sampling, and used for purposes beyond the intention (or non-intention) of their collection (Kitchin, 2014; Harford, 2014). This is further coupled with ethical considerations of privacy surrounding the volumes of data generated by people's everyday engagement with digital platforms (Kitchin, 2013; Zwitter, 2014; Mooney et al., 2017).

While new data sources, approached responsibly, provide some interesting new avenues of research (Kitchin, 2013), traditional datasets continue to have an essential role to play. Traditional data sources provide clear advantages in being collected/generated intentionally with forethought to data quality (at least for particular uses) in terms of accuracy, completeness, sampling and representativeness. A very welcome development is that we have also seen a move towards increasingly open data among traditional data sources (Arribas-Bel, 2014). Many government agencies have made their datasets – including large volumes of spatially-linked data – increasingly available through online portals. This has particularly been true at the municipal level, with a growing amount of open access (spatial) data for the analysis of urban contexts. The municipality of Amsterdam has exemplified this move providing a wide variety of spatial data freely online (Amsterdam Gemeente, 2019c). Beyond government sources, other useful examples have arisen such as the user-generated OpenStreetMap platform (see OSM, 2020). While there are opportunities for a further democratization of data, the burgeoning open data revolution has provided a boon for GIS researchers.

Who owns the city? Applied methods

In this textbox, I present an outline of the key steps in carrying out my example GIS research. While many studies involve more complicated analyses, this example provides a useful illustration of the structured steps in applying GIS towards answering my spatial research question. (In this example, I refer to ArcGIS and its tools, a common GIS software package, however, other open source alternatives such as QGIS could be similarly applied.)

Step 1   Acquiring and getting acquainted with the data.

My process began with downloading all the data I needed. Of course, some initial understanding of the data had already been necessary, however, this step also involved further reading over documentation as well as opening up and exploring the data in the GIS software.

Step 2   Data preparation.

When working with secondary sources, there is invariably data preparation required. In this case, the data was relatively well organized, however, I still needed to select out the subdataset I was going to focus on: *BGT-wegdeel*. I also clipped the dataset to the Amsterdam city boundary, since this was my study area. I did this using ArcGIS's *Clip* tool. As Amsterdam was covered by four separate files in the BGT, I subsequently also merged these into one file, using the *Merge* tool.

Step 3   Defining streetscape land-uses.

I then needed to apply my operationalization of the streetscape categories I was interested in. I did this through adding a new field and using the *Field Calculator* function to define combined categories based on the more detailed variables from the BGT data (see: operationalization table). I saved a new layer (*BGT-streetscape*) with my operationalized categories, excluding all unnecessary data.

Step 4   Combining with neighborhood layer.

As I was also interested in summarizing data at the neighborhood level, I added a neighborhood layer acquired from the Amsterdam data portal (Amsterdam Gemeente, 2019c). I then used the *Union* tool to combine this with my *BGT-streetscape* layer. In this way the streetscape areas were divided up by neighborhoods. I then used the *Dissolve* tool to aggregate the data as one polygon (i.e. shape) per land-use per neighborhood.

Step 5   Generate descriptive statistics on streetscape land-uses.

My next step – working with the attribute table rather than the spatial data – was to calculate land-use areas using the *Calculate Geometry* function. These could then be used to create summary statistics of the different land-uses for the city overall and per neighborhood.

Step 6   Visualizing the results.

The final step was to create output maps and a graph to visualize the findings (presented in subsequent textbox). The communication of findings through maps is a crucial part of GIS research and careful consideration should be applied in choosing effective symbology.

The GIS toolbox

Every methodological approach has its own toolbox of standard methods for analysing and understanding the world around us. While these may reflect common 'tools of the trade', they should in no way be the only methods at hand. Indeed, it is important to question one's own methodological bias. My discussion above on valuable advances in qualitative and mixed methods GIS approaches makes precisely the case (as does this book) for the advantages of approaching a topic from different methodological and disciplinary angles. It is nonetheless essential to become acquainted with the common – if only partial – toolbox of the GIS researcher. At its root, GIS software provides a set of tools focused on:

a   organizing data,
b   processing, preparing, inputting and storing data,
c   performing analyses on the data and thereby generating new information, and
d   visualizing data, primarily through maps.

Some of the common GIS software used are provided by private companies, such as ArcGIS or MapInfo, while others are free and open-source, such as the QGIS or GRASS applications.

It is difficult to find an overview of the basic spatial analysis – or 'geoprocessing' – tools in GIS given its structure as a 'package' of diverse tools available within a GI system. Some are simple manipulations applied to geographic data, others are more complex functions, and some may be very specific niche analyses. It is frequently the simple tools that prove the most useful for a GIS researcher: the building up of many simple analysis steps can deliver fruitful insights into the data. I present here what can be thought of as a *very incomplete* sampler of common tools. Among the 'basics' of the GIS toolbox are processes of:

- *Selecting* data, either by location or by specific attributes, or in relation to other data layers.
- *Overlaying* layers of data to understand where something co-occurs, or doesn't, in space.
- *Proximity* measures to understand what is near to something.
- *Network analyses* to understand travel across space.
- *Remote sensing analyses* to extract useful information from imaging (i.e. satellite images).
- *Spatial statistics* to explore **spatial patterns** and their statistical relationships.
- *Visualization* tools for generating maps, symbolizing and communicating data.

Moreover, it is important to emphasize that GIS research is versatile and may involve applying tools beyond the standard packages of GIS software. Examples include deriving key spatial variables from GIS analysis that are then used for regression modeling carried out in standard statistical software (see Arundel & Ronald, 2017; Arundel & Hochstenbach, 2019), or making use of a qualitative text analysis software to extract data for input into GIS mapping (see Kwan, 2008; Brown et al., 2017). The preceding textbox provides a concrete application of several GIS tools in addressing my example focus on the division of space in Amsterdam's streetscape.

Who owns the city? GIS analysis results

Through the GIS analysis described in the previous textbox, I was able to calculate different shares of the streetscape land-uses in Amsterdam based on my operationalized categories. The key findings are shown in the two final maps presented below. The first set of maps (figure 11.1) shows the land-use divisions in the Amsterdam streetscape. This is presented in two parts. The top map depicts the full study area examined. The object of study, consisting of narrow 'strips of land', is challenging to depict clearly in a full map (particularly when printed in a smaller format), therefore the inclusion of the second inset-map gives a better idea of the divisions in more detail for a central area of the city. The map also provides the key descriptive statistics through a pie-chart embedded in the map. The symbology choices applied intuitive color classes to match common depictions in transport mapping or roadspace colorations.

Looking at these first maps, we can see that most streets reflect a mix of car- and pedestrian-assigned uses, while certain larger streets also include separated bike paths (i.e. primarily assigned to bicycle use). Many areas are also designated as fully pedestrian and these also occur in larger zones such as public squares. Turning to the total sum of different land-uses across the city reveals a significant dominance of two categories of land-uses. Automobile space represents a clear majority of the streetscape, with 53.7% of the area either designated for 'car travel', 'car parking', or part of a mixed space that includes cars. The subcategory of car travel takes up the largest share here, with 41.6%. Pedestrian use then comes in second, with 37.8% of the streetscape, followed by space primarily assigned for bicycle use (6.8%) and finally transit space (1.7%). This indeed presents an interesting finding with over half of all 'streetscape' space in the city of Amsterdam designated for cars. On the one hand, this could be considered a disproportionate claim given their small share of trips made: only 21% of commuting trips (Harms & Kansen, 2018) and 19% of all trips by residents (Amsterdam Gemeente, 2019a). On the other hand, weighing the relationship between modal shares and what represents a 'just' land-use allocation is more complex than direct percentage comparisons – while this is beyond the focus of the methodological example, Nello-Deakin (2019) provides an interesting overview of this debate.

The second set of maps (figure 11.2) looks at neighborhood-level shares of streetscape area designated for automobile use (car travel, car parking, or car mixed) (top) and designated primarily for either pedestrian or bicycle use (bottom). This provides a further interpretation of relative differences across Amsterdam neighborhoods. Overall, the pattern reveals an expected differentiation between less car-dominated central neighborhoods and outskirt areas that are more so, although there remain many exceptions to this pattern in the data. Here, we also need to be aware in interpreting the map critically of significant differences in neighborhood size where large low-density and industrial areas disproportionately dominate. While I don't delve deeper

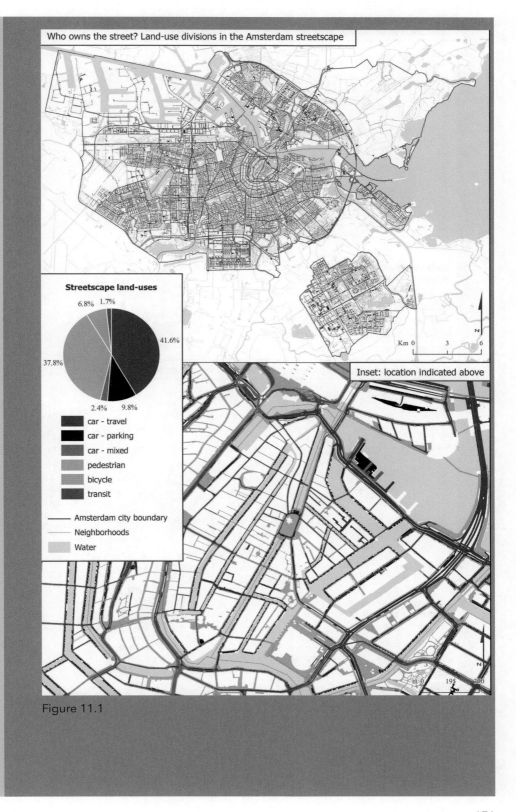

Who owns the street? Land-use divisions in the Amsterdam streetscape

INSET

Km 0   3   6

Inset: location indicated above

Streetscape land-uses

6.8% 1.7%

41.6%

37.8%

2.4% 9.8%

- car – travel
- car – parking
- car – mixed
- pedestrian
- bicycle
- transit

—— Amsterdam city boundary

---- Neighborhoods

Water

m 0   195   390

Figure 11.1

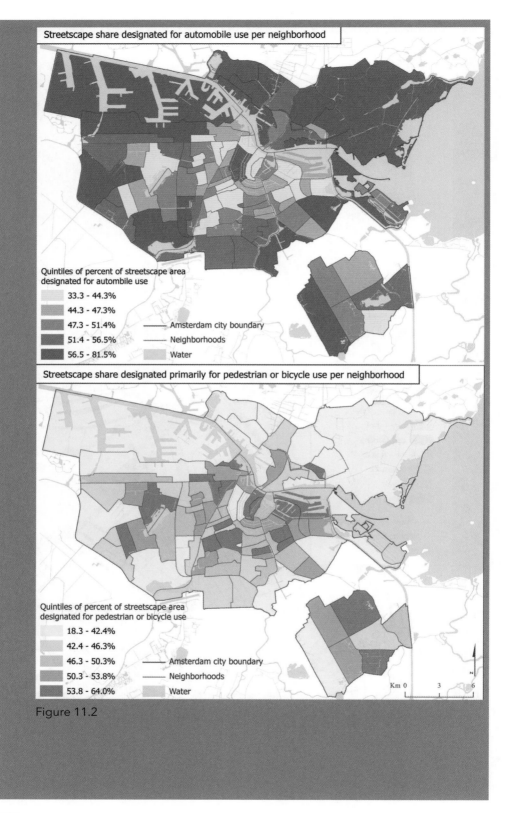

Streetscape share designated for automobile use per neighborhood

Quintiles of percent of streetscape area
designated for autombile use

33.3 - 44.3%
44.3 - 47.3%
47.3 - 51.4%   Amsterdam city boundary
51.4 - 56.5%   Neighborhoods
56.5 - 81.5%   Water

Streetscape share designated primarily for pedestrian or bicycle use per neighborhood

Quintiles of percent of streetscape area
designated for pedestrian or bicycle use

18.3 - 42.4%
42.4 - 46.3%
46.3 - 50.3%   Amsterdam city boundary
50.3 - 53.8%   Neighborhoods
53.8 - 64.0%   Water

Km 0   3   6

Figure 11.2

here, the neighborhood level assessment would also provide further opportunities to link up this streetscape data to other datasets. Given that there is a wealth of data available at the neighborhood level in the Netherlands, relationships between neighborhood characteristic and streetscape designated uses could be investigated, for example, how local socio-economic characteristics might relate to automobile dominance in the streetscape and associated issues of environmental justice.

As with all research, it is essential to also consider its limitations. In this example, these results are based on the official land-use designations and there are clear caveats that need to be recognized. While the data allows a determination of spatial divisions in official use designations, it both ignores more detailed nuances of shared spaces and does not reflect common informal claims to space. Firstly, local streets that would in reality include cars and cycling uses, were assigned to the car category (although these are separated out as a mixed car space in the subcategories). Relatedly, the official designation of many park paths are shown as exclusively pedestrian space, but this ignores their frequent use also by cyclists (in certain areas). Finally, within pedestrian space many more detailed elements are not included, for example bike parking areas or informal appropriations of sidewalks in front of buildings by residents (such as placing benches or planters). These are not included in the BGT data but would be expected to have substantial cumulative impacts. In this example, it appears that the data for Amsterdam, tends to underestimate the share of space that would be used by bicycles and overestimates the share of space for pedestrians – although in measuring the share of space used primarily or jointly by cars, such issues are less problematic. Nonetheless, the results presented here offer a useful exploratory example of applying a GIS approach to the question of *who owns the city*, focused on the space that makes up the streetscape of Amsterdam. In a more extended study, limitations could be (partly) tackled through further complementary research, including analyzing other secondary data sources such as detailed satellite imagery, or the collection of relevant primary data. This could also invole a valuable mixed methods approach to complement official space designations with more qualitative understandings of how spaces are used (or appropriated) by everyday users. Finally, while the example above is a useful way of thinking about how to examine 'who owns the street' in terms of the spatial allocation across different user groups, further considerations are needed in understanding how to evaluate what represents a 'just' share of land-use allocation (see Nello-Deakin, 2019).

Conclusion

In this chapter, we have examined how *space matters* and argued for the opportunities in understanding the world around us through a spatial lens. While space matters everywhere, I contend that cities present a context where spatial divisions and interactions are particularly intensified. Most areas of research that consume scholars in urban studies imply, directly or indirectly, significant spatial dimensions. GI science and systems present an invaluable approach to uncovering how the 'where' can help us to understand 'what happened, when it happened, how it happened, and why it happened' (Campbell & Shin, 2012). Being a critical GIS researcher also involves a reflective understanding of how such approaches constitute knowledge and particularly how they can engage jointly with other methods in getting a deeper understanding of the urban context. A well-rounded urban scholar is one that engages with a multitude of methods and this necessitates a recognition of the crucial role that space plays.

References

ACT (Amazon Conservation Team). (2019). *Sarayaku: In defense of territory*. http://amazonteam.org/maps/sarayaku

Amsterdam Gemeente. (2019a). *Amsterdam maakt ruimte: agenda autoluwe*. https://assets.amsterdam.nl/publish/pages/921204/agenda_amsterdam_autoluw.pdf

Amsterdam Gemeente. (2019b). *Catalogus Basisregistratie grootschalige topografie (BGT)*. https://www.amsterdam.nl/stelselpedia/bgt-index/catalogus-bgt/

Amsterdam Gemeente. (2019c). *Maps Data*. https://maps.amsterdam.nl/open_geodata/

Arribas-Bel, D. (2014). Accidental, open and everywhere: Emerging data sources for the understanding of cities. *Applied Geography, 49*, 45–53.

Arundel, R., & Hochstenbach, C. (2019). Divided access and the spatial polarization of housing wealth. *Urban Geography*, 1–27.

Arundel, R., & Ronald, R. (2017). The role of urban form in sustainability of community: The case of Amsterdam. *Environment and Planning B: Urban Analytics and City Science, 44*(1), 33–53.

Brown, G., Strickland-Munro, J., Kobryn, H., & Moore, S. A. (2017). Mixed methods participatory GIS: An evaluation of the validity of qualitative and quantitative mapping methods. *Applied geography, 79*, 153–166.

Campbell, E. J., & Shin, M. (2012). Geographic information system basics. https://2012books.lardbucket.org/books/geographic-information-system-basics/

Cope, M., & Elwood, S. (eds.). (2009). *Qualitative GIS: a mixed methods approach*. New York: Sage.

Craig, W. J., Harris, T. M., & Weiner, D. (eds.). (2002). *Community participation and geographical information systems*. Boca Raton, FL: CRC Press.

Elwood, S., & Leszczynski, A. (2018). Feminist digital geographies. *Gender, Place & Culture, 25*(5), 629–644.

ESRI (Environmental Systems Research Institute). (2019a). *Story Maps Gallery*. https://storymaps-classic.arcgis.com/en/gallery/

ESRI (Environmental Systems Research Institute). (2019b). *End of the Line*. https://storymaps.esri.com/stories/2017/dc-transit/index.html

Feddes, F., & de Lange, M. (2019). *Bike City Amsterdam: How Amsterdam Became the Cycling Capital of the World*. Amsterdam: Nieuw Amsterdam.

Frame, G., Ardila-Gomez, A., & Chen, Y. (2017). The kingdom of the bicycle: what Wuhan can learn from Amsterdam. *Transportation Research Procedia, 25*, 5040-5058.

Ghose, R. (2017). Defining Public Participation GIS. In *Comprehensive Geographic Information Systems*, 431.

Goodchild, M. F. (1992). Geographical information science. *International journal of geographical information systems, 6*(1), 31–45.

Gargiulo, I., Garcia, X., Benages-Albert, M., Martinez, J., Pfeffer, K., & Vall-Casas, P. (2020). Women's safety perception assessment in an urban stream corridor: Developing a safety map based on qualitative GIS. *Landscape and urban planning, 198*, 1–13.

Harford, T. (2014). Big data: A big mistake?. *Significance, 11*(5), 14–19.

Harley, J.B. (1989). Deconstructing the map. *Cartographica 26*, 1–20.

Harms, L., & Kansen, M. (2018). Cycling Facts. *Netherlands Institute for Transport Policy Analysis. The Hague*. http://revista.dgt.es/images/Cycling-facts-2018.pdf

Kitchin, R. (2013). Big data and human geography: Opportunities, challenges and risks. *Dialogues in Human Geography, 3*(3), 262–267.

Kitchin, R. (2014). Big Data, new epistemologies and paradigm shifts. *Big data & society, 1*(1), DOI: 2053951714528481.

Korzybski, A., 1931. A non-Aristotelian system and its necessity for rigour in mathematics and physics, Paper presented before the American Mathematical Society at the New Orleans, Louisiana, meeting of the American Association for the Advancement of Science December 28, 1931. Reprinted in Science and Sanity, 1933, 747–761.

Kwan, M. P. (2002). Is GIS for women? Reflections on the critical discourse in the 1990s. *Gender, Place and Culture: A Journal of Feminist Geography, 9*(3), 271–279.

Kwan, M. P. (2008). From oral histories to visual narratives: Re-presenting the post-September 11 experiences of the Muslim women in the USA. *Social & Cultural Geography, 9*(6), 653–669.

Longley, P. A., Goodchild, M. F., Maguire, D. J., & Rhind, D. W. (2015). *Geographic information science and systems*. John Wiley & Sons.

McLafferty, S. L. (2002). Mapping women's worlds: Knowledge, power and the bounds of GIS. *Gender, Place and Culture: A Journal of Feminist Geography, 9*(3), 263–269.

Mennis, J., Mason, M. J., & Cao, Y. (2013). Qualitative GIS and the visualization of narrative activity space data. *International Journal of Geographical Information Science, 27*(2), 267–291.

Mooney, P., Olteanu-Raimond, A. M., Touya, G., Juul, N., Alvanides, S., & Kerle, N. (2017). Considerations of privacy, ethics and legal issues in volunteered geographic information. In *Mapping and the citizen sensor*, Foody, G., See, L., Fritz, S., Mooney, P., Olteanu-Raimond, A., Costa Fonte, C., Antoniou, V. (eds.) London: Ubiquity Press, pp 119-137.

Monmonier, M. (2018). *How to lie with maps*. Chicago: University of Chicago Press.

Nello-Deakin, S. (2019). Is there such a thing as a 'fair' distribution of road space?, *Journal of Urban Design, 24*(5), 698–714.

O'Sullivan, D. (2006). Geographical information science: critical GIS. *Progress in Human Geography, 30*(6), 783–791.

OSM [Open Street Map]. (2020). *Open Street Map*. https://www.openstreetmap.org/

PDOK (Publieke Dienstverlening Op de Kaart). (2019). *PDOK: Datasets*. https://www.pdok.nl/datasets

Rijksoverheid. (2019). Basisregistratie Grootschalige Topografie. https://www.geobasisregistraties.nl/basisregistraties/grootschalige-topografie/basisregistratie-grootschalige-topografie

Saharan, T. (2018). T. *'Slum' and the City Subtitle: Exploring relations of informal settlements comparatively in Chennai, India and Durban, South Africa*. PhD Dissertation. University of Amsterdam. https://hdl.handle.net/11245.1/899ed5ab-e703-46f9-a829-202f912313a2

Schuurman, N., & Pratt, G. (2002). Care of the subject: Feminism and critiques of GIS. *Gender, place and culture: A journal of feminist geography, 9*(3), 291–299.

Sheppard, E. (2005). Knowledge production through critical GIS: Genealogy and prospects. *Cartographica: The International Journal for Geographic Information and Geovisualization, 40*(4), 5–21.

Tobler, W. R. (1970). A computer movie simulating urban growth in the Detroit region. *Economic Geography 46*, 234–40.

van Gent, W. P., Boterman, W. R., & van Grondelle, M. W. (2016). Surveying the fault lines in social tectonics; Neighhood boundaries in a socially-mixed renewal area. *Housing, Theory and Society, 33*(3), 247–267.

van Maarseveen, M., Martinez, J., & Flacke, J. (Eds.). (2019). GIS in Sustainable Urban Planning and Management: A Global Perspective. Boca Raton, FL: CRC Press. http://oapen.org/search?identifier=1002491

Zwitter, A. (2014). Big data ethics. *Big Data & Society, 1*(2), DOI: 2053951714559253.

12 Methods for studying urban biodiversity

Gerard Oostermeijer

Introduction

Cities as habitats for wild species

The world's first cities were created thousands of years ago, after the first agricultural revolution (Morris, 2013). Undoubtedly, various plants and animals immediately started living with humans amongst their dwellings. As cities are dominated by hard substrates like bricks, concrete, and asphalt, many wild species inhabiting them, such as the rock dove, peregrine falcon and butterfly bush, originate from rocky landscapes. Other species, such as rats, mice, and gulls, are opportunists, foraging on the leftovers and storages of human society. **Ruderal plants** have settled – often next to **ornamental plants** – in urban green spaces such as parks, (façade) gardens, tree wells, and road verges.

Urban ecology and evolution

There is increasing evidence that urban populations of several species differ from natural ones (Schilthuizen 2019). Apparently, the urban environment exerts strong natural selection, because this is a prerequisite for rapid evolutionary change. Temperatures are higher within cities, for example, creating the Urban Heat Island effect (Landsberg, 1981; Ceplová et al., 2017). Sound and chemical pollution are other environmental **drivers** that can result in changes in bird song (Slabbekoorn & Boer-Visser, 2006) and insect pheromones (Henneken & Jones, 2017). The inherent small size and fragmentation of urban green spaces (UGS) can lead to changes in dispersal traits of urban plant populations, because small rather than high dispersal distances are advantageous (Cheptou et al., 2008). Theoretically, urban populations require isolation from natural ones to avoid too frequent immigration of non-adaptive gene variants. This immigration may disturb the process of evolutionary adaptation to the urban environment. Nonetheless, insights from conservation biology (e.g. Haddad et al., 2015, Thompson, Rayfield & Gonzalez, 2017) have convinced urban ecologists that all urban green spaces should be connected

This general idea, now well-embedded in urban planning, will perhaps need to be adjusted when more insight is obtained on evolution in the urban ecosystem, and the roles of isolation versus connectivity.

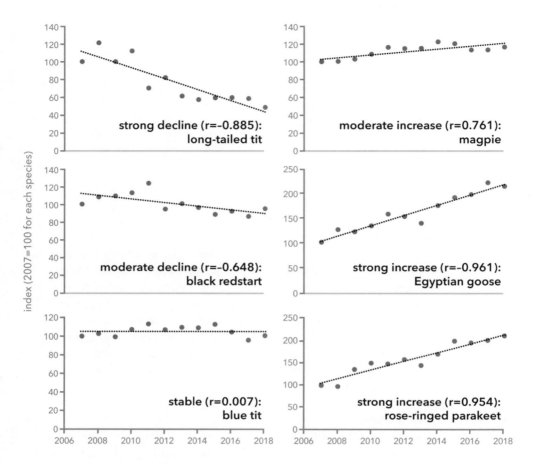

Figure 12.1:   Population trends of urban bird species from the Dutch bird monitoring project MUS (Monitoring Urban Species). Different species show different trends, but because potential causal factors were not included in the monitoring project, it is difficult to determine which cause is responsible for a particular species. The strong increase of the two invasive non-native species – Egyptian goose and rose-ringed parakeet – was expected, as these are good competitors for nesting space and suffer less from pathogens than the native species.

Novel ecosystems and biodiversity conservation

Although its biodiversity originates from natural habitats, the urban ecosystem does not have a natural analog, and is hence entirely novel (Kowarik, 2011). As a consequence, species conservation – a key concept in natural habitats – seems out of place. Because urbanization increases globally, multiple conflicts exist with biodiversity conservation (Kowarik, 2011). This is due to the general observation that species diversity of urban habitats is significantly lower than in natural environments. However, as diversity in non-urban habitats is dwindling even as it increases in the city, as was observed in our study on bees and hoverflies in Amsterdam (see case study), the abovementioned general difference perhaps applies less and less. At the same time, urban evolution leads to unique biodiversity that is also worthy of conservation.

Flower, bee and hoverfly diversity of urban and agricultural habitats

UvA Master's student Joan Casanelles compared abundances and diversity of flower-visiting bees and hoverflies at five **sampling** sites in each of three habitat types in the city of Amsterdam: urban parks, unmanaged urban green spaces (UGS) and farmland in a peri-urban agricultural landscape (Figure 12.1). Our main hypothesis was that urban habitats would harbor greater biodiversity than agricultural habitats, even though the latter comprise more continuous 'green space'. We expected that the more intensive land use of agricultural land would have a negative effect on insect abundance and diversity.

Figure 12.2: Map of the green structure of Amsterdam showing the five study sites for each of the three habitat types along the urban–rural gradient studied by UvA-IBED Master student Joan Casanelles. Dots: agricultural sites; squares: city parks; diamonds: unmanaged UGS.

The importance of biodiversity in the city

Biodiversity is an extremely broad concept, comprising more than just the number of species in a given area. It has a number of hierarchical levels:

1 *Genetic diversity* within and among individuals, populations, regions, and species,
2 The number of species (*species richness*) and the **relative abundances** *of different species* in a *community*. Taken together, species richness and relative abundances form the α-diversity *of a specific location*, such as the diversity of urban green spaces like parks. The differences in species composition and abundances *among locations* is called β-diversity;
3 All the *interactions* among species in communities, such as the interactions between plants and their pollinators, or the *food web* (also called trophic) *interactions*, e.g. soil fauna and invertebrates decomposing dead plants and animals so that the nutrients can be taken up by plants, herbivore insects eating from these plants, which are eaten by small birds, which are hunted by birds of prey. Any **taxonomic group** (or *taxon*, pl. *taxa*), or combinations thereof (to reflect components of the food web, for example) can be used to study **urban biodiversity**. Examples of *taxa* are bees, vascular plants, orchids, butterflies, flies, hoverflies, lizards, reptiles, and birds.
4 The total set of interacting populations, species and communities in a city make up the *urban ecosystem*, which uses available resources but also produces *ecosystem services* to humans, such as pollination of crops in urban gardens, storage and purification of water, and attractive environments in which inhabitants recreate.

Instead of conserving individual species that have moved into and adapted to the city, it seems better to focus on promoting sustainable biodiversity, ecosystem processes, and services in cities. In addition to the argument that other organisms have every right to settle in among and adapt to humans, there are several reasons to want higher urban biodiversity. First, biodiverse ecosystems function better and are more productive and stable (Tilman et al., 2014). Second, there is increasing evidence that humans feel better, and are both physically and mentally healthier, when living in a biodiverse city or neighborhood (Taylor & Hochuli, 2015; Sandifer et al., 2015).

General research aims and important questions

Sustainable conservation and management of urban biodiversity requires
a thorough understanding of the patterns that have formed over time and the factors causing them,
b analysis of **abiotic** and **biotic drivers** of population growth (or decline) of urban species,
c insight into functional traits that promote survival in the urban ecosystem, and
d assessment of the effectiveness of different methods to increase biodiversity or use it to improve the functioning of the urban ecosystem and the well-being of its inhabitants.

Urban biodiversity research has so many facets that there are as many research questions as there are researchers. From the author's perspective, intriguing and important specific questions are:

- How does the urban landscape differ from the (semi) natural, and how does this affect the survival of species or functional species groups?
- Which species live in and have adapted to the city? Are these merely a random selection of the species inhabiting natural ecosystems or do they represent specific habitats or possess specific functional traits?
- Which environmental factors (abiotic and/or biotic) form important selective forces in the adaptation of species to the urban environment?
- Are fragmentation and connectivity opposing forces in urban evolution?
- Can (and should) the urban ecosystem be modified to increase biodiversity?
- When setting targets for the urban ecosystem, should we aim for the best functionality, the highest biodiversity, or optimal human benefits?

Although many questions can be asked, this chapter in this multidisciplinary book will focus on the basics, i.e. methods to measure urban biodiversity, so that we obtain scientifically reliable data to answer them. More detailed questions on ecology and evolution require more advanced methods, which go beyond the scope of this book (see Schilthuizen, 2019). Hence, in the next section, we will look at approaches to describe and analyze species diversity and abundances, accompanied by a case study on plant and insect diversity along the urban–rural gradient in Amsterdam, presented in case study.

Describing biodiversity

Monitoring with a purpose

Many define monitoring as long-term collection of data at a certain time-interval (Lindenmayer et al., 2012). The main problem with this definition is that it doesn't mention any aim (Niemelä 2000). As a result, many biodiversity monitoring programs are initiated to 'detect trends'. These objectives can be loosely regarded as conservation-related (Hellawell, 1991). Too often, when a (significant) trend is detected, the researchers have to speculate about the possible causes. A frequent outcome is 'climate change', because that is an expected possibility, and hence considered most likely. We have to keep in mind, however, that when two variables change at the same time, they can be correlated even without any causal relationship (Araújo et al., 2005).

To avoid such speculations, it is wise to set up monitoring projects with the aim of answering clear, pre-formulated questions (or testable hypotheses). This ensures that

a attention will also be given to collecting data on potential causal factors, and
b that the monitoring doesn't have to last indefinitely, but can be stopped when the questions have been answered.

The past decades, millions of plant and animal records have been collected in an unstructured manner, often by citizens during other outdoor activities (Isaac et al. 2014). In particular in cities, records are often biased – for example, because they were only collected in larger parks, and are hence hardly suitable for answering specific questions. We used cumulative data from the Dutch National Database Flora and Fauna (NDFF) to relate biodiversity for several taxa in Amsterdam city parks to the use of these parks for large cultural events, but this failed due to the biased and unstructured nature of the available records (de Herder et al., 2018).

In the following sections, I will discuss approaches to study biodiversity in urban environments. A number of *taxa* (i.e. groups at variable levels in the scientific hierarchical classification of all living organisms, such as species, genera, family, and order) will be highlighted that have individuals observable without expensive tools, which makes them suitable for research by professional biologists as well as students and **citizen scientists**.

Determining species richness and abundances of 'observable' taxa

Plants

Because they are easily identified, and because they form food and habitat of many other species, plants are highly suitable for biodiversity research. With improving identification apps, also starting (citizen) scientists can make plant lists without spending hours on identification, although this is still error-prone and cannot match the speed of experienced biologists.

Plant species richness or community species composition can be used as response or predictor variables in studies on UGS, e.g. on management effects, relationships with area, or in analyses of animal habitat suitability.

Plant species richness can be determined with several methods. Because the aim is a comprehensive species list, studying plots of a given size is not appropriate, because these are only subsamples of the UGS, and will show considerable species overlap. Larger sampling units, such as distinct habitat types in parks (lawns, grasslands, roughs, tree stands), are more appropriate (Hermy & Cornelis, 2000). With the Tansley scale, a complete species list of the entire sampling unit can be made, with a very simple abundance score (rare, occasional, frequent, abundant, codominant, or dominant) for each species (Begon, Harper & Townsend, 1996). This yields data on species richness, composition and abundances, so that plant communities can be identified and Shannon-Wiener diversity indices (integrating species richness and abundances) calculated (Begon et al., 1996; see box).

To establish correlations between plant and animal abundances, vegetation can also easily be sampled along animal monitoring **transects** (see below). The latter are usually subdivided into sections of 10–50 m, which can serve as plot lengths of a certain width (1.5–2.5 m) for vegetation descriptions. In such large plots, the Tansley scale is very useful to estimate the abundance of each species. We used this method in a countrywide study to determine vegetation-based ecological indicator values of butterflies, based on the transects of the national butterfly monitoring scheme (Oostermeijer & van Swaay, 1998).

When the aim is to monitor changes in species composition over a longer time period, e.g. in relation to management, or after sowing different seed mixtures, standard vegetation decriptions (known as 'relevés') of permanent quadrats/plots are most commonly used across the globe, and also in cities (e.g. Frey & Moretti, 2019). Using a plot area considered appropriate for the habitat type (i.e. 4 m2 in grasslands, 100 m2 in forest), percent cover and mean height are estimated for each vegetation layer (trees, shrubs, herbs, bryophytes, and litter) and for the total vegetation (Westhoff & van der Maarel, 1973; Hermy & Cornelis, 2000). Subsequently, a list of *all* plant species (flowering *and* not-flowering) in the plot is made, recording for each species its percentage cover (vertical projection) of the plot, and the most advanced phenological stage. Most statistical (plant) community analyses (Oksanen et al., 2017) are based on this type of 'relevé data'.

Insects

The huge diversity of insects is reflected in the large number of sampling methods (Ausden & Drake 2006), of which we will discuss the most commonly used. These aim to capture insects occupying specific vegetation strata, such as the soil surface, the herb, shrub or tree layers. Note that sampling of insect groups (taxa) which don't have easily visible and identifiable species usually involves killing a (considerable) number of individuals with ethyl acetate, formaline, or salt water. This is unfortunately unavoidable, because many taxa can only be identified under a microscope. Research of insect diversity hence comes with substantial moral/ethical concerns (Fischer & Larson, 2019).

Details about each method listed below (and more) can be found in Ausden & Drake (2006).

- *Direct (or manual) searching*, using either an insect net (flying insects) or a pooter (small vegetation-dwelling insects).
- Butterflies, bees, dragonflies, and hoverflies can be counted directly along *monitoring transects* of a fixed width and height, along which observers walk with a constant speed. Weather conditions need to meet minimum criteria, specified *a priori* (see also box).
- *Pitfall traps* are used for ground-dwelling insects, such as ants and carabid beetles. They are placed in series of five, placed at a minimum of 5 m from each other to prevent mutual interference.
- *Pyramid traps* are small, pyramid-shaped structures covered with light-impermeable cloth used to capture insect species emerging from a specific soil surface area. Invertebrates emerging from soil or vegetation under the trap walk towards the light and are captured in a funnel trap: a light-transparent bottle holding preservative liquid.
- Flying insects (hoverflies, bees, wasps, butterflies, moths, and some beetle families) can be sampled with a *sweep net*. Sampling effort can be standardized by using a fixed number of sweeps per site. This is a suitable method for sampling along line transects, e.g. along a fixed length in each different habitat type.

- Flying insects are often sampled with a '*malaise trap*', a tent with open side entrances into which passing insects fly. Insects fly upwards towards the light into a funnel trap (see pyramid trap). These traps are unfortunately prone to vandalism.
- Many insect studies use *sticky traps*, i.e. small (A4-size) plastic sheets covered with a sticky substance on which flying or jumping insects get stuck. A major drawback is that individual insects die slowly and potentially painfully. Moreover, they don't remain in their best shape, so that identification becomes difficult.
- *Pan traps* consist of a white or colored container holding water (with salt or another non-toxic preservative). The container is either placed on the ground or erected on a pole just above the vegetation. Flying insects attracted by the trap land in the water and drown. Because insectivores may feed on the catch, pan traps need to be emptied every few days.
- A recent development are *camera traps*, i.e. a camera aimed at a white or yellow sheet of water-resistant material. A photograph of the sheet is taken at a pre-set time interval, and all insects on the images remain alive (!) and are identified by automated image recognition algorithms (Kaffa & Vos, 2019). Bees, for example, can be identified by the venation of their wings (Steinhage, 2000).
- Tree/shrub-dominated habitats are the domain of *beating nets*, flat square or round sheets of cloth held in position under a shrub or tree branch whilst the branch(es) above it are beaten with a stick. All insects on these branches fall down onto the cloth, from which they can be collected with a pooter.

It will have become clear that most methods focus on flying insects, fewer on insects living in the vegetation, and fewer still on ground-dwelling insects. Hence, a broad view of insect diversity requires multiple sampling methods. Because weather conditions and sampling date both have a significant effect on insect activity and emergence time, it is also essential that sampling is carried out over a longer time period, e.g. from April to September. Only then can time series analyses correct for **sampling variance** (e.g. by weather variation from year to year). If sampling is only done from April to May, and spring starts late that year, insect abundances and diversity will probably appear low, but not due to habitat type or management. Many six-month Master's degree projects, such as that by Joan Casanelles (see case study), are limited to sampling until August. We must take into account that some taxa might be missed because of this.

At each site, two linear transects of 30 m long and 1.5 m wide were monitored by walking along them at a constant pace multiple times between June and August 2016, to assess the diversity of flowering plants and their insect visitors. Monitoring was only done under suitable weather conditions: no strong wind, less than 75% cloud cover, and temperature ≥18°C. In addition, the visiting sequence to each site was varied among sampling dates to ensure that the frequency of morning and afternoon hours was equal among the sampling locations. Each site was also sampled with an equal number of visits.

Regarding flowering plants, the main hypothesis was supported: both urban habitats were similar, but comprised significantly higher flower abundance (number of flowers counted along the transects) and diversity (number of flowering plant species counted along the transects) than the agricultural habitats (figure 12.2). Parks showed significantly higher abundances of bees and hoverflies together, but this was mainly due to larger bee than hoverfly numbers, which were similar across habitat types. The second highest abundances were observed in unmanaged UGS and the lowest at farmland sites. Hence, the main hypothesis was again supported by the abundance data.

The Shannon diversity index (which combines number of species and the abundance per species), did not differ significantly among parks and unmanaged UGS. Diversity in both urban habitat types was, however, significantly higher than at sites in the agricultural landscape (Figure 3). This was true for bees as well as hoverflies, although the latter were more diverse in parks than in unmanaged UGS.

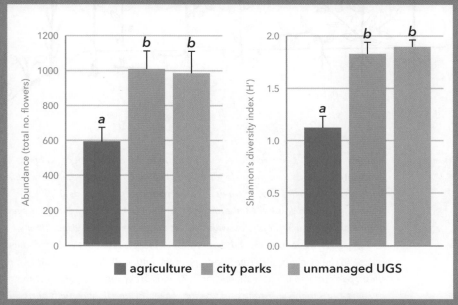

Figure 12.3: Mean flowering plant abundance (a) and diversity (b) in three habitat types along the urban-rural gradient in the city of Amsterdam. For a map of the five **sampling** areas for each habitat type, see figure 12.1. Error bars represent standard errors.

Birds

Because of their visibility, monitoring birds seems straightforward, but setting up a monitoring scheme to answer specific questions is difficult. The Dutch monitoring system for urban birds (MUS: Monitoring Urban Species: https://www.sovon.nl/en/MUS), maintained by the Dutch Centre for Ornithology SOVON, uses *point counts* at predefined locations along a walking or cycling route throughout a city. Citizen scientists spend 5 minutes at each point, counting all birds they see (except passing species without clear link to the city), and do this at 8–12 points in total, three times a year. Using this approach, trends between 2007–2018 could be established for 71 species, counted at 7134 points. Of these, 16 remained stable, 29 showed a moderate and 4 a strong decline, 16 a moderate and 6 a strong increase (figure 12.1, data downloadable from https://www.sovon.nl/en/content/stadsvogeltrends).

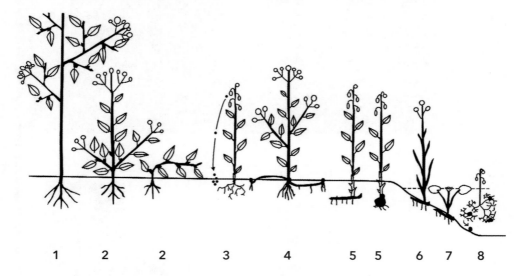

| 1 | 2 | 2 | 3 | 4 | 5 | 5 | 6 | 7 | 8 |

Figure 12.4:   *Raunkiaer (1934) classified life forms according to the placement of plants' overwintering buds. The main life forms are (1) phanerophytes, with overwintering buds >3 m above the ground (trees), (2) chamaephytes, with buds 0.30-1.5 m above the ground (dwarf shrubs), (3) therophytes, without buds, overwintering as seeds (annuals), (4) hemicryptophytes, with buds at or just below the surface (many herbs and grasses), (5) geophytes, with underground buds (perennials with rhizomes or bulbs), (6) helophytes, with rhizome-buds in the (inundated) substrate and emergent green parts (marsh or shore plants), and (7) and (8) hydrophytes, either with rhizome-buds in the substrate and floating leaves, or free floating with buds (turions) sinking to the bottom in winter.*

As mentioned above, what *caused* these trends remains a matter of speculation, because no potential causal factors were monitored. Hence, even though the long-tailed tit declined significantly, the researchers admitted that the underlying causes were 'a matter of speculation' (de Jong 2018). The project could have been more informative if the citizen scientists had also been asked to collect data on potential threats. Counts on prey abundance on trees or shrubs around point counts, done at every bird count, would have enabled the researchers to test the role of food availability, for example.

Alternatively, breeding territories can be mapped in fixed 'counting areas' of variable size (20–50 ha), providing detailed information on territory sizes and numbers. The Dutch Breeding bird Monitoring Program (BMP-A), Vergeer et al. (2016) doesn't include cities, though. It also doesn't measure any environmental variables. Observers can enter remarks on clear changes, but without predetermined structure these data remain largely anecdotal.

Bats

With colonies in buildings and trees, and their habit of hunting for insects attracted to artificial light, bats are also suitable for monitoring urban biodiversity. Identifying them requires a good *bat detector*. Because of this, bats seem less suitable for monitoring by citizen scientists than other groups. On the other hand, small bat detectors can now be attached to a smartphone and can even help to identify species. Because the number of species in cities is relatively limited, training laypeople is feasible, and even sound recordings produced by citizen scientists can yield large amounts of useful data (Newson, Evans & Gillings, 2015). Trained observers with a good bat detector can establish presence and abundance of species in specific areas. A monitoring project often uses monitoring transects subdivided into sections with a homogeneous habitat (Krebs, 2006).

The requirement for bat detectors is a limitation (as they cost money), but their use opens up another type of monitoring, i.e. using a *bat-logger*. This is a bat detector that continuously, or at certain time intervals, records the bat ultrasounds produced around it. They can be attached to trees in UGS at a height that reduces risks of vandalism or theft. Continuous bat activity monitoring is an interesting method to study, for instance, the effects of large events involving sound and light pollution on local bat populations.

Other small mammals

Besides bats, plenty of other mammals, such as hedgehogs, mice, shrews, squirrels, stoats, weasel, foxes, and badgers, live in cities. *Camera traps*, triggered by movement disturbing an infrared light beam, are increasingly used to determine their presence, and with multiple cameras in specific habitats, even abundances (Ehlers-Smith et al., 2018).

Rodents and shrews can also be monitored with (Sherman folding-type) *life traps* (Krebs, 2006). These can also best be placed along monitoring transects through several habitat types, so that differences in abundances can be statistically compared.

Functional groups

Thousands of species with specific ecology and detectability inhabit cities. Identifying the species captured or recorded is often limited by time, knowledge, or budget. To deal with this, organisms can be grouped according to functional traits. This is particularly useful for species-rich taxa such as insects, which can be grouped according to criteria such as feeding guild (i.e. carnivore, omnivore, or herbivore), or feeding mode (e.g. predator, nectar and/or pollen collector, sapsucker, or leaf chewer). To study pollination interactions, plants can be grouped into having 'open flowers', with readily accessible pollen and nectar, or 'tubular flowers', in which nectar is hidden at the bottom of a corolla tube of varying length (Fontaine et al., 2006). Flower-visiting insects can be grouped according to the length of their mouthparts, which determines on which flowers they can feed (Fontaine et al., 2006).

Plants can also be classified into Raunkiaer's (1934) life forms, based on the placement of buds at positions that allow them to survive periods unfavourable to growth (Figure 2). These work quite well within northwest Europe. At large geographical scales (e.g. for comparing urban vegetations across the globe), traits are added to the woody life forms to reflect differences in, for example, leaf size (Webb, 1959) or leaf consistency (Harrison et al., 2010). Relative abundances of life forms in plant communities generally reflect disturbance types and intensities, with therophytes dominating in the most disturbed (plowed, trampled) sites, hemicryptophytes in grazed or mowed grasslands, and phanerophytes with an understorey of geophytes in undisturbed forest. Understanding life forms allows us to comprehend, for example, why seed mixtures of disturbance-demanding therophytes (annuals) like poppies and corncockles do not last long after being sown into annually mown UGS, and are replaced by mowing-tolerant hemicryptophytes (mainly grasses).

DNA-based biodiversity assessments

Animals and plants leave traces of DNA in the environment. This *eDNA* can be used to establish their presence in a certain area, which works particularly well for species which are difficult to detect and sample (Stewart et al., 2017).

For taxa like insects or (soil) bacteria or fungi, species identification can be so time-consuming or even impossible that it is rapidly becoming faster, and hence cheaper, to extract DNA from entire sampling units (e.g. the contents of a pitfall or malaise trap or a soil sample) for *metabarcoding*: the detection of so-called barcodes, DNA sequences unique to particular species that can be used for their identification (Taberlet et al., 2012; Beentjes et al., 2019).

Spatial patterns: urban metapopulations

It is also useful to investigate spatial distributions of populations or gene pools of species, as these will provide information on connectivity within a city. In order to persist, populations should either be very large (if isolated), or connected with other populations of the same species through exchange of individuals or genes. In the latter case, there is a 'network' of populations, also known as a *metapopulation* (Hanski, 1999).

In order to determine whether or not urban species live in metapopulations, or even in discrete populations, data is required on migration rates of individuals or genes (in plants, genes can also disperse in pollen) among different habitat patches/ UGS. Gene flow can be inferred from genetic differentiation among populations (Meirmans & Hedrick, 2010). Using so-called assignment tests (Meirmans, 2012; Berry, Tocher & Sarre, 2015), the probability that a sampled individual originates from another population than it was sampled from can be determined, given that

a population sample sizes are large enough to reliably estimate **allele** frequencies and

b there is sufficient genetic variation and differentiation among populations (Meirmans, 2012).

Estimates of genetic differences among individuals and populations can be combined with field studies and GIS models to estimate the number of migrants in relation to landscape features determining connectivity (Klinga et al., 2019). For aquatic organisms, eDNA can be used to estimate abundances, for instance in canals and ditches that might serve as corridors (Stewart et al., 2017), and in terrestrial environments eDNA extracted from droppings/pellets can be used to estimate abundances and/or allele frequencies of certain mammals (e.g. rodents, badgers or martens) in corridors (Kohn et al., 1999).

In plants, connectivity through seed or pollen exchange can be estimated genetically by means of parentage analysis (Jones & Ardren, 2003). Movements of flower-visiting insects among populations or UGS (e.g. green roofs or parks) can be tracked by adding different colours of fluorescent dye to the anthers of flowers. The colours can be traced back on stigmas of visited flowers (in other patches) after dark, using a UV-torch, or – if sampled – under a fluorescence microscope (Van Rossum et al., 2011).

A good way of estimating whether or not species are able to maintain a viable metapopulation in a city is by first making a (validated) habitat suitability map, and subsequently determining which fraction of the habitat patches is occupied (patch occupancy: Hanski, 1999). In a viable metapopulation with frequent dispersal among populations, most of the suitable habitat patches will be occupied (i.e. there is high patch occupancy).

Spatial patterns and the theory of island biogeography

For many species, Urban Green Spaces are islands in a 'sea' ('matrix') of inhabitable stone and concrete. To what extent the matrix is experienced as inhabitable depends on the species; buildings are habitat for rock doves, but not for grassland plants.

If UGS are indeed comparable to islands, their biodiversity hypothetically shows distribution patterns comparable to islands. Island biodiversity patterns are explained quite well by the theory of island biogeography (MacArthur & Wilson, 1967; Marzluff, 2005). Large islands closest to the mainland tend to have higher species richness than small islands farther away, because island size and distance to the nearest **propagule** source control the extinction and colonization processes that determine species richness. Hence, it can be expected that urban UGS 'islands' also behave according to this theory (Marzluff, 2005; Breuste, Niemalä & Snep, 2008). Several studies support this 'urban island theory': the highest species richness is found in the largest UGS nearest to the natural landscape (e.g. Clarke, Fisher & LeBuhn, 2008; Fattorini et al., 2018).

Population genetic studies may also be used to test to what extent populations inhabiting UGS are isolated (Takami et al., 2004; Gardner-Santana et al., 2009) and, as discussed in the previous section, whether or not urban landscape features lead to more connectivity (Angold et al., 2006). At the same time, they can be used to assess the amount of gene flow from rural/natural to urban populations, which is important for the process of evolutionary adaptation to the urban ecosystem.

General conclusions

This chapter has hopefully made clear that there are many approaches to the study of urban biodiversity. Every plant or animal group (*taxon*) involves specific methods for collecting data.

Many biodiversity monitoring studies don't have clear aims. We have tried to emphasize the importance of formulating clear questions and testable hypotheses for each project. The methods chosen should depend on the questions asked. Following this approach, it is more likely that (potentially) important explanatory variables will also be monitored. We do not only seek statistically significant trends (Barlow et al., 2015), but also want to know what caused them.

Because monitoring spatial patterns and temporal trends in urban biodiversity requires lots of field observations, this research lends itself well for collaboration with citizen scientists and/or students. Because these groups have variable skills, their participation requires either 'foolproof' methods to collect reliable data in a structured way (see e.g. the MUS-example in 2.2) or intensive training sessions.

Once this additional step has been taken, however, studies of urban biodiversity can move beyond straightforward inventories, and even include more detailed ecological and even evolutionary research. We hope that this chapter has stimulated all those working in urban environments to include biodiversity in future studies and provided new research ideas to urban ecologists. In particular, we hope that it helps start many new collaborations between different categories of urban scientists (academic and applied researchers and students from different disciplins, NGOs involved in nation-wide monitoring of different taxonomic groups, city ecologists, citizen scientists etc.)!

In conclusion, we showed that urban habitats in Amsterdam show higher biodiversity for both flowering plants and the two main flower-visiting insect groups. The two factors were also correlated: more flowers and higher floral diversity also resulted in higher bee and hoverfly abundance and diversity. There was also a significant interaction in the analyses of variance, which indicates that insect diversity in each habitat depended on the flower abundance and diversity. Hence, agricultural sites with many flowering plants still attracted more insects. The study demonstrates that management of urban

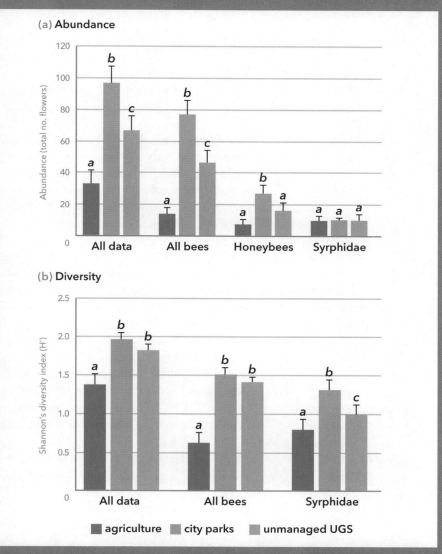

Figure 12.5: Bee and hoverfly abundance (a) and diversity (b) in three habitat types along the urban-rural gradient in the city of Amsterdam. For a map of the five sampling areas for each habitat type, see figure 12.1. Error bars represent standard errors.

green spaces that leads to higher plant diversity also has a beneficial effect on the insects that pollinate their flowers. At the same time, it illustrates that the larger expanses of 'green' space in the peri-urban agricultural landscape aren't necessarily home to many plants and insects. Here, management (of road verges as well as field and ditch margins) should be modified to create more habitat for wild flora and fauna!

References

Angold, P. G., Sadler, J. P., Hill, M. O., Pullin, A., Rushton, S., Austin, K., Small, E., Wood, B., Wadsworth, R., Sanderson, R., & Thompson, K. (2006). Biodiversity in urban habitat patches. *Science of the Total Environment, 360*, 196-204.

Araújo M. B., Pearson, R. G., Thuiller, W., & Erhard, M. (2005) Validation of species–climate impact models under climate change. *Global Change Biology, 11*, 1504-1513.

Ausden, M., & Drake, M. (2006) Invertebrates. In W. J. Sutherland (ed.) *Ecological census techniques: A handbook*, 2nd Edition. Cambridge: Cambridge University Press, pp. 214-248.

Barlow, K. E., Briggs, P. A., Haysom, K. A., Hutson, A. M., Lechiara, N. L., Racey, P. A., Walsh, A. L., & Langton, S. D. (2015). Citizen science reveals trends in bat populations: The National Bat Monitoring Programme in Great Britain. *Biological Conservation, 182*, 14-26.

Beentjes, K. K., Speksnijder, A. G.C. L., Schilthuizen, M., Hoogeveen, M., Pastoor, R., van der Hoorn, & B. B. (2019). Increased performance of DNA metabarcoding of macroinvertebrates by taxonomic sorting. *PLoS ONE, 14*(12): e0226527.

Begon, M., Harper, J. L., & Townsend, C. R. (1996). *Ecology, individuals, populations and communities*. 3rd Edition. London: Blackwell Science.

Berry, O., Tocher, M. D., & Sarre, S. D. (2015). Can assignment tests measure dispersal? *Molecular Ecology, 13*, 551-561.

Breuste, J., Niemelä, J., & Snep, R. P.H. (2008). Applying landscape ecological principles in urban environments. *Landscape Ecology, 23*, 1139-1142.

Ceplová, N., Kalusová, V., & Lososová, Z. (2017) Effects of settlement size, urban heat island and habitat type on urban plant biodiversity. *Landscape and Urban Planning, 159*, 15-22

Cheptou, P.O., Carrue, O., Rouifed, S., & Cantarel, A. (2008) Rapid evolution of seed dispersal in an urban environment in the weed *Crepis sancta*. *PNAS, 105*, 3796 -3799.

Clarke, K. M., Fisher, B. L., & LeBuhn, G. (2008). The influence of urban park characteristics on ant (Hymenoptera, Formicidae) communities. *Urban Ecosystems, 11*, 317-334.

de Herder, L., Steenvoorden, J., de Groot L., & Oostermeijer, J. G.B. (2018). *Evenementen en biodiversiteit in Amsterdamse stadsparken. Rapport IBED-UvA, Afd. Evolutie- en Populatiebiologie i.o.v.* Gemeente Amsterdam, Amsterdam.

de Jong, A. (2018). Stilaan minder staartmezen. *SOVON Nieuws 31*(1), 24.

Ehlers-Smith, Y. C., Ehlers-Smith, D. A., Ramesh, T., & Downs, C. T. (2018). Forest habitats in a mixed urban-agriculture mosaic landscape: Patterns of mammal occupancy. *Landscape Ecology, 33*, 59-76.

Fattorini, S., Mantoni, C., de Simoni, L., & Galassi, D. M.P. (2018). Island biogeography of insect conservation in urban green spaces. *Environmental Conservation, 45*, 1-10.

Fischer, B., & Larson, B. M.H. (2019). Collecting insects to conserve them: A call for ethical caution. *Insect Conservation and Diversity, 12*, 173-182.

Fontaine, C., Dajoz, I., Mériguet, J. & Loreau, M. (2006) Functional diversity of plant-pollinator interaction webs enhances the persistence of plant communities. *PLoS Biology, 4*, 129-135.

Frey, D., & Moretti, M. (2019). A comprehensive dataset on cultivated and spontaneously growing vascular plants in urban gardens. *Data in Brief, 25*, 103982, 1-26.

Gardner-Santana, L. C., Norris, D. E., Fornadel, C. M., Hinson, E. R., Klein, S. L., & Glass, G. E. (2009). Commensal ecology, urban landscapes, and their influence on the genetic characteristics of city-dwelling Norway rats *(Rattus norvegicus). Molecular Ecology, 18*, 2766-2778.

Glen, A.S., Cockburn, S., Nichols, M., Ekanayake, J., Warburton, B. (2013). Optimising camera traps for monitoring small mammals. *PLoS ONE, 8*(6), e67940.

Haddad, N. M., Brudvig, L. A., Clobert, J., Davies, K. F., Gonzalez, A., Holt, R. D., Lovejoy, T. E., Sexton, J. O., Austin, M. P., Collins, C. D., & Cook, W. M. (2015), Habitat fragmentation and its lasting impact on Earth's ecosystems. *Science advances, 1*(2), p.e1500052.

Hanski, I. (1999). *Metapopulation ecology*. Oxford Series in Ecology and Evolution. Oxford and New York: Oxford University Press.

Harrison, S. P., Prentice, P. C., Barboni, D., Kohfeld, K. E., Ni, J., & Sutra, J. P. (2010). Ecophysiological and bioclimatic foundations for a global plant functional classification. *Journal of Vegetation Science, 21*, 300-317.

Hellawell, J. M. (1991). *Development of a rationale for monitoring*. In F. B. Goldsmith (ed.) *Monitoring for conservation and ecology*. Conservation Biology series 3. Dordrecht, Netherlands: Springer.

Henneken, J., & Jones, T. M. (2017). Pheromones-based sexual selection in a rapidly changing world. *Current Opinion in Insect Science, 24*, 84-88.

Hermy, M., & Cornelis, J. (2000). Towards a monitoring method and a number of multifaceted and hierarchical biodiversity indicators for urban and suburban parks. *Landscape and Urban Planning, 49*, 149-162.

Isaac, N. J.B., van Strien, A. J., August, T. A., de Zeeuw, M. P., & Roy, D. B. (2014), Statistics for citizen science: Extracting signals of change from noisy ecological data. *Methods in Ecology and Evolution, 5*, 1052-1060.

Jones, A. G., & Ardren, W. R. (2003) Methods of parentage analysis in natural populations. *Molecular Ecology, 12*, 2511-2523.

Kaffa, C., Vos, R. (2019) Availability of insects as feed for meadow bird chicks assessed across years by batched image analysis of sticky traps. Preprint, bioRxiv, 24 pp, https://doi.org/10.1101/663591.

Klinga, P., Mikoláš, M., Smolko, P., Tejkal, M., Höglund, J., & Paule, L. (2019). Considering landscape connectivity and gene flow in the Anthropocene using complementary landscape genetics and habitat modelling approaches. Landscape Ecology, 34, 521–536.

Kohn, M. H., York, E. C., Kamradt, D. A., Haught, G., Sauvajot, R. M., & Wayne, R. K. (1999). Estimating population size by genotyping faeces. *Proceedings of the Royal Society of London, B 266*, 657–663.

Kowarik, I. (2011) Novel urban ecosystems, biodiversity, and conservation. Environmental Pollution, 159, 1974-1983.

Krebs, C. (2006). Mammals. In W. J. Sutherland (ed.) *Ecological census techniques: A handbook*. 2nd Edition. Cambridge: Cambridge University Press, pp. 251–364.

Landsberg, H. (1981). *The urban climate*. New York: Academic Press.

Lindenmayer, D. B., Gibbons, P., Bourke, M., Burgman, M., Dickman, C. R., Ferrier, S., Fitzsimmons, J., Freudenberger, D., Garnett, S. T., Groves, C., Hobbs, R. J., Kingsford, R. T., Krebs, C., Legge, S., Lowe, A. J., McLean, R., Montambault, J., Possingham, H., Radford, J., Robinson, D., Smallbone, L., Thomas, D., Varcoe, T., Vardon, M., Wardle, G., Woinarski, J., & Zerger, A. (2012) Improving biodiversity monitoring. *Austral Ecology, 37*, 285–294.

MacArthur, R. H., & Wilson, E. O. (1967). *The theory of island biogeography*. Princeton, NJ: Princeton University Press.

Marzluff, J. M. (2005). Island biogeography for an urbanizing world: how extinction and colonization may determine biological diversity in human-dominated landscapes. *Urban Ecosystems, 8*, 157–177.

Meirmans, P. G. (2012). The trouble with isolation by distance. *Molecular Ecology, 21*, 2839–2846.

Meirmans, P. G., & Hedrick P. W. (2010). Assessing population structure: F_{ST} and related measures. *Molecular Ecology Resources, 11*, 5–18.

Morris A. E.J (2013). *History of urban form before the industrial revolution*. London: Routledge.

Newson, S., Evans, H. E., & Gillings, S. (2015). A novel citizen science approach for large-scale standardised monitoring of bat activity and distribution, evaluated in eastern England. *Biological Conservation, 191*, 38–49.

Niemelä, J. (2000). Biodiversity monitoring for decision-making. *Annales Zoologici Fennici, 37*, 307–317.

Oksanen, J., Blanchet, F. G., Friendly, M., Kindt, R., Legendre, P., McGlinn, D., Minchin, P. R., O'Hara, R. B., Simpson, G. L., Solymos, P., Stevens, M. H.H., Szoecs, E., & Wagner, H. (2017). Ordination methods, diversity analysis and other functions for community and vegetation ecologists version 2.4-3. Available at: https://CRAN.R-project.org/package=vegan.

Oostermeijer, J. G.B., & van Swaay, C. A.M. (1998). The relationship between butterflies and environmental indicator values: a tool for conservation in a changing landscape. *Biological Conservation, 86*, 271–280.

Raunkiaer, C. (1934). *The life forms of plants and statistical plant geography*. Oxford: Oxford University Press.

Sandifer, P.A., Sutton-Grier A.E., & Ward, B.P. (2015) Exploring connections among nature, biodiversity, ecosystem services, and human health and well-being: Opportunities to enhance health and biodiversity conservation. *Ecosystem Services, 12*, 1-15.

Schilthuizen, M. (2019). *Darwin comes to town: How the urban jungle drives evolution*. Picador, London.

Slabbekoorn, H., & Boer-Visser, A. (2006). Cities change the songs of birds. *Current Biology, 16*, 2326–2331.

Steinhage, V. (2000). Automated identification of bee species in biodiversity information systems. *Computer Science for Environmental Protection, 1*, 4–6.

Stewart, K., Ma, H., Zheng, J., & Zhao, J. (2017) Using environmental DNA to assess population-wide spatiotemporal reserve use. *Conservation Biology, 31*, 1173-1182.

Taberlet, P., Coissac, E., Pompanon, F., Brochmann, C., & Willerslev, E. (2012). Towards next-generation biodiversity assessment using DNA metabarcoding. *Molecular Ecology, 21*, 2045-2050.

Takami. Y., Koshio, C., Ishii, M., Fujii, H., Hidaka, T., & Shimizu, I. (2004). Genetic diversity and structure of urban populations of Pieris butterflies assessed using amplified fragment length polymorphism. *Molecular Ecology, 13*, 245–258.

Taylor, L., & Hochuli, D.F. (2015) Creating better cities: how biodiversity and ecosystem functioning enhance urban residents' wellbeing. *Urban Ecosystems, 18*, 747–762

Thompson, L., Rayfield, B., & Gonzalez, A. (2017). Loss of habitat and connectivity erodes species diversity, ecosystem functioning, and stability in metacommunity network. *Ecography, 40*, 98–108.

Tilman, D. Isbell, F., & Cowles, J.M. (2014) Biodiversity and Ecosystem Functioning. *Annual Review of Ecology, Evolution, and Systematics, 45*, 471-493.

Van Rossum, F., Stiers, I., Van Geert, A., Triest, L., & Hardy, O. J. (2011). Fluorescent dye particles as pollen analogues for measuring pollen dispersal in an insect-pollinated forest herb. *Oecologia, 165*, 663–674.

Vergeer, J. W., van Dijk, A. J., Boele, A., van Bruggen, J., & Hustings, F. (2016). *Handleiding Sovon broedvogelonderzoek: Broedvogel Monitoring Project en Kolonievogels*. Sovon Vogelonderzoek Nederland, Nijmegen.

Webb, L.J. (1959) A physiognomic classification of Australian rain forests. *Journal of Ecology, 47*, 551-570.

Westhoff, V., & van der Maarel, E. (1973). The Braun-Blanquet approach. In: R. H. Whittaker (ed.) *ordination and classification of communities*. The Hague: Junk Publishers, pp. 617–726.

Williams, N. S.G., Morgan, J. W., McDonnell, M. J., & McCarthy, M. A. (2005). Plant traits and local extinctions in natural grasslands along an urban–rural gradient. *Journal of Ecology 93*, 1203-1213.

13 Action research in the city: developing collaborative governance arrangements for the urban commons

Joachim Meerkerk and Stan Majoor

Introduction: Making the city together through action research

In the context of dominant market logics and systemic democratic shortcomings, our research began with the question of how to engage a more inclusive group of stakeholders in order to collaboratively tackle an array of urban issues. 'Making the city together' resonates with the concept of *collaborative governance*. This suggests that, in order to better solve complex policy problems, a variety of stakeholders should engage in a process of collective decision-making. More horizontal and equal relationships can then foster more consensus-oriented and deliberative ways of policy making (Ansell & Gash, 2008; K. Emerson, Nabatchi & Balogh, 2012; Healey, 1998, 2010). Our action research method aims to develop and improve collaborative governance arrangements and applies the same concept of horizontal and equal relationships to efforts directed at involving stakeholders to jointly develop solutions to challenges in urban consumption spaces.

By conceptualizing consumption spaces as a common resource, we classify the complexity of stakeholders' challenges as a *commons problem*. Such complexity can be seen as a function of a diverse community of actors – which may be a mix of residents, entrepreneurs, civil servants, civil society professionals, and real estate owners – whose individual and collective decisions and actions affect the value and accessibility of this common resource for others (e.g. due to how they run their businesses, organize community or cultural activities, invest in public facilities, clean the streets, introduce zoning policies, or maintain their real estate). These dynamics resemble the open access and subtractable nature of a common resource as outlined by Nobel Prize laureate Elinor Ostrom (Oakerson & Clifton, 2017; Ostrom, 2010) and exemplify how the effects of each actor's decisions and actions result in stakeholders' interdependency. The concept of the **urban commons** – i.e. the collective management of common resources by an urban community of stakeholders (Bollier, 2014; Ostrom, 1990) – frames the coordination that is required because of this interdependency as a form of collaborative governance (Foster & Iaione, 2016).

Action research acknowledges the need for an immersed practice of policy analysis and innovation in such complex situations. It recognizes policymaking as a dynamic and contingent phenomenon that is construed in the continued interactions of a variety of stakeholders – each of whom has his or her own interests, values, and practices – as they negotiate, deliberate, make agreements, struggle for power, **co-create**, share (e.g. information or responsibilities), et cetera. In order to analyse the situation, develop new insights and improving interventions, action researchers tap into the pervading 'relational knowledge' and develop 'temporal solutions' to fit an emergent context (Bartels & Wittmayer, 2018).

The specificity of our method of action research is that it offers an approach to constructing or enhancing collaborative governance arrangements related to the collective management of common resources. By conceptualizing societal challenges as a coordination problem between multiple stakeholders, each of whom is dependent on the same shared resources, we believe we can offer a perspective that has broad application and is particularly relevant given the density and diversity of populations in urban contexts (Parker & Johansson, 2012). We also believe that our action research approach can be adapted to and used in other contexts (such as the projects described in other chapters in this volume; see also the discussion in chapter 16).

Our methodology focuses on analysing the actual situation in order to identify obstacles or unexploited opportunities for collaboration. Using this analysis, we then **co-design** and experiment with strategies and interventions to help bring about or enhance collaborative governance arrangements. The ensuing research – and theory development – is thus intertwined with concrete practices (Dick, Stringer & Huxham, 2009; Kemmis, McTaggart & Nixon, 2014) with the aim of creating experimental learning experiences in order to both develop practical improvements and contribute to policy making, organizational change and systemic innovations (Bradbury, 2015). This is a challenging endeavour in which we not only combine different qualitative methods, but are also – perhaps more than in other methods – confronted with a variety of normative and political questions and dilemmas (Bartels & Wittmayer, 2018; Bradbury, 2015; Wittmayer & Schäpke, 2014).

In this chapter we first offer our reflections on both the attitudes and routines that are needed to cope with the challenges of action research (1.1) and the types of activities an action researcher should expect to undertake (1.2). By describing how we apply a conceptual model, we then hope to give insight into how our action research method shapes the dialectical relationship between theory and practice (2). To illustrate our points, we use examples from our ongoing action research study on the *Zero Waste Lab Plein '40-'45* in the borough New West in Amsterdam.[1]

---

[1]   The project is funded by a four-year SIA–RAAK grant (National Taskforce for Applied Research). The case study of Plein '40-'45 is also part of the Interreg Europe ABCitiEs program.

Zero Waste Lab Plein '40-'45

Plein '40-'45, a square in the borough of New West, is home to one of the busiest street markets in Amsterdam. With an assortment of low quality and cheap products, the market caters to residents' needs in this underprivileged part of the city. Although an important social and economic hub for many, the market's image is predominantly defined by the litter and large amounts of waste it produces on a daily basis. Our action research started with our interest in the ambition of stallholders to both self-organize the reduction of plastic on the market and to develop a circular waste-management system, i.e. the Zero Waste Lab Plein '40-'45. Accordingly, we teamed up with Redouan Boussaid, a civil servant responsible for building strategic coalitions with key stakeholders to tackle current issues on the square.[2]

1   Performing action research: Becoming a contributive actor

Unlike more conventional forms of research, action researchers actively participate in the practices they study (Bradbury, 2015; Kemmis, McTaggart & Nixon, 2014; Stringer, 2007). Action research is therefore related to **ethnographic** approaches (see chapter 3 in this volume) that aim to create more experience-near understandings of practices (Geertz, 1974). However, instead of viewing the researcher's own participation as an instrument in acquiring a more informed understanding, action researchers see themselves as co-owners of the practices they collaboratively design (Bartels & Wittmayer, 2018; Bradbury, 2015). Action research can thus be defined as a way of doing research that seeks transformative change by engaging in a simultaneous process of taking action and doing research, linking both aspects together through critical reflection (Bradbury, 2015; Wittmayer & Schäpke, 2014).

Through their specific competences, action researchers contribute as active members in order to find solutions to challenges in complex settings, such as those that arise in the context of collaborative governance. For instance, an action researcher may: analyze practices and processes, and offer reflections that enable reflexivity;[3] offer and broker knowledge; facilitate group processes of co-creation and experimentation; mediate between different world views, perspectives, and interests; or advocate for change and innovation (Foster & Iaione, 2016; Wittmayer & Schäpke, 2014).

2   The case description in these segments is based on the firsthand experiences of author Joachim Meerkerk, who began conducting the action research in February 2018 and had been active on the square in other roles since early 2017. A key partner in the action research is Redouan Boussaid (referred to simply as Redouan hereafter), who is the area manager of Plein '40-'45 for the Amsterdam municipality.

3   The difference between 'reflection' and 'reflexivity' is to be understood as 'looking back at one's actions' versus 'considering one's actions as part of a system or culture that shapes and directs these actions'. The remainder of this chapter should clarify how both concepts play important and distinct roles in action research.

Although these sort of contributions require the performance of specific activities, the fundamental principle of action research lies in the building of reciprocal relationships and partnerships in order to create sufficient space and assent for the researcher to operate (Kemmis, McTaggart & Nixon, 2014). In the subsections below, we first introduce the four attitudes and routines we find crucial to realising such collaborative partnerships with stakeholders in action research (1.1) and then elaborate on the daily activities action researchers can expect to perform in their work (1.2).

1.1 Attitudes and routines of action researchers

1.1.1 Becoming a partner

Becoming an active partner in a project and co-creating with others requires the establishment of mutual trust and commitment. How one chooses to build such interpersonal relationships depends on the context of the case and, of course, on the character of the researcher (Kemmis, McTaggart & Nixon, 2014; Wittmayer & Schäpke, 2014). Both literature and our own experience have confirmed the importance of the three aspects described below.

Firstly, the researcher's *intrinsic engagement* with the practice, and sincere interest in the goals and ambitions of the stakeholders, are distinct prerequisites. While the emancipatory impact of action research is an important legitimation of its participative approach (Bradbury, 2015; Kemmis, 2010), the researcher's ability to actually interfere in people's lives depends on his or her aptitude both for developing qualitative relationships and for gaining the trust and cooperative willingness of others (Clinton, 1991; Kemmis, McTaggart & Nixon, 2014; Wittmayer & Schäpke, 2014) – for example, through collaborative problem definition (Benham & Daniell, 2016; Bradbury, 2015; Goebel, Camargo-Borges & Eelderink, 2019). Moreover, action researchers ask participants to be open about their aims and motives, and to invest their time and energy in introducing the researcher to their world. In our experience, this is only feasible when the researcher is genuinely motivated. Instrumentalization is easily recognized and dismissed.

Secondly, and relatedly, *commitment* is key. The practices through which action researchers work are closely connected to the concrete lives of the stakeholders (Stringer, 2007). This places additional importance on the researcher's willingness to invest his or her own time in getting to know the involved stakeholders, e.g. by learning about their needs and ideas, and building personal relationships. 'Being there', as opposed to simply 'collecting data', therefore plays an important role. Moreover, 'staying there' – i.e. showing one's allyship over a longer period of time and following through on one's promise not to disappear – is equally important.

Lastly, relationships must be *reciprocal* (Kemmis, McTaggart & Nixon, 2014). Case partners are often entrepreneurs or professionals and, by nature and understandably, they are frequently critical and demanding of the partners with whom they work. An action researcher's ability to acknowledge and answer their partners' 'what's in it for me' question, along with a hands-on attitude, is essential for maintaining his or her position as a trusted ally.

1.1.2 Demarcating tasks and responsibilities

A clear and mutual understanding between the researcher and the primary stakeholders regarding roles, tasks and expectations is vital. As an inherently collaborative venture, action research implores the researcher to become part of the community and the community members to help co-create the research project (Benham & Daniell, 2016; Bradbury, 2015; Jones & Bryant, 2016; Kemmis, McTaggart & Nixon, 2014; Miller, 2013). An important functionality of this collaborative character is the complementarity of stakeholders' diverse knowledge and expertise, including that of the action researcher. In their relationships with stakeholders, it is important for researchers to discuss and demarcate tasks and responsibilities, not only to avoid false expectations, but also because clear positionings contribute to the effective use of the involved partners' distinct capacities, competences and expertise. Notably, the details of how tasks are divided and interpreted are very much context dependent, requiring the researcher to inquire as to the capacities, competences and positions of stakeholders within a community (Wittmayer & Schäpke, 2014).

1.1.3 Partnership: co-creating results on three levels

Action research aims to be transformative. Accordingly, it not only aims to change specific practices, i.e. 'how things are done', it also seeks to simultaneously address the systemic context that orients, directs and shapes these practices (Kemmis, McTaggart & Nixon, 2014; Stringer, 2007; Wittmayer & Schäpke, 2014). Action researchers who wish to enable collaborative governance arrangements must therefore work to establish parallel, synchronized and synergetic change on three levels: practice, policy and theory. In other words, while working to develop practical solutions to the issues at hand, the action researcher is bound to encounter systemic obstacles that inform policy debates. Often, theory building – to form new insights – is then necessary to encourage transformation. This process is iterative and dialectical (Dick, Stringer & Huxham, 2009; Kemmis, McTaggart & Nixon, 2014).

1.1.4 Reporting and reflexivity

Recording the proceedings of a case can be a challenge for action researchers. Being immersed in the daily, operational grind often makes conventional methods of documenting, such as audio recording or even note taking, difficult if not disturbing to the work and/or involved stakeholders. Moreover, action researchers typically influence their case studies, thus becoming their own objects of study. Reflexivity, therefore, is an indistinguishable part of action research (Benham & Daniell, 2016; Bradbury, 2015; Goebel, Camargo-Borges & Eelderink, 2019; Wittmayer & Schäpke, 2014). To this end, we have adopted the habit of keeping a **logbook**, inspired by the concept of a reflexive journal or **diary** (as discussed in chapter 3). Our logbook not only contains notes and reports on what people have said and how they interacted, it also includes our own contributions, thoughts, considerations, and associations.

It is also a good place to sketch ideas and scribble reflections that are related to the research project but have a more general character.

Trust building

Initially, we spent our time walking around the market, chatting with stallholders, attending meetings and drinking coffee. We talked to people about their perceptions of the market's problems, how they viewed their fellow stakeholders and their activities, what they thought needed to be done, and their own roles in each of these aspects. Building trust was a challenge. While we certainly encountered enough ambition and positive energy, we were also confronted with stallholders' feelings of disappointment and betrayal towards the municipality. In order to build common ground, we teamed up with Redouan to hold a collective, after-hours meeting on the market square where we served soup and bread, and encouraged stallholders to share their concerns and ideas. During that meeting, we offered our feedback while grounding their interests and complaints in the concepts of the urban commons. By creating a space in which all sides – i.e. us as the researchers, Redouan as a civil servant, and them as the stallholders – jointly invested in understanding the other and finding mutual ambitions, we were able to cultivate a shared vocabulary and sense of partnership.

Later in the process, the inherent fragility of trust became more apparent when the principal researcher attended a public meeting intended to inform stallholders about the future of the market, organized by the Markets Bureau – a relatively new and special municipal department established for the management of street markets. At the time, the relationship between the Markets Bureau and the stallholders was colored by conflict and distrust. There had been disagreements between both sides regarding various plans and incidents, resulting in each seeing the other as an implicit enemy. Having worked with the stallholders intensively in the weeks prior, we (the researchers and Redouan) entered the meeting, informally conversing among them. Devoid of underlying motives, we sat down next to the stallholders, only to notice that the meeting was set up with stallholders on one side of the room and the Markets Bureau representatives on the other. We quickly got the sense that this had caused the Markets Bureau people to perceive us as being 'on the side' of the stallholders. Afterwards, our suspicions were confirmed by an email addressed to Redouan, whom they had explicitly accused of being 'for' the stallholders. It took us researchers quite a while to neutralize this situation and position ourselves as partners who support not one or the other stakeholder, but rather the collaboration between them.

Over time, we clearly saw the importance of organizing extensive introductory talks with the various stakeholders. Only after reflecting on the position we had found ourselves in – i.e. our perceived bias for the stallholders – did we realize that, while we had already been working with the Markets Bureau throughout several meetings, we had never technically introduced ourselves, nor given them the opportunity to explain their position or practices. Ultimately, a lengthy conversation allowed us to eliminate mutual unfounded presuppositions, and to identify the common goals and ambitions that then became the starting point for further collaboration.

Reflecting on roles and positions
A prerequisite for the self-organization of a market waste system is a collective of willing stallholders. However, because the small group of stallholders who initially took the initiative to organize the collective actually lack the time and skills, this has proven difficult. As a result, our role as researchers has become central: together with Redouan, we strive to offer the necessary support by developing strategies, and inventing and carrying out ancillary activities. We also assist by writing concrete plans and pursuing various avenues of correspondence when necessary. Redouan helps by facilitating waste-collection capacities and by making other means available. Importantly, we have made a concerted effort not to take the project over, but rather to assist the stallholders, who we believe should remain the owners of the initiative. Accordingly, we frequently encourage reflexive conversations between the initiating stallholders, Redouan and ourselves, discussing who should, for example, take the initiative, formulate principal ambitions and ideas, consult with and inform other stallholders, or make arrangements with various stakeholders. For instance, the organization of a survey that asked stallholders for their top five complaints and ideas started with the initiating stallholders' sense of urgency to strengthen the legitimacy of their representative role. As researchers, we suggested a two-question survey to ask what other stallholders felt could be improved so that these issues could then become a part of their 'collective agenda'. Redouan made cards the stallholders could easily fill out, with one question on each side. Together, we handed out the cards and collected them afterwards. Then, although we went through and discussed the responses as a group, the initiating stallholders prioritized the feedback and eventually returned to the market to share 'their' results with the community.

1.2   Activities of action researchers

As mentioned above, the activities of an action researcher are immersed in the case study's daily practices and proceedings, and aim to acquire an informed understanding of the 'happenings' – both for the researchers and the other involved actors – and to create transformative change (Benham & Daniell, 2016; Bradbury, 2015; Kemmis, McTaggart & Nixon, 2014; Stringer, 2014). Based on our experience and the literature, this subsection distinguishes the five main activities associated with our form of action research (Wittmayer & Schäpke, 2014). Although we describe them separately here, in practice these activities often overlap.

The first and probably most fundamental activity is *making **observations** and keeping fieldnotes* of what is going on (see also paragraph 1.1.4). While there are many different methods of pursuing the immersed and integrated nature of data collection that is typical of action research – see, for example, the plethora of tactics described in the handbooks and case studies mentioned in this chapter – it is important for researchers to remain sensitive, flexible, and creative in order to adjust their research methods to the local context and perceptions of stakeholders. After all, an action researcher's worst-case scenario would be to ultimately find that nothing has changed and that he or she has been ostracized from the community, despite his or her most creative, facilitative and artistic efforts (Chambers, 2015; Stefanac & Krot, 2015; Wakeford, Pimbert & Walcon, 2015). Throughout the research process, fieldnotes, observation, documentation, and all other forms of recording what is encountered – e.g. collecting images and stories – form the crucial foundation of action research (R.M. Emerson, Fretz & Shaw, 2011).

These materials then become meaningful through *interpretation and analysis*, for which the use of a conceptual model should be applied to guide the action researcher. More on the role of a conceptual model can be found in section 2. Interpretation and analysis are done both after the fact, when the researcher is back at his or her desk, and on the spot in the moment. Subsequently, sharing one's observations and providing partners with meaningful interpretations of their actions or theoretically informed accounts of their practices – i.e. the activity of *feedback and reflection* – can also help the researcher's stakeholders to gain new insights into and ideas about how to act in specific situations or how to better organize and improve their project.

Similarly, *offering knowledge* also helps the action researcher to assist participants in creating a different and more informed understanding of both their own actions and those of others, and of the context in which they operate (Freire, 2000). In this sense, sharing one's knowledge is integral to the transformative power of action research (Kemmis, McTaggart & Nixon, 2014). An action researcher must not only have a large reservoir of knowledge related to their case study, but, again, they must also have the sensitivity, flexibility, and creativity necessary to both connect and associate such knowledge with real-time practices, and to find the right moment to communicate such ideas (Aragón & Castillo-Burguete, 2015). Indeed, we believe that a creative repertoire and the ability to recognize these 'teaching' moments are amongst the core competences an action researcher develops through experience.

Finally, the activity of *developing new insights, ideas and theories* beyond the case study helps the researcher spur progress and innovation. Although this type of academic 'craftsmanship' requires a level of concentration often associated with isolation and drudgery (Glaser, 1978), as action researchers ourselves we have found that continuously moving back and forth between the work on the street, our bookshelves, and our laptops eventually pays off the effort of breaking that routine.

Conducting action research on Plein '40-'45

Our research has largely taken place in regular conversations and meetings. The backbone of our involvement has been centred around weekly appointments with Redouan, during which we exchange updates and reflections, or visit the market together. Most of the stakeholder meetings – except our individual introductory talks – have been specifically related to a project or activity and would have taken place even without our involvement. As action researchers, we consider it our job to listen in on, participate in, and sometimes co-organize these encounters with the aim of influencing the collaborative process. We focus on observing what is being said, and apply our conceptual model to interpret these observations (see section 2) and offer feedback, reflections and/or knowledge in order to help stakeholders improve the situation.

One example of how we have thus far influenced the collaborative process through action research is the regulation of plastic bags. To reduce litter and boost sustainability, Redouan initially told us that he wanted to convince the Markets Bureau to adopt regulatory rules that would prohibit the use of plastic bags. Besides Redouan's experience of this as a 'mission impossible', given his bad relationship with the Markets Bureau, we also gave him our feedback: such an ambition is actually inconsistent with the underlying goal of building a coalition of willing stakeholders to self-organize improvements for the market. We then offered Redouan knowledge in the form of research that shows that regulations are better upheld and easier to monitor when the stakeholders themselves design the rules and regulatory instruments (Ostrom, 2010).

Later on, Redouan told us that this moment had been a turning point in his perception both of the project and of his responsibilities. Making him fundamentally rethink his own approach, our 'intervention' had given him a practical strategy for realising his ambition of creating a more horizontal and co-creative way of working. Likewise, this insight became one of his main reasons for supporting the stallholders' efforts to build a market collective. Later on in the process, we gave the Markets Bureau similar feedback and offered the same knowledge, which – according to them – helped them realise that a repressive and authoritarian approach would not only fail to solve the market's problems, it would also be too expensive. Consequently, they changed their aim to focus on building and supporting the market collective and on opening up a dialogue about which rules to set and follow, predicated on a belief in the effectiveness of self-regulation.

Phases of action research

In order to guide and orient ourselves and other scholars in the complex endeavour of action research, we have distinguished seven phases in which the researcher's activities occur (Eelderink, 2020; Kemmis, McTaggart & Nixon, 2014; Stringer, 2014). It should be noted, however, that these distinctions are blurred in practice. In the enactment of action research, phases may actually overlap or are constituted by the same activity. Similarly, the chronological order is apt to change, certain phases may seem redundant or be hardly recognizable, and a researcher may go back and forth between the various phases. Nonetheless, we believe our distinctions can help action researchers establish and refine their research strategies. Given the participatory nature of action research, these different activities should be interpreted accordingly.

Phase	Activity
Presearch	Setting the stage by getting acquainted with the stakeholders and initial orientations, e.g. through document analysis, preliminary **interviews**, or informal meetings.
Fieldwork preparation	Focusing further research by means of an initial analysis based on the presearch phase, e.g. by identifying issues, stakeholder mapping, composing topic lists, or designing workshops.
Fieldwork	Data and information gathering via participation in the case study with the help of a range of qualitative and possibly quantitative tools.
Analysis	Identifying and describing in detail the issues at play, and building argumentation for resolving interventions and employing specific strategies.
Design	Co-designing interventions and strategies for improvement, e.g. through consensus building, the prototyping of instruments and policies, and by formulating goals or evaluative criteria.
Experimentation	Iteratively realising and implementing the intervention, facilitated by an experimental learning environment.
Output and evaluation	Evaluating concrete results and reflecting on the process, plus celebrating achievements and successes.

2 Using a conceptual model to foster systemic transformation

Our method aims to improve collaborative approaches to solving local issues and to bring about the systemic transformation necessary to sustain these solutions. With these goals in mind, our method makes use of a conceptual model to both help researchers construct an informed perspective (2.1) and to share this perspective with stakeholders in order to facilitate a space for collaborative learning and joint problem-solving (2.2). A conceptual model also helps researchers to reveal the systemic consequences of a potential intervention, and to identify where, when, and what kind of transformation is needed (2.3). While our particular model has been specially developed for our research project and conceptualizes efforts of collaborative governance in the context of the urban commons, the role our model plays in our method offers lessons that are more generally applicable.

2.1 Using a conceptual model as a perspective for change

Our facilitative and supportive role as action researchers – i.e. to inform, direct, and theoretically ground change – implies a basic level of impartiality. To this purpose our method strongly relies on a conceptual model that serves to normatively shape the researcher's perspective on both the practices and the opportunities for improvement. In other words, our model frames both how we see the world and how we aim to change it.

In our method, our conceptual model functions as a schematic account of the governance arrangements we encounter by structuring the influence of contextual factors into categories, i.e. the characteristics of a common resource, the attributes of the community, and the market, and the institutional context.[4] The model formulates a theory on how these aspects affect the (lack of) collaboration between the involved stakeholders, based on theories of collaborative governance and urban commons. This then determines how we value the process and the output of the governance arrangement and entails our model's normativity.

Like any other conceptual model, the models used in action research function as an informative guide for data collection: categories help researchers formulate helpful questions and interests to explore in the field. A model also helps order and interpret the researcher's data. Unusually, our method also uses the model as a tool in designing strategies and interventions for improvement – e.g. by formulating the requirements and principles these strategies and interventions should include by considering the contextual factors and normative goals. Moreover, the use of a conceptual model orients action researchers by helping them interpret what is going on in the moment-to-moment interactions they encounter in the field. In our experience, the more we have internalized our model as a natural way of seeing the world – without continuously and dogmatically reviewing its technical terms and definitions – the better we have been able to understand the practices we engage in, and the more it has enabled us to immerse ourselves and be contributive partners.

---

4   Our model is based on the Institutional Analysis and Development Framework. For an introduction to this framework, see Ostrom (2010) and McGinnis (2011).

2.2 Using a conceptual model to create collaborative learning spaces

A conceptual model is also used as an instrument to establish common ground between researchers and stakeholders. In our study, to clarify the underlying assumptions and ambitions of our involvement, we started by discussing our model's normative stance with the involved actors. We have also used our model in the reflections we offer in order to help stakeholders achieve a deeper and more explicit understanding of their own ambitions and actions, and their relationships with other stakeholders (Dick, Stringer & Huxham, 2009). As such, a model also facilitates a shared vocabulary and mutual understanding amongst stakeholders, which then allows them to conceptualize their individual views and stories in similar terms and concepts, opening up a communicative space and possibilities for a joint learning process (Burns, 2015; Kemmis, McTaggart & Nixon, 2014). As facilitators of this process, action researchers use a conceptual model to design the learning architecture that explains how a collection of stories are related, how different actors listen to others' stories, and what needs to change in pursuit of certain goals.

Importantly, while others are often equally interested in fleshing out the underlying principles and dynamics, the use of conceptual models is the habitat of academic researchers and does not necessarily work as a clarifying tool for everyone. Consequently, collectively developing stakeholders' stories that resonate with the content of the model may be more effective at establishing joint involvement and ownership than attempts to share a conceptual model in its abstraction (Burns, 2014).

2.3 Using a conceptual model to spur systemic change

Action research aims to establish transformative change by creating an interactive and dialectical relation between practice and theory (Dick, Stringer & Huxham, 2009; Kemmis, McTaggart & Nixon, 2014), another ambition for which a conceptual model plays a pivotal role in our method. Firstly, a conceptual model helps stakeholders create a deep and reflexive understanding of how their actions and those of others are shaped by an underlying system of discourse, conventions, and relationships – including power structures. An understanding of these social constructs opens up the possibilities for sustainable change (Kemmis, McTaggart & Nixon, 2014) by offering insights into the interconnectedness of the factors at play and thereby revealing a systemic dimension.

Secondly, a conceptual model helps researchers expose and situate the knowledge gaps that inevitably emerge throughout their work in the field. In such cases, further theoretical exploration – i.e. theory building – can help address this type of obstacle through systemic transformation in order to better facilitate the desired practical solutions. Indeed, the dialectical process between practice and theory means also that a conceptual model will evolve over time. While this is not specific to action research, action research does establish this element more intentionally and integrated than most conventional research methods (Kemmis, McTaggart & Nixon, 2014; Raelin & Coghlan, 2006).

Experimental learning on collaborative waste-management

A new waste-management system is a cooperative endeavour. While stallholders can do a lot on their own, there are limits to their capabilities. A circular system starts at the source with proper disposal and sorting, but also requires, for example, a larger, integrated logistical system. Changes to the waste-management system also affect the interests of others and are subject to different municipal domains, policies and regulations. Even if collaboration were not technically necessary for practical reasons, it would still help avoid the potential hindrances caused by those who are reluctant to change. Plein '40-'45 is awash in frustration: the relationships between stallholders and the Markets Bureau are riddled with conflict, the municipality's central policies directly contradict some of the solutions devised by the market's own self-organizers, and collaboration between different municipal departments is often stymied by poor communication, complex hierarchical structures, and budget issues.

Building on the widely shared desire to make the collaboration work, we suggested the establishment of an experimental learning space to facilitate the construction of new processes and relationships. As we write this chapter, we are still in the midst of collaboratively designing this experimental learning space, which itself is, interestingly, already an experimental endeavour. To achieve more effective internal collaboration, for example, different municipal entities must first know who is doing what. As we work to puzzle that out, new communicative spaces are already opening up. For instance, by discussing the design of the waste-management system that the stallholders had developed in cooperation with Redouan, it became clear that the ambitions of the Markets Bureau were remarkably similar. The conflict then, we collectively concluded, was actually a result of the stallholders' ambition to move 'too quickly', in the eyes of the municipality. Suddenly, both sides realised that a difference in tempo had been the cause of the opposition and hostility – a great starting point for recalibrating their relationship.

Another problem that has arisen in the realisation of a new waste-management system is bureaucratic: the Markets Bureau is not open to discussing the amount they charge for waste disposal, even if the new system is self-organized and would reduce volume. Similarly, they have refused to discuss individually adjusting the fee to address the fact that costermongers produce 90% of the waste. In their words, the fee is determined by the policies of another department and is the consequence of past political choices. Moreover, they argue that because central policies are the result of a democratically elected council and designed to protect citizens' equal rights and treatment, they are not open for discussion. From our perspective, the municipality's rigidity on this front can also be seen as way of avoiding risk or complexity. In the new, experimental learning environment, we sit down with both sides to jointly investigate the applicability of these kinds of arguments and, whenever relevant and possible, find alternative strategies. In an open discussion with the stakeholders, we help them unravel the complexity behind their arguments in order to open up space for alternatives – which may then result in a need for additional theories or theory building. In our case, we are working to promote the democratic legitimacy of collaborative governance arrangements beyond the mere consent and support of representative bodies. Our efforts, we believe, could change the dynamics between the different actors. Over time, we hope our experiment will demonstrate whether this belief is correct based on the success of future stakeholder collaborations.

3 Conclusions

While action research is a challenging approach that brings academic researchers out of their 'armchair' comfort zones and into messy realities, we are convinced it is well worth the effort. In this chapter, we have tried to provide informative, initial insights into what an action research project entails. Above of all, we hope to have shown the adequacy of action research in complex urban environments, such as in those involving collaborative governance arrangements.

Our experiences have taught us that the use of a conceptual model is crucial in developing an effective action research method. Firstly, because it prevents the researcher from getting lost by acting as a beacon in the messy reality that is the field. And, secondly, because it plays a dominant role in establishing the transformative change for which we as action researchers strive.

We hope this chapter has made it clear that conducting action research demands intrinsic motivation and sincere engagement. Action researchers need to adopt a great sense of reflexivity in order to simultaneously contribute to real life practices and deal with the ethical and political questions that invariably arise throughout the process. Moreover, action researchers should not forget that the practices in the field are leading, and that they must flexibly and creatively adjust their research methods to fit the local context and stakeholders' perceptions.

References

Ansell, C., & Gash, A. (2008). Collaborative governance in theory and practice. *Journal of Public Administration Research and Theory, 18*(4), 543–571.

Aragón, A. O., & Castillo-Burguete, M. T. (2015). Introduction to Practices. In H. Bradbury (ed.), *The SAGE Handbook of Action Research*, 3rd edition. London: SAGE Publications Ltd., pp. 13–16.

Bartels, K. P. R., & Wittmayer, J. M. (2018). Introduction: Action Research in Policy Analysis and transition research. In K. P. R. Bartels & J. M. Wittmayer (eds.), *Action Research in Policy Analysis: Critical and Relational Approaches to Sustainability Transitions*. London: Routledge, pp. 1–17.

Benham, C. F., & Daniell, K. A. (2016). Putting transdisciplinary research into practice: A participatory approach to understanding change in coastal social-ecological systems. *Ocean and Coastal Management, 128*, 29-39.

Bollier, D. (2014). *Think like a commoner: a short introduction to the life of the commons*. Gabriola Island: New Society Publishers.

Bradbury, H. (2015). How to Situate and Define Action Research. In H. Bradbury (ed.), *The SAGE Handbook of action research*, 3rd edition. London: SAGE Publications Ltd., pp. 1-9.

Burns, D. (2014). Systemic action research: Changing system dynamics to support sustainable change. *Action Research, 12*(1), 3-18.

Burns, D. (2015). How Change Happens. In H. Bradbury (ed.), *The SAGE Handbook of Action Research*, 3rd edition. London: SAGE Publications Ltd., pp. 434-445.

Chambers, R. (2015). PRA, PLA and Pluralism: Practice and Theory. In H. Bradbury (ed.), *The SAGE Handbook of Action Research*, 3rd edition. London: SAGE Publications Ltd., pp. 297-318.

Clinton, R. L. (1991). Grassroots development where no grass grows: Small-scale development efforts on the peruvian coast. *Studies In Comparative International Development, 26*(2), 59-75.

Dick, B., Stringer, T. E., & Huxham, C. (2009). Theory in action research. *Action Research, 7*(1), 5-12.

Eelderink, M. (2020). *Handboek Participatief Actieonderzoek: Samen bouwen aan een betere wereld*. Amsterdam: Uitgeverij SWP.

Emerson, K., Nabatchi, T., & Balogh, S. (2012). An Integrative Framework for Collaborative Governance. *Journal of Public Administration Research and Theory, 22*(1), 1-29.

Emerson, R. M., Fretz, R. I., & Shaw, L. L. (2011). *Writing Ethnographic Fieldnotes*, 2nd editon. Chicago: University of Chicago Press.

Foster, S. R., & Iaione, C. (2016). The City as a Commons. *Yale Law & Policy Review, 34*(2), 281-349.

Freire, P. (2000). *Pedagogy of the Oppressed*, 30th Anniversary edition. Translated by M.B. Ramos. New York: The Continuum International Publishing Group Inc.

Geertz, C. (1974). "From the Native 's Point of View": On the Nature of Anthropological Understanding. *Bulletin of the American Academy of Arts and Sciences, 28*(1), 26-45.

Glaser, B. G. (1978). *Theoretical sensitivity: advances in the methodology of grounded theory*. Mill Valley: Sociology Press.

Goebel, K., Camargo-Borges, C., & Eelderink, M. (2019). Exploring participatory action research as a driver for sustainable tourism. *International Journal of Tourism Research*.

Healey, P. (1998). Building institutional capacity through collaborative approaches to urban planning. *Environment and Planning A, 30*(9), 1531-1546.

Healey, P. (2010). *Making better places: the planning project in the twenty-first century*. Hampshire: Palgrave Macmillan.

Jones, R., & Bryant, C. R. (2016). Participatory action research for rural and regional development. *Geographical Research, 54*(2), 115–117.

Kemmis, S. (2010). What is to be done? The place of action research. *Educational Action Research, 18*(4), 417–427.

Kemmis, S., McTaggart, R., & Nixon, R. (2014). *The Action Research Planner: Doing Critical Participatory Action Research*. Singapore: Springer Science+Business Media.

McGinnis, M. D. (2011). An Introduction to IAD and the Language of the Ostrom Workshop: A Simple Guide to a Complex Framework. *The Policy Studies Journal, 39*(1), 169–183.

Miller, T. R. (2013). Constructing sustainability science: Emerging perspectives and research trajectories. *Sustainability Science, 8*(2), 279–293.

Oakerson, R. J., & Clifton, J. D. W. (2017). The Neighborhood as Commons: Reframing Neighborhood Decline. *Fordham Urban Law Journal, 44*(2), 411–450.

Ostrom, E. (1990). *Governing the Commons: The Evolution of Institutions for Collective Action*. Cambridge: Cambridge University Press.

Ostrom, E. (2010). Beyond markets and states: Polycentric governance of complex economic systems. *American Economic Review, 100*(3), 641–672.

Parker, P., & Johansson, M. (2012). Challenges and Potentials in Collaborative Management of Urban Commons. In T. B. Valic, D. Modic, & U. Lamut (eds.), *Multi-Faceted Nature of Collaboration in the Contemporary World*. London: Vega Press Ltd, pp. 92–113.

Raelin, J. A., & Coghlan, D. (2006). Developing managers as learners and researchers: Using action learning and action research. *Journal of Management Education, 30*(5), 670–689.

Stefanac, L., & Krot, M. (2015). Using T-Groups to Develop Action Research Skills in Volatile, Uncertain, Complex, and Ambiguous Environments. In H. Bradbury (ed.), *The SAGE Handbook of Action Research*, 3rd edition. London: SAGE Publications Ltd., pp. 109–117.

Stringer, T. E. (2007). *Action Research*, 3rd edition. Thousand Oaks: SAGE Publications, Inc.

Stringer, T. E. (2014). *Action Research*, 4th edition. Los Angeles: SAGE Publications, Inc.

Wakeford, T., Pimbert, M., & Walcon, E. (2015). Re-Fashioning Citizens' Juries: Participatory Democracy in Action. In H. Bradbury (ed.), *The SAGE Handbook of Action Research*, 3rd edition. London: SAGE Publications Ltd., pp. 230–246.

Wittmayer, J. M., & Schäpke, N. (2014). Action, research and participation: roles of researchers in sustainability transitions. *Sustainability Science, 9*(4), 483–496.

14 Streetlabs as a co-creative approach to Research Through Design[I]

STBY (Nina Stegeman, Geke van Dijk, Bas Raijmakers)

Introduction

Research Through Design is a form of qualitative research into people's behaviors and motives that is integrated in the design and development of new products, services, and systems. The integration of 'understanding' through research with 'creation' through design accelerates innovation, and is particularly valuable when an organization wants to explore the potential of new innovative directions with many unknowns. **Co-creative** Streetlabs with local residents offer a valuable practical approach to Research Through Design, as they enable a joint exploration of urban questions about the use of public space, such as improving bike parking, creating more space for pedestrians, and co-creating traffic policies. National and local governmental organs, including the City of Amsterdam, are increasingly interested in this method because of its highly participatory character. Through co-creation they can actively involve citizens in decision-making about innovation projects. As specialists in Research Through Design, STBY has frequently been asked by local governments to carry out Streetlab projects regarding urban space design and to actively involve the users. In this chapter, we will show how to use Research Through Design as a method by means of its application in a Streetlab on co-creative urban space design in Amsterdam. We will use the case of the redesign process of the Haarlemmerstraat and Haarlemmerdijk to illustrate what this method demands and what it can achieve. Other examples and broader discussions of Research Through Design methods can be found in the suggestions for further reading at the end of the chapter.

I   This body of work has been developed in close collaboration with several project teams from the City of Amsterdam. Two people have in particular been frequently involved in this process – Maaike Nicolai-Geerling and Devi van Huijstee. We are thankful for their trust and commitment to giving local stakeholders a voice in the redesign of public space.

Redesigning a very busy urban area

The Haarlemmerstraat and Haarlemmerdijk in the city center of Amsterdam are currently very busy and even overloaded with cyclists, pedestrians, scooters, and cars. These two adjoining streets, which merge into each other at an intersection, are lined with shops and cafes that attract lots of people and tourists. Residents of the two streets live in houses above the shops. At the same time the Haarlemmerstraat/dijk is a busy main through road for cyclists in particular, as it connects the city center with the Western district of Amsterdam. Because of their multiple functions, these streets bring together a diverse group of users. The increasing crowd results in an unsafe traffic situation, and a livability that is under pressure.

To address this issue, the City of Amsterdam is working on both long and short term redesigns of the urban space. The long term redesigns will provide a structural solution to reduce traffic pressure, while the short term redesigns provide quick wins as a more temporary solution. Before implementing emerging ideas for these quick wins, the City wanted to involve local stakeholders in a collaborative process of prioritizing identified bottlenecks and examining the desirability and effectiveness of some ideas for short term redesigns. The City of Amsterdam asked STBY to support this urban design project by engaging local residents and businesses of the Haarlemmerstraat/dijk area in this prioritization and communal co-creation.

Streetlabs: a co-creative and collaborative approach

Over the past few years, STBY has been commissioned by various local councils in Amsterdam to support innovation projects around the use of public space by conducting design research. In some of these projects, we focused on the opportunities for improving bike parking in specific areas. In others, we focused on opportunities for creating more space for pedestrians. Working on projects with similar research questions allowed us to develop and improve a customized research method, called 'Streetlabs'. This co-creative and collaborative method is an approach to Research Through Design that creates a setting for different users to share their experiences and perspectives, in this case on using and redesigning a common public space. The Streetlab method is different from traditional public consultations where residents can only respond to ready-made plans from the City. Traditional consultations have limitations, because they are limited in their participative character. Inhabitants are only involved in innovation projects towards the end of the process, when not much can be changed. Furthermore, the participants who shout the loudest get most attention, while others remain quiet and unheard. That is why the City of Amsterdam was keen to explore alternatives to this traditional format. They expressed their need for an open conversation with different users of a neighborhood in a safe setting and equality for all.

In response to these requests STBY came up with the Streetlab method, a Research Through Design approach in which we both explore current situations and speculate about future situations, and we do this in a very co-creative and collaborative way. Co-creation and collaboration are important design elements that we use to make sure we understand the users whom our commissioners are designing for. During a Streetlab session, participants work in small groups to explore problem areas (the 'as is' situation) and opportunities for improving the public space (the 'to be' situation). The participants also share their visions for the specific street or neighborhood the research focuses on. These co-creative and collaborative sessions are open and constructive conversations on both what *could* be done and what *should* be done. We encourage people to speak from their own personal experience, and to avoid generic statements. Sometimes it is tempting for people to conclude that 'That's just the way it is', and that no solution can be optimal for all. This is why we have found the constructive and positive tone of the conversations during the Streetlabs to be special. Although people have different motivations and different needs, with the Streetlab approach participants are encouraged to find a common ground, a balance for a shared future.

Jointly considering short and long term redesigns

Questions that were specifically relevant to the Haarlemmerstraat/dijk Streetlab mostly related to priorities for short and long term redesigns of the public space area. Short term redesigns included quick wins that would improve the livability of the street during an interim period while a more substantial redesign would be prepared for the years after. These quick wins were focused around seven possible adjustments and redesigns: adjusting pedestrian crossings, keeping car traffic out of the street, new rules for loading and unloading of goods, reducing car parking spaces, new rules for scooter drivers, new bicycle parking facilities, and creating more space for pedestrians in the Haarlemmerstraat/dijk. The longer term redesigns were aiming to divert the main cycle through route from the street to reduce the traffic pressure. The City of Amsterdam was curious to learn from the opinions, preferences, and sense of urgency around the short term redesigns according to different users of the street.

Initial exploration and reframing

The initial stage of preparing for a Streetlab is a combination of immersion into the local area and engaging in exploratory conversations with the project team from the City of Amsterdam who commissioned the project. The design researchers need to develop a sensitivity for what is within their scope and what is not, and to prepare starting points that will trigger the required conversations between the participants.

Depending on the specific questions proposed by the project team, we sometimes choose a blended methodological approach to the Streetlab; we may first do an online survey among the wider community to prioritize topics that could be discussed, and then follow this up with in-person exploratory sessions with a smaller group of participants. While designing such a blended qualitative and quantitative research methodology, the first step is to distinguish the research questions you can best investigate through qualitative data from the questions you can better investigate through in-depth quantitative data (see also chapters 2, 3, and 5).

As the objective of Streetlabs is to collect stories and consider perspectives from different angles, diversity in the participant group is very important. That is why recruitment is an essential stage of a research project. Recruitment is time-consuming, but by recruiting the right mix of participants the quality of the insights is greatly enhanced.

Immersion in the local area and community

To kick off the research project, two of STBY's design researchers stationed themselves in a local cafe at the Haarlemmerdijk to first do some observations in the street, take photographs, get a sense of likely issues in the street, and compile first drafts for the design research questions.

Initial conversations with the project team from the City of Amsterdam helped us to define the scope of the Research Through Design project and its constraints, and to reframe the research questions. As the project team was already developing some initial ideas for possible short term solutions, and were keen to hear what local stakeholders would come up with, we decided that for this project a combination of exploratory Streetlab sessions with an online survey among a wider group of local stakeholders would be most effective.

The online survey investigated the urgency and priority of public space issues people experience in the area, and also their interest in some of the considered quick wins. Frequent users of the street, such as local residents and business owners, received a letter in which they were asked to participate in the online survey. We asked participants to indicate which of the suggested potential short term redesigns should be implemented first in order to create and improve the livability of the street. This survey offered a large group of people the option to consider potential changes and to communicate their preferences.

Recruitment for the Streetlab session that followed the survey was done via both the invitation letter for the survey and an additional **snowballing** method. By activating the personal networks of people in the area, an invitation for the Streetlab session was circulated. Because the survey reached a relatively large number of people, lots of people registered for the co-creative and collaborative session. Since only a limited number of participants could join the session, we selected a mixed group of participants based on demographics (e.g. gender and age) and relationship with the street (e.g. resident or local business). The selected participants received an invitation for the session at the Posthoornkerk.

Streetlab Facilitation

During the Streetlab sessions the participants sit in small groups around tables, with a mix of local participants and some professionals from the City. We always aim for a mixed group of 8–10 participants per table, to make sure all voices are heard and different interests are considered and discussed. The local participants can be inhabitants, shop owners or other local entrepreneurs, people who work in the streets, and frequent visitors such as shoppers and dog walkers. It is crucial that there is room for each participant to share his or her story, and that everyone feels they have been listened to. The Streetlabs method helps the participants, including civil servants who work in the particular city district, to discuss their views on the value of the joint use of public space, and to **co-create** a new shared perspective on future city living. Because the conversations are moderated by a neutral party, in this case STBY, participants can be confident in openly sharing what they have to say. Another important element in this respect is that the Streetlab sessions take place on 'neutral ground', a location in the area where everyone feels equal and free to speak out.

As moderators of the conversation, we have to make sure we gather enough data to perform a thorough analysis based on the stories and experiences collected from all perspectives – from people who pass through the street as pedestrians or cyclists as well as local shop owners, residents, and neighborhood visitors. It is not surprising that by bringing together the perspectives of different 'actors', who all share the same space, some tensions and conflicts of interest surface. For example, a shop owner may wish to increase the visibility of his or her business by placing an announcement board on the sidewalk. But for a parent with a stroller, that board may become an obstacle. While entrepreneurs see a busy street as a business opportunity, for inhabitants or visitors this might also be a hassle. These stories from different perspectives about the shared use of urban space is exactly the kind of data we are looking for. Visual tools, such as a streetview map and pictographic cards of key elements in public space, help to trigger these stories and explore problem areas. Once the current problem areas are collectively identified, we steer the conversation to how things could be different in the area and how the participants think their ideas could change future experiences. The ideas collected in the Streetlab are considered by the City for actual interventions.

Although the conversations in the Streetlab sessions are open and personal, we take care that the privacy and anonymity of the participants is taken into account throughout the process of the Research Through Design project. All introductions and interactions between the participants during the Streetlab sessions are on a first name basis, as are the stories and ideas represented in the final report. At the start of the Streetlab session, participants are informed about what is going to happen with the data gathered. At the end of the session we hand out consent forms to sign, so they can officially give permission to use what has been said. At the end of the design research project the participants usually receive a summary of the outcomes, so there is also a level of reciprocity.

Creating a communal spirit and exchange of ideas

The venue chosen for the Streetlab session in this project was the Posthoornkerk. This is an old semi-public church in the Haarlemmerstraat that no longer holds religious services and is currently used for a variety of occasions. Together with the project team from the municipality, we chose this location for the session because it is located in the area the research project focuses on, well known to people, and easily accessible. In addition, the Posthoornkerk is a comfortable location for the session because it has an open space that allows for both the plenary introduction and a set-up for intimate and safe conversations at several tables.

To create a communal spirit and set expectations of the participants in the Streetlab session, we gave a brief kick-off presentation in which we explained the objective of the session and the co-creative approach. Creating a communal spirit is especially important for this kind of Research Through Design, because we try to find common ground despite different experiences and perspectives of participants. That is why we make it clear to participants in the introduction that the session is not a complaint session, or an opportunity to push through ready-developed ideas, but rather a constructive conversation to jointly consider the range of perspectives of different users of the same public space.

At the start of the Streetlab session in the Posthoornkerk a STBY moderator also introduced a high level summary of the results of the online survey. These results indicated the priority of the issues in the Haarlemmerstraat/dijk of the 828 people that filled in the survey. By showing these first results in the kick-off presentation it became clear that the purpose of the co-creative collaboration session was not to focus on reiterating already well-known issues, but rather to explore potential solutions to these issues in the form of short term redesigns that could provide quick wins for the current situation in the Haarlemmerstraat/dijk.

Prior to the session we had already made a table layout, and divided the 32 participants over 4 different tables. This was to make sure that every table had a fair mix of participants, based on relevant profiles (e.g. residents vs businesses) and demographics (e.g. age and gender). Before diving into the in-depth conversations on the topics at hand, we devoted some time at each table for informal introductions by using introduction cards that were filled out by participants on arrival, which helped to keep the introduction round at the tables focused.

Orchestrating conversations around current situation (AS IS) and future situation (TO BE)

Every Streetlab concentrates on a predefined location, identifying concerns, preferences, and ideas that are specific to that location. These can be as specific as pointing out spots that people find highly suitable for bike parking facilities, or a specific traffic light that is dangerous for short-sighted people, or specific parts of the street where parents with a stroller cannot walk due to different objects that become obstacles.

In order to keep the conversations in a Streetlab focused and constructive, we create and bring a series of visual tools, or 'probes', to concentrate exchanges on the local situation. Probes are tangible artifacts like maps or labels, which are often used in the Research Through Design approach. These visual tools are an important design element that keep the conversation focused. Large maps of the street will be on the tables, often with both a detailed satellite image and a more minimal line sketch.

Figure 14.1: Maps and other materials we used for the Haarlemmerdijk/straat streetlab.

These maps give the participants the opportunity to point out and express their experiences and preferences in relation to the specific focus areas. In addition to these maps we use laser-cut objects such as bicycles, bicycle stands, pedestrians, cars, scooters, and crossings that can be used to reenact situations and experiences of participants, or to set up imagined redesigns of an area and gather feedback from the participants on those ideas.

While orchestrating the conversations at the tables around the current situation – the lived experience today as it is – we steer away from generic opinions and beliefs and towards actual activities and routines of participants, as these are more indicative of the use of urban spaces than mere generic intentions. Although people have different motivations and different needs, with the Streetlab approach they are encouraged to find a common ground, a balanced vision for a shared future. Most people love the places where they live, work, and visit, and they care deeply about their local environment. Interestingly enough, the same factor that may cause conflicts of interest – the fact that different users have different needs – is also the factor that makes the city a great place.

Figure 14.2: Haarlemmerbuurt stories on the map.

The stories about the current situation (as is) also provide a starting point for conversations around the future situation (to be); about what could be different. By jointly reflecting on the stories shared, and by coming up with alternatives for the current situation, we co-explore imagined future situations. The moderators know the limits of what could be done, and what the opportunities are according to the municipality, and make sure to thoroughly explore these. At the same time the moderator encourages participants to think without limits, as long as the ideas suggested have roots in their actual experiences in the current situation. By simultaneously opening up the discussion (diverging) and grounding the ideation in lived experiences (converging) the joint process of ideation and reflection gradually moves towards a few recurring themes that all participants see as the most important ingredients for future urban designs.

Generating new ideas and opportunities while avoiding known limitations

In advance of the Streetlab session in the Posthoornkerk, the STBY team was informed by the project team of the City of Amsterdam about the limits of what could be done and the opportunities to explore during the session. We invited the project team and some of their colleagues to our studio for what we call an 'expert meeting', in which we collectively identified these opportunities and limits.

A tool we often use during these meetings is the 'know/don't know matrix':
- Top left: things we ask our clients to brief us on, so we do not explore anything they already know during the Streetlab session.
- Top right: things we discuss in-depth with our clients to optimally inform our Streetlab preparation. These are the things we will chase during the session and definitely find answers to.
- Bottom right: things we cannot predict, but usually do come up from these sessions, and which in the end might be of high value for the project.
- Bottom left: things that may come up from the session, but are actually already known. The client may have forgotten to brief us on these. During the analysis these things will be filtered out.

Know / Don't know matrix

	...what I know	...what I don't know
I know...	**Don't** spend time exploring this	**Investigate** themes that are immediately relevant
I don't know...	**Limit** time and energy spent on this	**Explore** surprising new themes thay may come up

Figure 14.3: Know/don't know matrix.

Documentation and analysis of the stories and ideas collected

During the co-creative collaboration session, the moderators take notes on Post-its, and also record the conversation at each table (see also the discussion on **fieldnotes** in chapter 3). These notes and recordings are very helpful to guide a structured documentation of what has been said and shown by the participants. The conversations from the different tables are documented in a similar format, which supports pattern recognition and the clustering of emerging themes. While analyzing, the **saturation** of recurring stories and the repetition in the emerging insights are a sign that enough data has been collected. **Triangulating** the results across the different tables in the Streetlab session also increases the confidence in the results. The design researchers, who each facilitate a table during the Streetlab session, iteratively review and discuss the emerging insights and jointly formulate the resulting opportunities and recommendations.

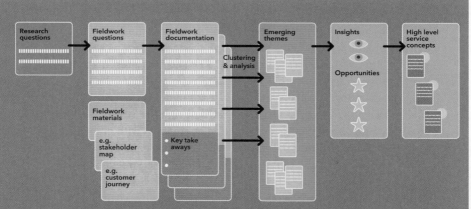

Figure 14.4: How we usually document and analyze exploratory research processes such as Streetlab projects.

Emerging themes, key insights, and opportunities

What stood out from the Streetlab about the Haarlemmerstraat/dijk was that for many participants, the topics of safety and making more room for pedestrians in the street had highest priority. From the analysis of all the feedback, three main principles emerged. The first involved speed-inhibiting measures, which could be thresholds, ridges or cobblestones placed just before crosswalks, requiring cyclists and scooters to reduce their speed. The second principle involved the removal of parking spaces to make more space for loading and unloading goods in the street. The third principle involved making more room for pedestrians in general by adjusting sidewalks.

Both the outcomes from the online survey and the co-creative session gave useful directions in the prioritization of key insights and opportunities of the research project. The outcomes of the survey indicated which issues had to be addressed first and which were less urgent, according to the participants. The most urgent issues were then discussed in detail during the Streetlab sessions.

In the report, we centered the key results around seven short term redesigns, the so-called quick wins. While keeping the report as concise, visual, and empathic as possible, we conveyed the feedback from participants on the short term redesigns to the project team from the City of Amsterdam. In addition, we illustrated the ideas and suggestions that came up for improving the livability conditions of the area with quotes and pictures. In this stage, the photographs taken of the Haarlemmerstraat/dijk at the very beginning of the project were very useful to substantiate some of the key insights. For easy reference, the recommendations for the project team were also incorporated in a visual overview.

Delivering the results

The final stage in a Streetlab project is the delivery of the results to the project team that commissioned the Research Through Design project, as well as sharing the key outcomes with the local community. STBY usually presents and discusses an extensive report with the project team. This report includes the key insights from the discussions in the Streetlabs and also a series of design inspirations – visuals that express the direction of the ideas generated during the Streetlabs. These visuals are often photographs of the current situation augmented with graphic animations to express envisioned future redesign of the urban space. In the final delivery session with the client team, we are the representatives of the Streetlab participants, making sure that their voices are heard and that their perspectives are well understood by the project team. We also make sure to develop an engaging visual summary that can be shared with a wider network of internal and external stakeholders, and the local community who took part in the design research by filling out the survey or joining the collaborative Streetlab session. The distribution of this summary is usually done by the City, as they often combine this with an announcement of planned interventions.

Sharing results with both project team and local stakeholders

In a new session with the client team and a mix of stakeholders from the City of Amsterdam, we discussed the results from the Streetlab and the recommendations for the short (and long) term urban redesign in the area. This created a clear connection between the insights generated and the design solutions that were being considered.

As a follow-up to this meeting we started preparing an information meeting for local residents and businesses, in which we communicated the results of the project together with the project team. This final session was again organized in the Posthoornkerk, the same venue where the co-creative and collaborative session was held. The knowledge generated by STBY was used by the project team to create a new street design that was presented during the assembly. The results of the research project were shared with inhabitants, shop owners, visitors, and people who work in the streets, followed up with a Q&A from the City of Amsterdam.

Subsequently, people attending this session could ask further questions and engage in conversations with each other and civil servants in smaller groups about the intended redesigns of the urban space. People gathered around tables with large maps of the area. Each table represented another section of the Haarlemmerstraat/dijk at which specific short term redesigns could be discussed. Civil servants and STBY researchers facilitated this discussion in which people could also do some suggestions relevant to the plans. Examples of discussions and suggestions were put on the map of Haarlemmerstraat/dijk.

Implementation & Reflection

This Streetlab method has proven to be very useful for urban (re)design projects, because of its highly local focus and collaborative, co-creative approach. The projects concentrate on a particular location, identifying insights that are specific to that location. These insights can be as specific as pointing out spots that people find highly suitable for bike parking facilities, or a specific traffic light. In this way, the Streetlab method offers a customized application of general policies and practices. It is based on lived experiences and personal storytelling, and not on generic opinions and beliefs.

This method is relevant for local governments, because it provides better internal confidence for making considered decisions. They can listen and learn from experiences and preferences of local residents and businesses at an early stage, before plans are fully drawn up. During the co-creative and collaborative sessions, the participation of 'fresh contacts' from neighborhoods (rather than just reaching out to the usual suspects) is a valuable addition. Moreover, as the conversations around the table are actively facilitated across internal and external stakeholders, creating a more mutual conversation takes place without slipping into the traditional 'us vs them'. The Streetlab method navigates political discussions that are stuck by bringing power to people who take lived experiences as the basis of their argument.

The Streetlab method is relevant for neighborhoods and participants because they are sincerely listened to and the setting provides a concrete opportunity to give suggestions for improvement. Because the sessions have the format of a conversation between people, it gives a better sense of what other people in the area prefer. It also gives a better sense of what local governments are planning and what the room for local customization is. Participants experience a different way of how to speak with the municipality. They experience a conversation that is more based on ideas of the commons than on political ideas. The municipality and its citizens are taking responsibility together for a public good – the public space.

One of the key challenges that the Streetlab method faces lies in the assumptions that both many residents and civil servants have about conventional public consultancies. The traditional way of consulting the public about intended changes in urban space design often takes part at a late stage of the design process when visitors can only object to the plans, instead of contributing to the direction of those plans at an earlier stage. The effect of this is that these sessions often trigger heated debates and many frustrations, and that only very few people go. During the preparations for the early stage co-creative and collaborative Streetlabs, we regularly need to get these existing assumptions out of the way before people are interested in taking part. Once they have, they see the difference and are very positive about it. The position of STBY as a facilitator – that is, steering away from politics and power struggles and instead focusing on sharing, listening and collaboration – is crucial. The civil servants cannot at this moment take up this in-between position, but they recognize that an experienced agency can.

The application of the Research Through Design method is not limited to street redesign. STBY uses Research Through Design to connect organizations with the lives and experiences of their target groups. This helps our clients to innovate their service offering, making it more valuable for both their users and their business. Our projects generate rich, visually illustrated, and engaging materials that bring real people into the heart of service innovation processes. In our work we engage with key issues in contemporary society, technology and business working on themes such as future society, intelligent systems, sustainable development, and agile collaboration.

Increased confidence on new interventions

With the input from the Streetlab on the Haarlemmerstaat/dijk, the project team from the City of Amsterdam were in a more informed position to effectively design new alternatives for an improved urban space. Several interventions will be implemented and carefully monitored in 2020.

Some examples of implemented redesigns in the Haarlemmerstraat/dijk are: elevatinging the cross roads to slow down cyclists and other users to make them more considerate towards pedestrians; removal of all parking spaces in order to create more room for pedestrians; more spaces for the loading and unloading of goods (which can be used for car parking after 4pm); and more facilities for bicycle parking and green.

Recommendations for further reading

Dorst, K. (2016). *Designing for the common good*. Amsterdam: BIS.

Miller, S. (2017). Empathic Conversations. *Medium*. https://medium.com/@STBY/empathic-conversations-aa8a26dde65a#.y4u2s5zer.

Nesta (2014). DIY Toolkit: Practical tools to trigger and support social innovation. https://diytoolkit.org/tools/.

Schaminee, A. (2019). *Designing with and within public organisations*. Amsterdam: BIS.

Stickdorn, M., Hormess, M. A., Lawrence, A., & Schneider, J. (2018). *This is service Design Doing: Applying service design thinking in the real world*. Sebastopol, CA: O'Reilly Media. Also accessible at https://www.thisiss

15 *Too many cities in the city?* Interdisciplinary and transdisciplinary city research methods and the challenge of integration

Machiel Keestra and Nanke Verloo

Introduction: Interdisciplinary, transdisciplinary and action research of a city in lockdown

As we write this chapter, most cities across the world are subject to a similar set of measures due to the spread of COVID-19 coronavirus, which is now a global pandemic. Independent of city size, location, or history, an observer would note that almost all cities have now ground to a halt, with their citizens being confined to their private dwellings, social and public gatherings being almost entirely forbidden, and commercial areas being nearly devoid of visitors. Striking as these apparent similarities are, closer scrutiny would reveal important differences between cities and within cities – differences that can be highly relevant to consider when scholars are assessing the responses of cities to this pandemic or trying to predict the consequences of those responses.

For example, the public health systems in some cities are better prepared than in others for coping with the increasing number of patients in life threatening conditions. Multigenerational households, which are associated with a greater risk for elderly members, are not equally common in all cities. Tourist destinations have taken a more severe economic hit from the lockdown than those cities which are economically less dependent upon this particular source of income. Communal celebrations in one city will result in a higher number of contagions and perhaps even deaths in this situation, whereas that same social fabric generally does contribute to a population's health.

The pandemic has also had unprecedented effects on differences and inequalities within cities. In cities in the United States, neighborhoods primarily inhabited by African Americans have been disproportionately affected by COVID-19 due to living and health conditions, yet also due to the fact they disproportionately perform vital jobs. Parks and green spaces are crowded, while city centers like Amsterdam's Red Light District have suddenly lost the bustle of tourism, providing opportunities for citizens to reoccupy scarce public spaces and reclaim **ownership**.

Clearly, such differences between cities are in many cases only discernible to the eye of an expert, possessing the necessary background knowledge to interpret the perceptible local changes caused by the global pandemic. Typically, drawing upon his or her disciplinary training, the expert also knows how to further probe the impact of the pandemic in an appropriate way. However, compared to the usual application of expertise, this crisis situation might, in an unusual way, test even experts.[1] For the pandemic has created a unique situation, imposing unfamiliar constraints on the health, economic, social, and other conditions of cities, constraints that interact in sometimes unexpected ways with each other. Such interactions in turn force experts to collaborate across the boundaries commonly associated with disciplines, their concepts, theories, methods, and assumptions (Klein, 1996).

Take for example the picture below of the Amsterdam Mercator square – a picture that we used for a workshop on **interdisciplinarity** not too long before the pandemic was recognized. As we'll describe in the next section, this picture is interpreted differently by experts in city planning, history, and computational analyses, compared with the interpretation of behavioral and cultural scientists.

Figure 15.1: Mercatorplein in Amsterdam, Fall 2019 (Image by Eva Plevier). Note that the picture was taken before the coronavirus pandemic was publicly recognized and measures were taken.

[1]   Some research suggests that expertise is brittle as soon as it is applied to unusual, atypical cases, where common answers and approaches do not apply. Important as it is, expertise does indeed have some disadvantages, one of them being that experts tend to apply their usual approaches even in circumstances when this applicability is questionable (cf. Lewandowsky & Thomas, 2009; Keestra, 2017).

Yet all experts would need to drastically revise their disciplinary interpretation and the research questions provoked by the picture as soon as they learned that it was taken during the pandemic while the government implemented a social lockdown policy to mitigate the virus spread, since historical, social, and architectural influences partially gave way to the impact of the pandemic. Any interdisciplinary process poses a similar challenge and requires a similarly open mindset, albeit in less unprecedented circumstances.

These brief **observations** of how a virus pandemic can have differential impacts upon various cities, and what this exceptional situation might mean for the application of city methods, allow us to draw a few consequences for the current context of this chapter on interdisciplinary and **transdisciplinary** research. First, whenever we are investigating a complex and dynamic phenomenon it is by no means easy to determine which disciplinary perspectives are required to do justice to it. Indeed, the choice of useful disciplines can only be made after an initial overview of the situation and a preliminary selection of what appear to be the most important features of the situation. *Relevance* is key in guiding this selection process and scholars must remain open to the possibility that they may need to revise their earlier assessments of what is relevant and what is not. Second, if scholars from different disciplines were to study different features of a city in isolation, their '**multidisciplinary**' account would miss important dynamic and complex interactions, such as those between a city's demographics and geographical situation, its governance and economy. In other words, it is the *integration* of the perspectives of different disciplines that is crucial, as only then are such interactions taken into account. Indeed, this integration between disciplinary perspectives is what distinguishes an interdisciplinary from a multidisciplinary account. Thirdly, in addition to checking the relevance of disciplines and aiming for their integration, the outcome of interdisciplinary and transdisciplinary research has typically *limited generalizability*. Since a city is sensitive to a multitude of internal and external dynamical factors, in ways that partly rest upon its socio-cultural history, its investigation will often have the nature of a **case study** rather than be capable of leading to law-like insights (Krohn, 2010; Menken & Keestra, 2016).

As can be seen from these three characteristics of ascertaining the relevance of different disciplinary contributions, the challenge of their integration, and the limited generalizability of their results owing to the specificity of interdisciplinary (ID) and transdisciplinary (TD) research, such research into 'real world problems' is clearly distinct from most monodisciplinary research.

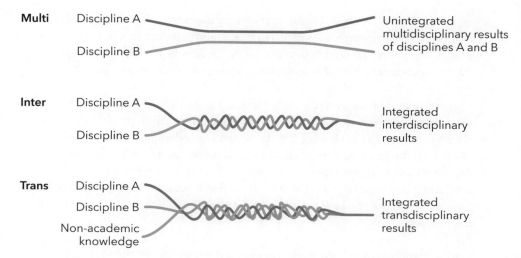

Figure 15.2:   Multi-disciplinarity entails no integration of the contributions of different disciplines. Interdisciplinarity is characterized by such integration. Transdisciplinarity further includes the integration of non-academic contributions. (From Menken & Keestra, 2016)

A consequence of this distinction is the absence of a general ID/TD methodology that can guide specific case studies. By contrast, the collaboration implied in such research requires researchers – and stakeholders, if they are involved – to reflect upon their potential contribution and the implicit assumptions associated with that. We will elaborate on this in the next section. Next, we offer several typologies of integration that urban scholars could employ for their research projects, after which we will offer a few brief analyses of initial collaborations of urban research. Finally, we discuss in more detail the process of the interdisciplinary research project. This will include a brief reflection upon the decision-making process that is implied in such projects. In sum, we aim to provide some guidance in conducting an ID/TD project, albeit not in the form of a definite methodology.

Setting the stage: establishing an ID/TD research team

As mentioned above, determining which perspectives are relevant for a given project is an important task, perhaps even more so when the study results should assist government officials and politicians in taking measures. Scholars, irrespective of their discipline, might feel justified by their integrated insights in proposing a particular public policy or city planning. However, the impact of such proposals on a particular community will also be complex and dynamic, and can provoke unexpected positive or negative responses or even civil disobedience, impeding the effectiveness of the intervention.

In order to increase the *social robustness* of their knowledge-based intervention proposal, the research team should therefore invite relevant stakeholders or community representatives to participate in the project. In doing so they recognize that stakeholders – such as citizens, shop keepers, tourists – perhaps have specific experiences with the city that are not yet covered in research (for examples of transdisciplinary research, see chapters 13, 14, and 16). In addition, the normative-pragmatic choices that need to be made cannot be fully justified by knowledge claims, but require forms of community deliberation (Nowotny, 2003).

Integrating the perspectives of stakeholders in a project turns it, in fact, into a transdisciplinary one, with effects on all research stages – from problem definition, via the collection and analysis of data, to integrating and implementing the results of the project (Hirsch Hadorn et al., 2008). **Action research** goes one step further. Actionable knowledge requires integration of stakeholder perspectives while conducting the research project in such a way that it generates options for action for those stakeholders who have to cope with the problem situation (Bradbury-Huang, 2008; Keestra, 2019).

Having mentioned above the limited generalizability of interdisciplinary and transdisciplinary research, generalizability is further challenged when stakeholders are involved and actionability is adopted as a research criterion. If the results of scientific research are typically generalizable over numerous comparable situations but not directly applicable in real world situations (for example because laboratory conditions are meticulously controlled or human subjects are carefully selected), for inter- and transdisciplinary projects the reverse often holds. Avoiding the abstraction and isolation of the research object increases the applicability of the research output to the specific object under scrutiny, while constraining its applicability to objects that might appear to be comparable yet are potentially very different (Krohn, 2010).

A consequence of these preliminary observations is that interdisciplinary and transdisciplinary research projects usually cannot rely upon given theoretical frameworks or methodological apparatuses. Instead, such projects require from the very start that participants engage in team reflection upon their own and others' perspectives on the research problem, are open to reconsidering the relevance of their and others' potential contributions, and are also ready to adjust the definition of the problem they aim to investigate (Looney et al., 2014). Disciplinary and extra-academic experts alike must be prepared to engage in a metacognitive and reflective team process, as represented in the figure below.

If a group of researchers has been able to agree upon their research problem and has reached a consensus about the mix of disciplinary perspectives – how to continue once that phase has been completed? With integration apparently being such a crucial step in the project, what choices have to be made, what options are available? What kind of results might the research group be expected to produce?

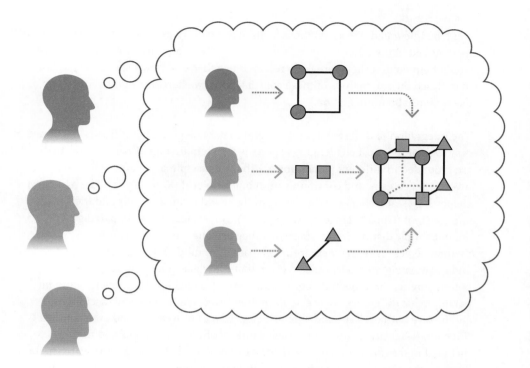

Figure 15.3:   An interdisciplinary team of experts develops together a more comprehensive understanding of a phenomenon – represented by the three-dimensional cube composed of the different elements each of them contributes. Their team metacognition and philosophical reflection upon their interdisciplinary collaboration facilitate the process of their development of an interdisciplinary integration of their distinct mental representations of the phenomenon. (From Keestra, 2017).

Integrating disciplinary perspectives

In this book, myriad methods are discussed by scholars working in various fields ranging from fields in the social sciences (geography, planning, anthropology) to the natural sciences (biology), mathematics (computational science), humanities (history and cultural studies) economics, architecture and action research. When starting from a real-world problem, the selection of relevant perspectives, the number of methods or datasets to be used, as well as the decision about their adequate integration, are constrained by the nature of this problem.

For the purpose of this book, we organized a workshop on interdisciplinarity with urban studies scholars that included a thought experiment in order to explore such decision-making. We invited them to discuss a given picture (see picture 1 and the picture on the cover of this volume) showing an urban streetscape, and imagine a research project based on their own discipline by following the question-based set-up of our volume: what do I see, how can I understand, what do I miss, and why does it matter? Then they were asked to share their approach with a researcher from another field and imagine how their two – at times, vastly different – approaches could be integrated. We asked them to discuss the overlaps in their approaches, what they missed in the other's approach (or perhaps their combined approaches), what would help them if they were to do research together, and how they would go about that. Based on our analysis of these conversations, we here distinguish four types of discussions about integration.

The integration of different disciplines and methodological approaches is not always easy. One of the most challenging aspects is the combination of perspectives that are grounded in different **paradigms** or different disciplinary matrices to describe, investigate, explain, and communicate about the world (Kuhn, 1970). The paradigm shapes how researchers see the nature of the world more generally and their place and role in it (Guba & Lincoln, 1994, p. 107). Importantly, though, paradigms are not simply distinct in the sense that they use qualitative or quantitative methodologies, as researchers from one paradigm might still use both qualitative and quantitative methods. Indeed, given that every discipline nowadays displays both theoretical and methodological pluralism, it is obvious that, notwithstanding paradigmatic differences between disciplines, every combination of disciplines will involve both overlaps and similarities as well as differences and even conflicts (Menken & Keestra, 2016). Since such conflicts often entail values and norms included in these disciplinary matrices, it can be very challenging for researchers to overstep the corresponding boundaries. In that situation, differences often extend to disagreement about central questions like the problem definition, assumptions about appropriate knowledge, how insights can and should be produced, what the researcher's role is in relation to the field, and the final objective and goal of research. We therefore first consider the option of non-integration.

Conflicting perspectives – no integration

Take the example of the conversation between two urban researchers. One is a planner doing **institutional analyses** from a **critical theory paradigm** and the other is a computational scientist studying behavior in the city through sensing using a **positivist paradigm**. When they view figure 15.1, they both see something different, as their different paradigms shape how they perceive and understand the world. The planner sees the historical buildings of the Amsterdam School of architecture of the early twentieth century in relation to the more recent interventions in public space; the planner immediately thinks critically about this historical progress and sets out to study the political economy of postmodern renewal and its history by using cadaster data to understand the economic changes. What the computational analyst sees is an empty square that is underused, which he blames on an inadequate design. The analyst proposes to study what elements or features of the urban space would make the square more attractive to users using **street-level imagery** and computational techniques that show how people make use of, or refrain from using, the square. The two researchers are thus both interested in the interventions that produced the public space, but they have competing assumptions about which kinds of data are adequately representing the experiences of the users. The planner insists that technological approaches overlook the real experiential knowledge of the people using the square on an everyday basis, since images can't provide understanding of the reasons why they use the square or not, and do not take account of the socio-economic and historical context. The computational scientist disagrees: he believes that images of the square can be used to ask people in a random sample online what they like or dislike about the square and in so doing collect the user knowledge required. The kinds of knowledge they intend to produce and their objectives also differ: the planner wants to make a critical analysis of the socio-economic and political decisions behind the interventions of the square, the computational analyst wants to make the square more attractive to users. If they were not interested in adjusting their perspectives, they would not be able to bridge their differences because they do not agree on the problem definition, the appropriate data, the knowledge necessary for knowing the square, nor about the kind of knowledge they want to produce and the objective of such a study. Hence, integration seems absent, rendering this potential project multidisciplinary and not interdisciplinary.

Narrow multidisciplinarity with potential for integration

The second typology we identified in our workshop is a shared perspective between two different approaches, characterized by comparable methods used by the same or related disciplines as they work together in a project. Whenever collaborating disciplines are relatively close to each other in terms of their relevant theories, methodologies, or results, we might refer to that situation as 'narrow' multidisciplinarity or interdisciplinarity, in contrast to 'wide' interdisciplinarity, which would include more diverging disciplines (Newell, 2007). In a narrow multidisciplinary approach, disciplines, their assumptions, norms, and (implicit) paradigms typically lie close to each other, making the task of establishing a common research question or integrating their methods or results fairly easy. However, such 'narrow' collaboration would rarely lead researchers to confront their assumptions, rethink their knowledge, or push the fields in unexpected directions – perhaps contributing to its cost-effectiveness.

Let's look at the conversation between the same computational analyst and a GIS specialist looking at the image of the biker (see figure 1.1 in chapter 1 of this volume). They both observe a biker doing something that is not planned for: he is riding on the tramrails. Their shared problem definition is that there is a mismatch in the way space is allocated to different users. Their problem definition is also the hypothesis that they want to test by complementing each other's findings. The computational scientist uses 'real time data' of videos of user movements and the GIS specialist uses 'representative data' via quantitative spatial data sets. They argue that their approaches complement each other easily because they share the same **post-positivist paradigm** that seeks to produce evidence-based policy evaluations, in this case of spatial designs – making this an example of 'narrow' interdisciplinarity. As they are researching a shared hypothesis they do engage in a process of mutual learning about the allocation of space, but they do not proceed to reinterpret their data as they merely supplement their findings with other results that increase the validity of their tests. This could be a valuable outcome for short-term policy evaluations because results and insights gain in validity and robustness when confirmed by different tests (Wimsatt, 2007). However, given the fact that this multidisciplinary approach does not yet integrate disciplinary distinct approaches, it is not likely to generate new or unexpected findings that could alter our understanding of the city or, in this case, the use of public space.

Wide multidisciplinary with potential for integration

A wide multi-disciplinary approach brings together researchers from disciplines that diverge more in terms of the theories they uphold, their methods, results, etcetera. To the extent that integration takes place between these perspectives, we can distinguish between multidisciplinary and interdisciplinary collaborations, as was represented in figure 15.2 above (Menken & Keestra, 2016). Nevertheless, the researchers still have to overcome differences and work together towards a process of mutual learning by discussing similarities and differences with regard to their paradigms and their approaches to collecting data in order to co-produce a shared problem definition and objective. Such a multidisciplinary research is sometimes carried out according to a phase model when the different parts of the multi-method approach are conducted subsequently or separately from each other, without the researchers needing to reinterpret their own approach or knowledge. Hence, this approach is a partial form of integration.

An example of such a multidisciplinary approach was developed in a conversation with a scholar using urban **ethnography** and a classical economist looking at the picture of the biker. The economist did not show an interest in the biker but in the historical buildings behind him. He imagined that a lot of public money was invested in maintaining this cultural heritage and wondered whether that money was well spent? To answer that question, he would study the changes in the value of the housing prices surrounding the historic building. He would trace land registry data and data from real estate agents since the period of public investment in the building. He warned that this could not be researched in just one setting, so he would do a quasi-experiment comparing the change in property value after public investments in cultural heritage in similar cases across the country. He hypothesized that if property values were found to rise after public investments in a representative number of similar cases, you could argue that these investments were worthy and effective.

The paradigm of the economist conflicts with the paradigm of the urban ethnographer, who would also be interested in understanding the (unintended) effects of certain policies, like investments in cultural heritage, but would take a profoundly different approach. She insists that the economical focus overlooks the more subjective reasons why people choose to buy a property and what they are willing to pay for it. The economic value focus is also problematic from her perspective because it excludes the value of cultural heritage to people who do not have the resources to buy property in this area. She also considers the fact that there are many other factors that shape the property value, like the rise of Airbnb in the city center of Amsterdam or the fact that the popular Nieuwmarkt square is around the corner. The economist responds to this last argument by explaining his control variables, which should balance out the effect of other influences beyond the public investment in cultural heritage. The identification of similar cases should also deal with these external influences. This might be convincing, but it does not deal with the two prior concerns of the ethnographer.

They agree that it would be useful to work together: the economist would run his analyses regarding the changes in property value and subsequently the ethnographer would do fieldwork and **interviews** in order to understand the more subjective reasons why property owners invested in the property around the historic building. The economist warns against a 'hypothetical bias' when asking whether, for example, people value the church or not: if you ask people whether the church is important, they will always say yes. The ethnographer would, however, not do a survey in which people were asked whether the church was important, but in-depth **interviews**, to understand all the reasons why and the process of *how* people choose to buy a property there (see chapter 5). It is possible that people do not mention the church at all, in which case that is a valuable result in itself. Additionally, the ethnographer would carry out further research beyond interviewing the residents by performing **participant observations** in the space in and around the church, to include visitors who might value the church but do not live in the area. They imagine that an additional critical analysis, using statistical (chapter 2) or **GIS** data (chapter 11), of the socio-economic make-up of property owners and social renters in the area might provide alternative insights in the various ways in which the church is valued by residents in relation to unequal housing opportunities for Amsterdam residents.

Through working together and engaging with each other's viewpoints, the differences between the economist and ethnographer turn into respect and appreciation for each other's approaches. Their findings complement one another because they provide another insight on the same object. However, the two do not go as far as reinterpreting their own ways of knowing, nor do they integrate the two qualitatively different perspectives in a single yet more comprehensive view. If they were to carefully integrate their methods and insights, this would not just have an impact upon their research but also upon their potential policy advice, making it more – socially and scientifically – robust than merely adding together their perspectives.

Interdisciplinarity – seeking integration between perspectives

What makes an interdisciplinary project different from a multidisciplinary project is the extent to which the disciplines and related methodologies become integrated throughout the process of doing research. Participating researchers in an interdisciplinary project engage in an iterative process of mutual learning and decision-making. Given the difficulty of these processes, it can be helpful when a 'real-world problem' serves as a boundary object. The photos of the square and the biker functioned as such boundary objects in our workshop, encouraging conversations about what each participant observed, how they would define the problem, what they would do to study that problem or phenomena. During these conversations the epistemological and ontological assumptions became tangible, and overlaps and differences became visible.

Even when scholars participate in interdisciplinary projects, they do not always have to have a complete consensus about paradigms or assumptions, let alone share the same paradigm. Differences can invite participants to consider how they might fill a gap in each other's approaches. A way to start imagining interdisciplinary opportunities might thus begin by jointly answering the question 'What do I miss?' as an interdisciplinary team. Clearly, the result of such a conversation can be an even more challenging methodological and theoretical pluralism than the pluralism that is already present within a single discipline. Eventually, resulting insights should lead to a more comprehensive insight by integrating various perspectives on the same problem or phenomenon. That also means that initial outcomes might contest each other. Such contestation could invite all participants to adjust their approaches or methodologies, collect more data, reinterpret their analysis, or even reconsider their epistemologies.

While looking at the image of the Mercator square (figure 15.1), a group of scholars from the fields of cultural analysis, geography, planning, history, and computational analysis observe that the square is recently renovated but, at the time of the photograph, quite empty. Their local knowledge informs them that this square is actively used on days with better weather, especially the fountain, which is a place for children and families to gather and play. After sharing what they observe, they come to agree that it would be interesting study the seeming tension between the built environment and its use or users. They wonder why the square is not used more on other days and what effects the design of public space has on the inclusivity of a space. Each scholar approaches the definition of this problem from the perspective of their own discipline: the historian would reconstruct the architectural history, the cultural analyst would study the **aesthetics** of the public space, the geographer would study the everyday uses of the square, the planner is interested in the policy and planning process behind the current built environment, and the computational analyst would study the use of the space through remote sensing. Discussing how they would approach the square differently allows them to co-produce a problem definition that remains general enough to include different disciplinary perspectives but specific enough to share a common goal.

To integrate the disciplinary perspectives the participants need to rethink what is missing in their own approach and what the other approaches may contribute. They ask themselves, 'What do I miss?' By thinking through what their own approaches overlook or ignore they start to imagine the contributions of other disciplines to their findings. For example, the planner would not be able to make sense of the subtle ideological backgrounds of design aesthetics that the study of the cultural analyst would make visible. Conversely, the cultural analyst needs the study of the planner and the geographer to understand the actual planning process of the design and the intentions behind it, as well as the everyday uses and experiences of citizens. The historian would place the overall analyses in a historical perspective that shows how the progress of policies, architecture, and socio-economic changes affects the city and its users.

The participants use different approaches that influence the way they develop their insight. For the cultural analyst – taking a critical theory paradigm – the question of representation is less important. He could make a semiotic analysis (see chapter 7) of what the aesthetics of the design communicate and make an argument about the in- and exclusive meaning of the design. His analysis, however, would be strengthened by data from the historian, planner, and geographer, which show how the space was historically (see chapter 6) or institutionally (see chapter 8) produced, how planners intended the design, and how it is used on a daily basis (see chapters 3, 4, and 5 for methodologies that allow for such data). These data could validate the analysis of in- or exclusion via a close reading of the square's aesthetics, but they could also contrast with it. In that case, the cultural analyst is challenged to open his mind to another interpretation of the aesthetics based on a different set of data.

Simultaneously the planner, geographer, and data scientist should stay open to a different type of learning that is not based in empirical data but in close reading of design aesthetics in its historical and cultural context.

If the scholars are able to integrate their ways of learning about the square, they would integrate different knowledges or perspectives to inform and contribute to their analyses. That way, they engage in a process of mutual learning. For example, the data about everyday use might be developed through a combination of data collection methods - interviews, participant observations and remote sensing. Together these data sets might offer the planner an insight about the unintended consequences of planning process of the design and the contingency of some previous findings concerning the use of the square. The cultural analyst might change his reading of its aesthetics upon listening to interviews with citizens about their appreciation of the space. The historic trajectory might reveal that over time the city has been investing in this space to regenerate it from a relatively marginalized neighborhood to a more affluent area. And that trajectory might be placed in a critical perspective by a geographer using quantitative analyses (see chapter 2) to show how that process of gentrification has excluded low-income families. Such process of mutual learning could provide valuable information for policy makers to rethink the practice of spatial planning and the way it affects in- or exclusion in the city.

Interdisciplinary research as an iterative process of mutual learning

The examples above highlighted how interdisciplinary research typically implies a process of mutual learning in the participants – and the same holds for transdisciplinary and action research. We noted how the perspective each participant brings along can be different from that of others with regard to important, often implicit, assumptions about what the fundamental characteristics are of a city, of knowledge, of scientific methodology, of adequate interventions, and so on. Integrating such different perspectives requires an individual and team process of metacognition and reflection, as we noted above, preparing for different degrees of collaboration and integration.

Unsurprisingly, the consequence of these challenges is that the interdisciplinary research process is typically different from a mono- or multidisciplinary research process. Although the specific nature of interdisciplinary research can be observed at all phases of the research process, its impact is especially large in the initial phase of the research process, when the research problem and questions are determined. A monodisciplinary research question is also usually formulated in its preliminary phase in agreement with the – implicit – concepts, assumptions, and methods of that discipline. Consequently, the specification of a theoretical framework in such cases creates no tension with such an initial research question, as both question and framework are constrained by those same concepts, assumptions, and methods. Yet when a theoretical framework is developed for an interdisciplinary research process, the integration of multiple perspectives will have an impact upon the preliminary research question, which will have received different formulations and interpretations from all disciplines. For the integration of these perspectives a research question must be formulated that is sustained by each perspective, adjusting perhaps all of the question's initial monodisciplinary formulations.

Obviously, once participants have jointly determined their interdisciplinary research problem, it is implausible that this can be investigated by methods stemming from only a single discipline. Something similar holds for the integration of the data that result from carrying out their interdisciplinary research. Such research will yield an unusual combination of kinds of data, the integration of which must be determined by the participants with an eye on their problem.

As a consequence, the interdisciplinary research process has the shape of an iterative decision making process (Newell, 2007) during which participants are not able to follow their usual linear research process. Instead, at different phases of this process they must make decisions while taking into account an unusual combination of approaches, which has specific implications for each process phase. Yet the specific nature of this process is particularly visible with regard to research question, as is visible in the question's two-tiered development in the model of interdisciplinary research below (Menken & Keestra, 2016).

This formal description of the specific nature of the interdisciplinary research process and its challenges in terms of metacognition and reflection does not, perhaps, sufficiently capture how difficult it can be for a research team to reach the consensus required for bringing their project to fruition. Let us therefore close this chapter by briefly shedding some light on how such a consensus might be reached. Particularly in those cases when integration cannot be established with the help of a shared model or theory, participants must engage in a reflective dialogue to develop common ground and integrate their perspectives (Bammer, 2014; Eigenbrode et al., 2007). A dialogue like the one we facilitated with the authors of this volume engages the participants in reflecting on their (often implicit) assumptions and paradigms and uses a boundary object like a picture to confront participants with the differences between what they see and how others view the same picture, how they define the problem, and what they would do to research it. Such a dialogue can facilitate this process of joint metacognition and reflection, as represented in figure 15.3 above. Students and scholars can use a variety of other tools to facilitate such reflective dialogue.[2] During the dialogue, researchers hopefully come to recognize the value of

---

2   Online tools to facilitate reflective dialogue – and other collaboration tools – can be found at the websites of e.g. Transdisciplinary-Net (https://naturalsciences.ch/topics/co-producing_knowledge), Integration and Implementation Science (https://i2s.anu.edu.au/resources/subject/collaboration/), Science of Team Science (https://www.teamsciencetoolkit.cancer.gov/) and the Association for Interdisciplinary Studies (https://interdisciplinarystudies.org/the-scholarship-of-interdisciplinary-teaching-and-learning/).

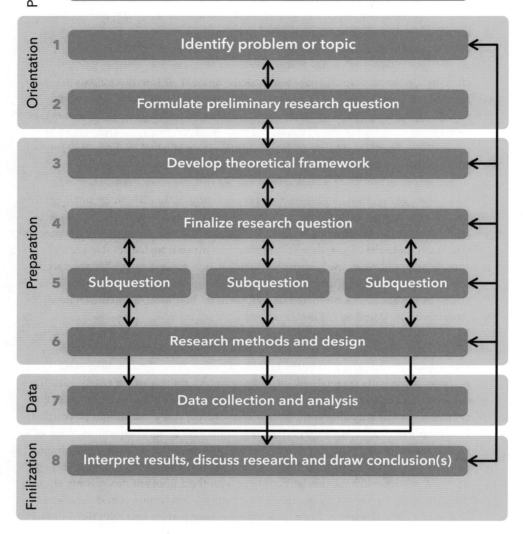

Figure 15.4:   *The Institute for Interdisciplinary Studies' model for interdisciplinary research. In this model for the interdisciplinary research process, the different steps (the blue boxes in the middle of the figure) reflect the tasks that must be completed in a specific research phase (indicated in the left margin). Although one may sometimes need to return to a previous step, the order of steps is more or less fixed and one should not skip a single one. As an obvious example, one cannot analyze data that are not yet collected. However, it is important to realize that one needs to think one step ahead (i.e. one should know how to analyze data before one starts collecting them). For this reason, several steps have been grouped together in the following phases of the interdisciplinary research process: Orientation, Preparation, Data collection and analysis, and Finalization. (From Menken & Keestra, 2016).*

each other's starting points and appreciate each other's guiding examples[3] of valuable research while seeking maximal coherence between them and preparing themselves for joint decision making on important steps of the research process – like the definition of the research problem and question (Keestra, 2017).

Although this is not the place to elaborate further on that process, this brief sketch does convey that interdisciplinary – and transdisciplinary or action – research brings further challenges for participants in addition to those commonly faced in disciplinary or multidisciplinary research. Because of this, this research process is perhaps not only more demanding in terms of personal and team engagement, but generally also more time consuming, at least in its initial phase. Given the current research climate, this will for many present a major obstacle to getting involved in this type of research. We hope to have made clear, though, that the extra efforts are worth investing in this mode of research. In addition to the mutual learning that benefits each participant, the results of such research are generally more robust and will hold under varying conditions, making their implementation often more successful than results which are obtained under much less comprehensive conditions. Moreover, both research institutions and individual researchers are increasingly convinced that innovation and creativity are less likely to emerge within isolated disciplines than from collaborations at the intersection of disciplines (Milman et al., 2015; National Academies of Sciences, 2004). This will be no different for city research: inviting participants to move beyond disciplinary horizons and engage in unfamiliar options in urban terrains that are jointly explored will make us as researchers and practitioners better equipped to deal with complex situations like the current pandemic, which are increasingly challenging our urban environments.

References

Bammer, G. (2014). From toolbox to big science project. A bold proposal. In M. O'Rourke, S. Crowley, S. D. Eigenbrode, & J. D. Wulfhorst (eds.), *Enhancing communication & collaboration in interdisciplinary research* (pp. 386-406). Los Angeles (CA): Sage Publications.

Bradbury-Huang, H. (2008). Quality and "actionability": What action researchers offer from the tradition of pragmatism. In A. B. Shani, S. Albers Mohrman, W. A. Pasmore, B. Stymne, & N. Adler (eds.), *Handbook of collaborative management research* (pp. 583-600). London: Sage Publications.

Eigenbrode, S. D., O'Rourke, M., Wulfhorst, J. D., Althoff, D. M., Goldberg, C. S., Merrill, K., ... Winowiecki, L. (2007). Employing philosophical dialogue in collaborative science. *BioScience, 57*(1), 55-64.

Guba, E. G., & Lincoln, Y. S. (1994). Competing paradigms in qualitative research. In N. K. Denzin & Y. S. Lincoln (Eds.), *Handbook of qualitative research* (pp. 105-117). Thousand Oaks (CA): Sage Publications.

---

3   Note that 'paradigma' in Greek means also 'example'. Kuhn also refers to paradigms as 'accepted examples of scientific practice' (Kuhn, 1970, p. 10).

Hirsch Hadorn, G., Hoffmann-Riem, H., Biber-Klemm, S., Grossenbacher-Mansuy, W., Joye, D., Pohl, C., ... Zemp, E. (eds.). (2008). *Handbook of transdisciplinary research*. Dordrecht: Springer.

Keestra, M. (2017). Meta-cognition and reflection by interdisciplinary experts: Insights from cognitive science and philosophy. *Issues in Interdisciplinary Studies, 35*, 121-169.

Keestra, M. (2019). Imagination and actionability: Reflections on the future of interdisciplinarity, inspired by Julie Thompson Klein. *Issues in Interdisciplinary Studies, 37*(2), 110-129.

Klein, J. T. (1996). Crossing boundaries: *Knowledge, disciplinarities, and interdisciplinarities*. Charlottesville, VA: University Press of Virginia.

Krohn, W. (2010). Interdisciplinary cases and disciplinary knowledge – epistemic challenges of interdisciplinary research. In R. Frodeman, J. T. Klein, & C. Mitcham (eds.), *The Oxford handbook of interdisciplinarity* (pp. 31-49). Oxford: Oxford University Press.

Kuhn, T. S. (1970). *The structure of scientific revolutions* (2nd, enlarged ed.). Chicago: University of Chicago Press.

Lewandowsky, S., & Thomas, J. L. (2009). Expertise: Acquisition, limitations, and control. *Reviews of Human Factors and Ergonomics, 5*(1), 140-165.

Looney, C., Donovan, S., O'Rourke, M., Crowley, S., Eigenbrode, S. D., Rotschy, L., ... Wulfhorst, J. D. (2014). Seeing through the eyes of collaborators. Using toolbox workshops to enhance cross-disciplinary communication. In M. O'Rourke, S. Crowley, S. D. Eigenbrode, & J. D. Wulfhorst (eds.), *Enhancing communication & collaboration in interdisciplinary research* (p. 220-243). Los Angeles (CA): Sage Publications.

Menken, S., & Keestra, M. (eds.). (2016). *An introduction to interdisciplinary research. Theory and practice*. Amsterdam: Amsterdam University Press.

Milman, A., Marston, J. M., Godsey, S. E., Bolson, J., Jones, H. P., & Weiler, C. S. (2015). Scholarly motivations to conduct interdisciplinary climate change research. *Journal of Environmental Studies and Sciences*, 1-12.

National Academies of Sciences (2004). *Facilitating interdisciplinary research*. Retrieved from Washington, DC: https://www.nap.edu/download. php?record_id=11153

Newell, W. H. (2007). Decision making in interdisciplinary studies. In G. Morçöl (ed.), *Handbook of decision making* (p. 245-264). New York: Marcel-Dekker.

Nowotny, H. (2003). Democratising expertise and socially robust knowledge. *Science and Public Policy, 30*, 151-156.

Wimsatt, W. C. (2007). *Re-engineering philosophy for limited beings*. Piecewise approximations to reality: Harvard University Press.

16 Exploring city science

Caroline Nevejan[I]

Introduction

This chapter introduces and explores city science as a research practice, discourse, and possibly a research paradigm in its own right. **City science** is used here as a container term to refer to research that happens in, with, and for the city and which is transdisciplinary through all phases of the research process and potentially affects all phases of the policy process (Nevejan, 2018). This chapter aims to give evidence for the need to address city science as a research practice in which science, policy, and design merge in the local context of challenges that cities face in the twenty-first century with accelerating dynamics of climate change, financialization, and increasing inequalities worldwide. The focus of this exploration is on the research relations between European cities and European universities, with Amsterdam and the research into City Rhythm as case for detailed elaboration (Nevejan, Sefkatli & Cunningham, 2018).

The awareness of the potential value of collaboration between cities and universities is growing in many places. Universities are part of the social realities of cities and need to show their value to society beyond the publication indexes that rule academic careers. Cities engage more and more with evidence-based policymaking and cities are confronted with increasingly complex and even wicked problems, and they need research to help solve these situations. However, processes for establishing trust and truth are different between science, academia, and the politics and bureaucracy that characterize city management. Cities need to solve issues fast because politicians are only in office for four years. Civil servants in the city, on the other hand, are trained to evade risk and uncertainty and are eager therefore to protect the status quo. In contrast, academic and scientific researchers need time to develop their research and, by definition, research will question a status quo. Because the need to face cities

---

I   Author wants to thank Scott Cunningham for reviewing this text, Pinar Sefkatli for providing the illustrations, and Nanke Verloo and Luca Bertolini for editing this book which has the potential to significantly improve research in/with/for/on cities.

challenges in integral and transdisciplinary ways increases dramatically, new avenues for collaboration emerge.

This chapter identifies issues and methodologies that are indispensable for city science research projects and discusses the hindrances that one needs to overcome in such projects. The first section positions the need for city science in the current social, economic, ecological, and technological developments in Europe and in global dynamics. The second section sketches current developments in the relation between cities and universities and offers an overview of current collaborations between universities and municipalities in Europe. The third section describes the research process of city science, its transdisciplinary nature, how this affects research designs and highlights specific elements in the character of city science. The conclusion explores the future of city science.

The need for city science

Cities have become complex systems in which the human experience is changing. With the introduction of information and communication technologies, globalization has acquired new speed and scale to conquer the world. In the last 50 years, cities have become complex systems in which infrastructure, social structures, ecological dynamics, and ICT have become interwoven in such a way that an intervention in any of these three fields affects all other fields. An ICT connection in a remote place, as simple as a phone, changes the nature of the place because its connections to the outside world significantly increase possibilities for access to news, entrepreneurship, and education. In larger cities ICT is part of all elements of daily life from food to education, from transport to medical care.

For a long time, the human being was the measure of all things, and human experience was firstly defined by this sense of physical context. With the development of sciences, human experience was extended with different concepts of measuring; measures to assess quality of goods, of activities, of distance and proximity, of different functions of the body, nature and more. Human experience is increasingly defined by the result of measurements and, as such, the measurable human being as a concept has emerged. Today, with live data streaming around the world, we are confronted with the concept of the measurable human kind.[2] To give a simple example, the live data streams about where traffic jams are happening now instantly affects the choice of route for many travelers in the area. One can imagine other data streams affecting the behavior of thousands of people in real time. One can speculate that the COVID-19 crisis is the first in which real-time data have the potential to report on a global scale, in direct relation to personal well-being, about the state of infection of humankind. Such a data feed needs only a global app in which people upload their physical and social status in relation to the virus via a mobile phone. In such an app, a direct relation is generated between the body as local presence,

---

2   I introduced the concepts of *Homo Mensura, Homo Mensurabilis, Humanitas Mensurabilis* in the opening session of the UNESCO World Social Science Forum in 2013 in Montreal.

the body as measurement, and the body as part of a global transformation of humankind. Transformation in this sense means the sense of awareness, the sense of image of the self (i.e. me in comparison to the whole world or, for example, we here against them there), the sense of adapting to social and physical behavior, and the sense of accepting surveillance measures in pursuit of global health. Such surveillance measures nonetheless deeply affect societies and the functioning of democracy.

More and more people realize that climate change, financial markets, supply chains, culture, and education are global phenomena in which people are interdependent. In these settings each problem is deeply interlinked to many others (Castells, 1996; Gloerich et al., 2018). As a result, research practices cross disciplines; different knowledge practices need to work together to face the issues at hand. Information and Communication Technologies have significant influence on this new landscape. Because of the ubiquitous incorporation of ICT in vital urban processes, dynamics of power have acquired a new repertoire. More control, on the one hand, and more participation, on the other, bring new dilemmas to the surface. The speed and scale of data aggregation is of a different nature than the slower of processes which a human being needs to understand and accept. The speed of computation on the other hand, cannot compete with the speed of the creative mind. Cities have become communities of systems and people in which systems have acquired unanticipated agency (Nevejan & Brazier, 2011; Nevejan, 2012).

In communities of systems and people, new questions are posed about establishing trust and truth. Being and bearing witness has been a foundational dynamic for establishing trust and truth in the many centuries before us, but this is now changing because systems have acquired this unanticipated agency. Questions are raised about the governance of such communities of systems and people and what is needed for them to be able to function under democratic law (Oostveen, 2018). Executing research in cities that actually are constituted by communities of systems and people requires the researcher to include considerations of privacy, possible harm, strategies for being able to protect sources, and more.

Future research will increasingly involve the use real-time data across different social urban contexts. This will affect the operational bandwidth for the design of responsibility and for the accountability of the outcomes of research in a real-life context. The bandwidth of possible outcomes is easily affected by the vested interests of politicians, activists, businesses, residents, experts, or commercial researchers. Current academic and scientific methodologies are not yet fit for dealing with the speed and scale of current global data flows. The black box of financial markets or the spreading of fake news offer a glimpse into a dark future if we do not invent new ways for establishing trust and truth in the emerging data flows, so that they are transparent and comprehensible for many people in different societies around the world. Many businesses like to mine these data, yet few are doing this in lawful and respectful ways.

Future data methodologies will need to consider the local and the global, the social and the ecological, as being interconnected all the way through (Raworth, 2017). Such methodologies need to facilitate the deconstruction of data aggregation in order for people to understand and relate to real-life events. Such methodologies need to facilitate the systematic and transparent building of models to which stakeholders and other people contribute, to generate outcomes that are meaningful to them (Hermans & Cunningham, 2018). The need to rethink the relation between science and society in western democracies has acquired new urgency (Pamuk, 2017).

In the city as a complex system, in the city as a community of systems and people, there is a loss of the sense of causality that directly affects people's ability to steer towards their own well-being and survival. Human actions are informed by expected result, by a known cause and effect dynamic. In a complex system, however, it is not clear what the effect of one's actions will be. Even on the mundane level of separating household waste, for example, how does one know if the gathered plastic will be recycled? This affects the trade-offs for trust (Nevejan, 2007). In this complex environment, the need for a science that interacts with the complexity of the city – a science in which different kinds of knowledge and different practices interact – requires specific attention. Therefore, such a city science is transdisciplinary from the start.

Current collaborations between cities and universities

The relation between cities and universities has had a variety of configurations over the centuries in different cities in Europe. In the last few decades, alongside doing research and publishing about it, the focus of European universities has been directed to establishing national and international standards for scientific education and qualification. In the so-called Bologna process (1999), a variety of European governments had a series of meetings to ensure comparability between higher-education qualifications. This led to the establishment of the Lisbon Recognition Convention (2012), which has created a harmonized Bachelor and Master degree structure in all participating countries in Europe. In recent decades, the research programs of the European Commission have stimulated collaboration between universities in different countries and the participation of companies and societal organizations as well. Cities are playing an increasingly significant role in these research projects.

In 2020, it appears that in several European cities the collaboration between universities and municipalities has acquired new urgency. It also appears that cities and universities in Europe increasingly collaborate locally in a variety of ways, with significant results for both the cities' challenges and the universities' research. Such collaborations face similar challenges in all these western, eastern, northern and southern European cities. Structures of governance between university and municipality are complex, financing is hard to secure, and communication and learning between large organizations is difficult. Cities have limited agency in the political landscape of nation states and international cooperation, while universities have large international networks that can shed new light on local issues at hand. Current challenges may therefore benefit from close local collaboration between policy and research. Air quality, smart mobility, circular economy, equal opportunity, mental health, and citizen technology are just a few themes which cities and universities immediately agree are urgent and require such collaboration.

For universities it is important to show the (potential) societal impact of current research because, among other reasons, universities are dependent on public finance and graduates need to be able to significantly contribute to society. For municipalities it is increasingly important to develop evidence-based policy making in these times of social networks, fake news, and smart propaganda campaigns. The challenges cities are facing require inter- and transdisciplinary collaborations (see chapter 15). The energy transition, for example, demands engineering and ICT infrastructural research from STEM faculties[3] and from technological universities. The energy transition also needs economic and social innovation and behavioral changes to which the humanities and social sciences can contribute. It needs innovation in vocational training for all the people who will build the energy installations in homes. However, both the university and the municipality are organized as separate silos of expertise, whether in faculties and research groups or in municipal departments, and yet they need to collaborate to overcome the challenges they face.

The challenge for city science is to overcome the obstacles of university professors who need to publish in peer reviewed journals, and the obstacles facing cities, which need to be managed but do not have the time to wait years for results. In the last decade, many collaborations have been established. Both in the university and in the municipality these collaborations are driven by an increasing awareness of each other's value. Cities gather data professionally on demographics, health, education, economic dynamics, or the environment. The universities work internationally and are able to benchmark current local developments with developments occurring elsewhere. Universities collaborate internationally in developing methodologies that can be applied in multiple places. They analyze in a manner that enables lessons learned elsewhere to be applied locally. In the collaboration between municipality and university, a new relation between local and global is shaped.

The step from research outcome to implementation in a municipal or city context requires specific attention. Neither academic and scientific research, nor municipal policy practice, is fit for making such transitions or transmissions from research to practice. In this context, the discipline of design offers the research methodologies to bridge this gap.[4] Design is specialized in translating concepts to products and services that influence people's behavior.

---

3   Science, Technology, Engineering, and Mathematics Faculties.
4   See also chapter 14 in this volume on research via design (Bas Raijmakers, STBY) and chapter 13 on action research (Stan Majoor and Joachim Meerkerk).

In the table below the different steps in the research, design and policy process are shown in relation to one another. It shows the steps neatly one after another, which in reality hardly ever happens. Time constraints often make it necessary to execute different steps at the same time. In such trajectories, scientists and designers and policymakers align in every step they take and give feedback to each other all the way so they stay tuned with each other's work through the whole process. This requires solid orchestration, editorial and visualization skills of the research team involved as will be described in the next paragraph.

Figure 16.1:   *City Science: interactions between Research, Policy and Design. (Nevejan 2018). Visualization by Chin-Lien Chen, Office of CC.*

Research, Policy and Design

This graph offers an impression of the different steps that characterize classical trajectories in each of the fields of Research, Design and Policy in relation to one another. Different collaborations between science, policy and design happen. The first policy step, becoming aware, can be the result of a scientific study (step 1- 12), in the building of a new school for example. Sometimes the design interaction (step 8 and 9) happens before the scientific research and inspire it (step 3-7), as happens in the development of mobile phones for example. Policy usually has no time to wait for the science or design experts to contribute their solutions. They like to skip step 3 – 9 and decide as soon as possible how to solve an issue. For scientists it is hard to respect this haste, while designers are used to work for clients and guide them through the process.

Design as a discipline has developed an array of methodologies for working with insight and expertise between different kinds of knowledge and has also developed iterative processes that afford the different kinds of knowledge to contribute at the right time and in relation to others in appropriate ways (Lawson & Dorst, 2013).

City science, the research process

City science is a multi-actor process (Enserink et al., 2010). Stakeholders (citizens, businesses, organizations), experts (scientific, academic, professional, craft) and engaged people (politicians, civil servants, activists) all play different roles in the specific phases of both the research and the policy process. For the stakeholders especially, it is sometimes very complex to understand the processes of research and policy making. Moreover, stakeholders have limited agency in these contexts and yet must be brought into accommodation with the decisions being made around them (Hermans & Cunningham, 2018).

In urban democratic processes, the interaction between the expert, the engaged, and the stakeholder defines the quality of the outcome (Innes & Booher, 1999; Fung, 2006). Research not only contributes to the expertise of the expert but also to the expertise of others. It may affect stakeholders by, for example, changing the perception of a certain situation; it may affect relations between the engaged politician and the engaged activist because new facts are unveiled. In the collaboration between science and the city the interdependencies between experts, stakeholders, and engaged activists or politicians are a given and part of the rich context in which city science operates. However, these interdependencies can seriously jeopardize outcomes and therefore need to be addressed in the methodologies that are applied. Design, as a vital element of the research process, can facilitate the synergy between rigor in both science and policy[5]. Design brings structured creativity and commitment to end users at the heart of such collaborations (Nevejan, 2018).

---

5   See City Rhythm example, below.

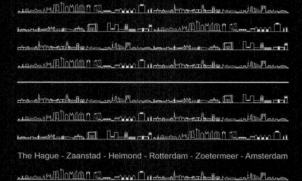

City Rhythm

Caroline Nevejan - Pinar Sefkatli - Scott Cunningham

The Hague - Zaanstad - Helmond - Rotterdam - Zoetermeer - Amsterdam

Figure 16.2: Visualization by Caroline Nevejan and Pinar Sefkatli.

City Rhythm – building an alliance

In the transdisciplinary research program City Rhythm, 6 cities, 30 civil servants, 60 students, 10 professors, 20 artists, and 25 data experts participated. The research included different disciplines: social sciences, philosophy, architecture, data science, and artistic research. The City Rhythm research is currently further elaborated upon in the NWO study Designing Rhythm for Social Resilience (2018–2023).

Peace Around the House
Data and Policy Cycle Workshop
14/10/2016
Samual Kaspers (Municipality
of Zaanstad) and Yosha Kramer
(Municipality of Zoetermeer)

Shopping Centre
Data and Policy Cycle Workshop
14/10/2016
Suzanne van den Berge
(Municipality of Rotterdam) and
Sandra Rob (Municipality of
Zaanstad)

Youth
Data and Policy Cycle Workshop
14/10/2016
Mieke ten Bosch (Municipality
of Zaanstad), Joost Hoedjes
(Municipality of The Hague)

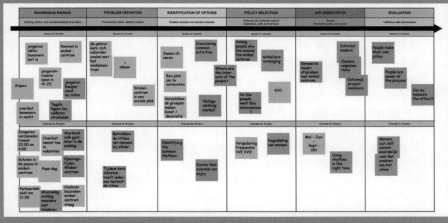

Figure 16.3: Visualization by Pinar Sefkatli, Fatiha Alitou & Caroline Nevejan.

Aligning scientific and policy agendas

Previous research on trust in neighborhoods had indicated that 'sharing rhythm' is a factor that enhances trust. By giving over 20 lectures in several cities in different municipal contexts, and with the support of the National Association of Municipalities of the Netherlands, I established the support of six cities because they all shared the need to enhance social safety in neighborhoods. As a result, the security and safety departments of these six cities committed to the research both in time, data and finance. With the help of civil servants the research agenda was finetuned and made specific. The cities therefore felt ownership and the research agenda became sharper.

City science follows classical phases in a research process. It sets an agenda, makes a research design, develops a theoretical framework, defines methodologies, executes the research, validates, falsifies, and evaluates. The specific nature of city science in these phases is articulated in the following section.

Agenda setting

In the agenda setting phase, the needs of the city are matched with questions that are interesting for science and academia. The needs of a city can be defined in different ways. They can be formulated by politicians, by management, and by professionals who are faced with new issues that arise or keep being unsolved. Preferably, a new research program is relevant for all layers of government, which opens up avenues for real commitment in time, data, and finance. With larger studies in particular such commitment is indispensable. Without this, a researcher risks losing cooperation and coming away empty-handed.

For a scientist or an academic it is complex to participate in agenda setting phases, as it raises career dilemmas. To participate in joint agenda setting efforts with a municipality requires time that cannot be spent on making publications. And yet this is the criteria upon which the quality of individual scientists is judged. Universities are internationally judged by the score of their publication index, and as a result their employees are accordingly judged upon the amount of scientific publications. Even though universities increasingly value societal impact as a rewarding factor in employees' evaluation, the pressure to publish too easily prevents academics and scientists from engaging with cities and spending time exploring and building a relation with the city to build future research upon.

However, when engaged with structural collaboration between policy and research, engagement with the city generates new research agendas all the time. In the research design, challenges between university and municipality are met by including specific design elements in the overall research design. Civic participation, open experiments, living labs, pilots, interventions, and events for reporting back can be conceived of in such a way that they fulfill both the university's standard of research as well as the municipality's need for policy input.

The research question

As result of the agenda setting workshops with the civil servants, we formulated the research question. This question has to be of relevance for both the university and the municipality. The principal investigator, with the research team, orchestrates the moments of catharsis of the different inputs and visualize this in such a way that, when giving lectures, it speaks to the different stakeholders and their colleagues in their different realms and disciplines.

Also the research question is visualized here in order to make the communication between participants better. The line accompanying the image below is: 'Any of the transitions in the image below are needed, yet it does not function like this now and we do not know how to make it work'. Figure 16.4 is the result of an interpretation of the civil servants focus groups.

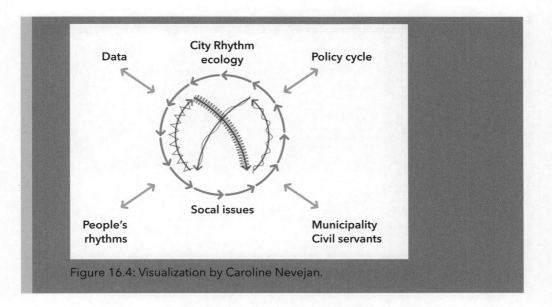

Figure 16.4: Visualization by Caroline Nevejan.

Research design

City science can generate complex processes with many stakeholders, experts, and otherwise engaged people participating at specific moments in time. Transparency and communication about the research process and about what is expected from whom and when, and with what result, is of vital importance.

Already for this type of communication, several professional languages are needed. Smart inter-cultural orchestrations help to facilitate this communication and contribute to its success: the language in the email, the visualizations of the process, the documentation of the process (including the recording of the sessions), the location with the food and drinks that are offered, the open conversation and time for translation between different realms, the time for chatter or taking a walk and learning to know each other's sensitivities. A research design needs to take this into account by adding empty time, orchestration time, and (perhaps unconventional) processes for documentation during the research. If this is not part of the design, frustration easily takes over.

In city science, the research design is iterative and needs to adapt all the time, and this needs to be communicated to those involved. City science projects are transdisciplinary and combine different kinds of knowledge in iterative research processes. Stakeholders, experts, and engaged people need to be aware of their roles and positions in the larger research process in order to be able affect the course of events. Therefore, the time for tuning between the different kinds of knowledge in preparation, executing, and validating the research, needs to be part of the research design. Not only must different kinds of knowledge come together, often also different kinds of experience must also meet.

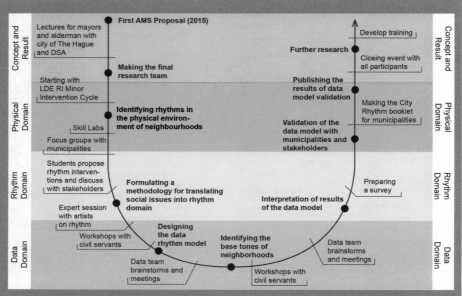

Figure 16.5: Visualization by Pinar Sefkatli.

Clarity of research design for navigation

The visualization of the research design helps the different contributors to navigate the larger context to understand their own position and contribution. In transdisciplinary teams one is continuously confronted with what one does not know. It is hard when one feels responsible for delivering good quality in an unknown context, which is why a shared image of what the team is doing and thorough documentation really help, especially when this image represents a timeline and participants can anticipate what will come next.

As a researcher one easily forgets to inquire, and thereby presumes to know the experience of others. Here, the identification and positioning of different key informants helps. They are engaged in the agenda setting, in the research design, in the execution of the research, in the analyzing and evaluating phases. They also offer advice and speak up when they are not asked to do so, helping the research team to navigate the complex landscape. In the case of City Rhythm there were key informants in rhythm studies, in municipal policy making, in data economy, in cultural expression, and – very importantly – in every borough where we worked. We spent a lot of time lost in translation, but the perseverance of all involved and their desire to understand each other and the work being done were key to the success of City Rhythm.

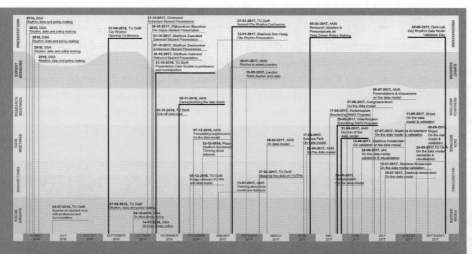

Figure 16.6: Visualization by Pinar Sefkatli.

Timeline: Orchestration of events

This graph was made in hindsight and shows different kinds of meetings we needed through the research process. Several times we had a large gathering in a conference setting with all stakeholders together. Other times we had different specialized working groups elaborate. It is an iterative process in which some milestones can be identified before, and some not at all. However, in the research design moments of validation, both for the university and for the city, are formulated in a clear manner. Orchestrating and directing this process with many stakeholders, requires great flexibility and leadership from the Principal Investigator and the core team.

When people with different kinds of knowledge need to collaborate, the sharing of values helps to facilitate the interaction. Formulating these values in the beginning of the project, as a distinct phase in the research design, helps individual contributors to steer towards synergy with others. During the process the making of 'boundary objects', like a model, a scenario, or a production plan, helps to let different perspectives surface (Leigh Star, 2010). These can easily function as milestones in the iteration as is shown in the graph of City Rhythm

Methodology

Because city science is transdisciplinary it uses mixed methods by definition. These methods include quantitative and qualitative methods, and can include scientific experiments, pilots and what are now called Living Labs (see chapter 13), design trajectories (chapter 14), surveys (chapter 2), data gathering methods (chapters 2, 3, 4, 5, 6), and more[6]. The 'research-through-design' nature of many city science projects

---

6   Depending on the research agenda and research design, methodologies from all sciences can be relevant to use in specific cases.

highlights the relevance of the societal context in which the behavior of people emerges in relation to the cities as communities of systems and people. Amid this complexity, research-through-design methodologies offer the development of series of interventions that can be influenced, monitored, and evaluated by all stakeholders. Complex societal and technological trajectories, such as the energy transition, climate adaptation, or the introduction of circular economy, can benefit from such an approach.

Visualizing 'work in progress' results

In transdisciplinary research, visualizations help to translate between different kinds of knowledge. Visualizing methodology and visualizing outcomes help to enable every discipline to offer their specific perspective. In City Rhythm, and as result of the intense work with the students, we were able to identify and test a methodology for rhythm analyses in the physical world, early on. By visualizing this methodology, the cities also saw the results of their work quite soon. Figure 16.7 is a visualization of the methodology for translating social issues into rhythm issues.

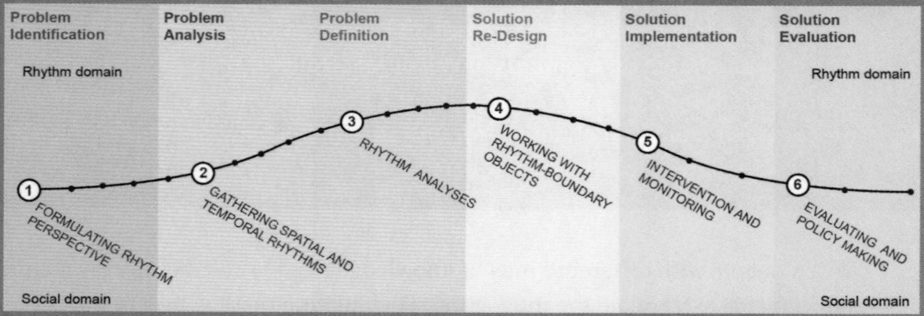

| Problem Identification | Problem Analysis | Problem Definition | Solution Re-Design | Solution Implementation | Solution Evaluation |

Rhythm domain

Rhythm domain

3

4

RHYTHM ANALYSES

WORKING WITH RHYTHM-BOUNDARY OBJECTS

5

1

2

INTERVENTION AND MONITORING

6

FORMULATING RHYTHM PERSPECTIVE

GATHERING SPATIAL AND TEMPORAL RHYTHMS

EVALUATING AND POLICY MAKING

Social domain

Social domain

Figure 16.7: Visualization by Pinar Sefkatli.

When using mixed methods, the relation among the methods and the different data sources needs to be validated at every step. To establish integrity in such trajectories requires the engagement of all involved. Though it might be in different manners and at different times, establishing the integrity of the research process is a structural concern to which all can contribute, as became clear in City Rhythm. The data scientist, the social worker, the artist, the tabla player, the professor, and the student jointly established this integrity by sharing presentations at milestones and reflecting upon these from their different perspectives. Again, orchestrating and directing this process requires great flexibility and leadership from the principal investigator and the core team.

Part of the methodology concerns documentation. Scientists, academics, and civil servants are used to only sharing knowledge in their own professional realms. They are not used to sharing their research outside of these circles. This needs to be addressed beforehand in the methodological starting phase and the choice of methods. When many people participate in a study, rigorous documentation is vital. One has to find ways that work in progress can be shared and collaboration can flourish. Chosen methods need to be evaluated from this perspective beforehand.

Executing research

When executing the research, all the above elements require attention. Different layers of governance, in and around the project, may require attention. Monitoring with representatives of stakeholders may help. Actual developments and shifting political agendas sometimes affect the research process as well. Diplomacy in the research requires constant attention.

As principal investigator it is quite intense to manage the feeling of uncertainty among so many people. Researchers want to be able to write their papers, civil servants want results for the politicians, students want their credits, professors have very little time, and many citizens do not believe it will make any difference what they do. It helps to include the different stakeholders, experts, and other engaged people in the analyses and to include members of the research team in managing this uncertainty. The creation of high quality 'boundary objects' that trigger imagination of possible outcomes from out different perspectives, also helps.

Design expertise offers significant added value here. To manage this uncertainty, it is important to develop creative ideas and start communicating at an early stage what is happening in the research. Orchestrating and celebrating throughout the whole process is vital for nurturing the engagement of all involved. In the case of City Rhythm, these kinds of considerations have been critical at every step of the research process: safeguarding students, developing transparency in algorithms, finding proxies that answered the question yet shielded privacy, and more.

When things get really complex, one still needs to take the trouble to pursue the understanding of stakeholders involved. Showing how choices are made, where uncertainty is creatively tackled, helps to empower all participants in the research to ask questions and contribute their insight. In this process it is of importance to trust and have respect for others expertise while at the same time demanding that people explain how they work and why they make the choices they make. Incommensurability, the fundamental not sharing of an understanding, characterizes such interaction (Kuhn, 2000). However, when being able to endure the un-comfortability of such encounters, new ideas may be born

Making boundary objects

The visualizations function as boundary objects in transdisciplinary contexts. Below, you see visual analyses of young people's presence at a square. When discussing these with residents and businesses it was found that between 17:00 and 18:00, when the young people came home from work and met for a chat before going home for dinner, there was also a lot of other activity which was experienced as 'too much'. This annoyance was projected onto the youngsters. As result of these analyses, the students advised to redirect the traffic so that the annoyance would disappear. The visualizations are made by the students.

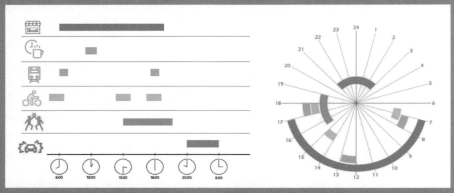

Figure 16.8a: Zaanstad, Circular and linear documentation of the ground rhythm of the neighborhood.

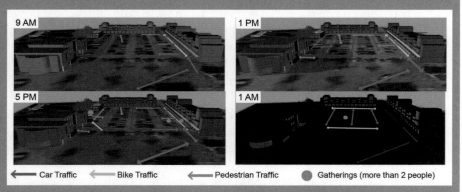

Figure 16.8b: Zaanstad, 3D visualization of Town Square with the documentation of arrows indicating the direction and intensity of each traffic flow.

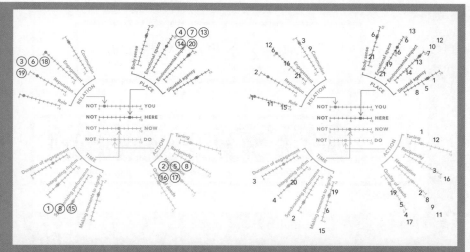

Figure 16.9a: The identification of proxies and datasets.

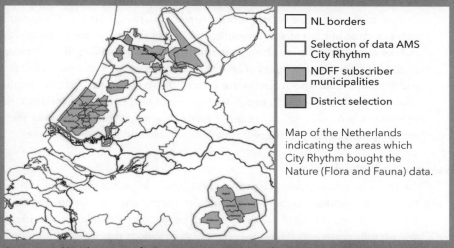

NL borders

Selection of data AMS
City Rhythm

NDFF subscriber
municipalities

District selection

Map of the Netherlands
indicating the areas which
City Rhythm bought the
Nature (Flora and Fauna) data.

Figure 16.9b: The map of where we get the data from.

Transparency of uncertainty and choices made

Even when knowledge is very specialized, it is possible to communicate the concepts, uncertainties and choices that can be made. Here are visualizations of the computer model that were discussed with the variety of stakeholders to get a better understanding with which data and why these data are chosen to work with and it gives a flavor of how the Hidden Markov Model in this case is constructed.

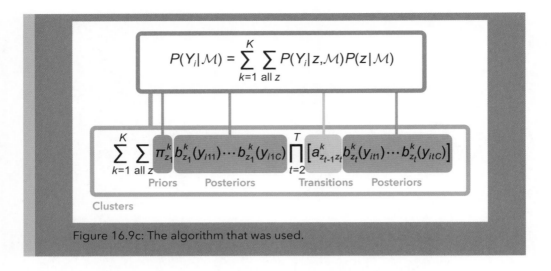

$$P(Y_i|\mathcal{M}) = \sum_{k=1}^{K} \sum_{\text{all } z} P(Y_i|z,\mathcal{M})P(z|\mathcal{M})$$

$$\sum_{k=1}^{K} \sum_{\text{all } z} \pi_{z_1}^k b_{z_1}^k(y_{i11}) \cdots b_{z_1}^k(y_{i1C}) \prod_{t=2}^{T} \left[a_{z_{t-1}z_t}^k b_{z_t}^k(y_{it1}) \cdots b_{z_t}^k(y_{itC}) \right]$$

Priors   Posteriors   Transitions   Posteriors

Clusters

Figure 16.9c: The algorithm that was used.

During all these intense social processes one has to make sure that the research is well done and of high quality and integrity. That is why these complex projects can only be done by a team in which all members take responsibility for the end result. In the City Rhythm, the interdisciplinary research team had specific meetings in which analyses and conclusions were formulated in such a way that all members of the research team could agree. These meetings happened before and after larger meetings where all stakeholders in the research were present. In this way the research team developed a new language for understanding City Rhythms.

Evaluating and validating

Given the transdisciplinary character of the research, in this phase every member of the research project has individual results and achievements that need to be met and there are shared overall research results that need to be formulated. Specific results and overall results and achievements need to be validated and evaluated. The timing of different outlets of the results in the different domains – science, policy, public space, and other stakeholders – needs attention.

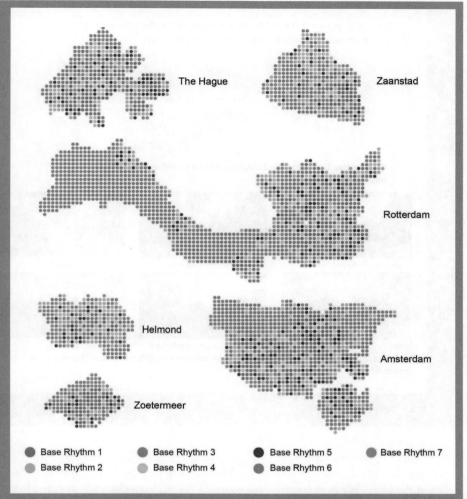

Figure 16.10a: Base rhythms.

Making results, daring to run

Ultimately, and by 'running with possible results' in which a more design-like approach of creative induction and deduction was applied, the research team developed a new language for understanding City Rhythm consisting of beats, base rhythms, and street rhythms. By subsequently making a model, which is informed by the new language and concepts, and running the model, the results allowed unforeseen conclusions to emerge. The research suggests that there are similar base rhythms for social safety in different cities and neighborhoods. This is only validated in an exploratory way, yet it already opens up new avenues for research and policy making as well.

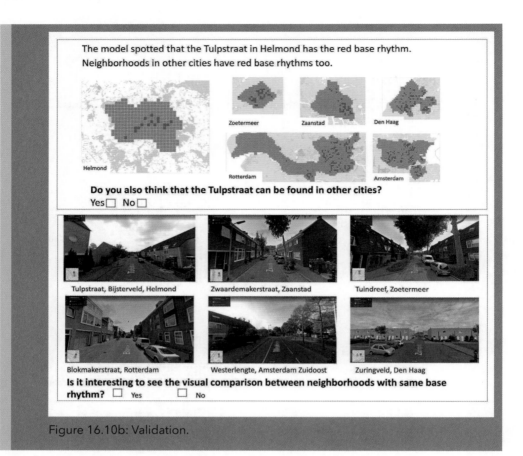

The model spotted that the Tulpstraat in Helmond has the red base rhythm. Neighborhoods in other cities have red base rhythms too.

Zoetermeer   Zaanstad   Den Haag

Helmond

Rotterdam   Amsterdam

Do you also think that the Tulpstraat can be found in other cities?
Yes☐ No☐

Tulpstraat, Bijsterveld, Helmond   Zwaardemakerstraat, Zaanstad   Tuindreef, Zoetermeer

Blokmakerstraat, Rotterdam   Westerlengte, Amsterdam Zuidoost   Zuringveld, Den Haag

Is it interesting to see the visual comparison between neighborhoods with same base rhythm? ☐ Yes   ☐ No

Figure 16.10b: Validation.

Results with different granularity offer specific outcomes for different members of the team. For example, for their journals the data scientists in the City Rhythm team need a different level of detail on the algorithm that has been used, compared to a civil servant from one of the cities. The architect and social scientist develop a different methodology from the computer scientist and they need to legitimize these findings in a different way.

In the iterative research process, validation and falsification happen at distinct moments in time. Documentation of the whole process has also been gathered. Due to the specific results and the overall results, and the documentation of the entire process, the ultimate validation and evaluation is a rich exercise. Members of the team have been observing each other during the research process and can now bear witness to the whole process.

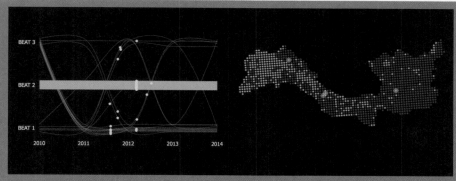

Figure 16.11: Rotterdam beat.

Sharing results

Moving images help us to understand dynamics. The making of these images also helped us to understand the outcomes much better. As result of the visualizations, the rhythm language for data was tried out. This visualization allows people to play with different base rhythms that emerge from data over five years and in three beats. Beats are understood as moments of transition. In a grid of 500 x 500 meters, the specific street rhythm within a base rhythm can be identified. The white dots on the map and the bolder line in the graph: in these three neighborhoods there was apparently a transition in 2011, after which the sphere for social safety remained the same (Boertjes, 2018).

Communicating results to the municipalities requires different skills: visualization, scenario building, and the writing of policy briefs. Next to the specific journals and the policy briefs for specific boroughs in municipalities, it is a challenge to communicate the overall results since none of the established channels are used to this kind of research. In the case of City Rhythm, a logbook of exploration was published and made available online (Nevejan, Sefkatli & Cunningham 2018). Making this logbook was useful to the researchers to engage all the findings, methodologies, and events with the initial research questions, and made it possible for the different domains to experience the other domains as well. The scientists published a chapter in a scientific book on Rhythm (Crespi & Mangahani 2020)

Discussion and future research

Increased complexity in cities requires new interaction between universities and municipalities, between research and policymaking. In order to safeguard independence from each other at the same time, methodology and validation require specific attention. Design, as the discipline that specializes in translating concepts into products and services that affect human behavior, is a necessary third partner in successful city science projects.

In summary, city science requires the coming together of different practices, experiences, knowledges, ontologies, and libraries. A research design that considers the formulation of values, the building of shared cultures of curiosity, the orchestration of respect for difference, the visualization of planning and outcomes, and an elaborate time design that allows for every participant to contribute to particular moments in the research process, is vital for success.

In cities, more crises are anticipated because climate change is expected to generate a series of unforeseen conditions that cannot be fully anticipated. These crises will simultaneously affect the social, infrastructural, ecological, and ICT domains. With the development of real-time data in large quantities, a new source of information becomes available for research and policymaking (see chapter 4). The current COVID-19 crisis is the first convincing global example of this new collaboration between science and policy, where different governments anticipate controlling the virus with new data management techniques. In the social sciences and humanities especially, this will generate new paradigms in which new methodologies for just-in-time research and just-in-time policy will work hand in hand.

In this crisis, the social sciences and humanities are entering a new zone of influence and validation. However, from a European liberal perspective, in which science and academia need to be independent, the political influence on research processes can have unanticipated and detrimental effects. The American National Foundation, the directorate for Social, Behavioral and Economic Sciences, is now formally monitoring the research proposals that are rewarded.[7] As is already the case in China, the relation between the SSH faculties and the government is intense. In Europe we embark on this collaboration with a civic society perspective, but this cannot be taken for granted and needs to be monitored carefully. This chapter argues that city science is a new field of research which we need to explore and monitor carefully, and which will generate significant results for both City and Science provided its autonomy and independence are not jeopardized.

References

Boertjes, E. (2018). *Dynamic City Rhythm data visualization*. Available at: http://www.bloomingdata.com/cr/ (accessed 17 May 2020).

Brazier, F., Oskamp, A., Prins, C., Schellekens, M., & Wijngaards, N. (2004). Law-abiding and integrity on the Internet: A case for agents. *Artificial Intelligence and Law, 12*(1-2), 5-37.

Castells, M. (1996). The rise of the network society, volume I. The information age: Economy, society and culture. Oxford: Blackwell.

---

7   In the summer of 2019 the International Conference on Computational Social Sciences (ICS2) was held at the University of Amsterdam. In the panel that was run by the National Science Foundation of the United Stated of America, these new American policies were announced. The European scientists in the session were very shocked.

Enserink, B., Kwakkel, J., Bots, P., Hermans, L., Thissen, W., & Koppenjan, J. (2010). *Policy analysis of multi-actor systems*. Eleven International Publ.

Fung, A. (2006). Varieties of participation in complex governance. *Public administration review, 66*, 66-75.

Gloerich, I., Hart, J., Lovink, G., Nevejan, C., & Verkerk, I. (2018). *Flying Money 2018: Investigating Illicit Financial Flows in the City*, Institute for Network Cultures, Amsterdam.

Innes, J. E., & Booher, D. E. (1999). Consensus building and complex adaptive systems: A framework for evaluating collaborative planning. *Journal of the American planning association, 65*(4), 412-423.

Hermans, L., & Cunningham, S. W. (2018). *Actor and strategy models*. Oxford: Wiley Blackwell.

Kuhn, T. S. (2000). *The road since structure: philosophical essays, 1970-1993, with an autobiographical interview*. University of Chicago Press.

Lawson, B., & Dorst, K. (2013). *Design expertise*. Routledge.

Leigh Star, S. (2010). This is not a boundary object: Reflections on the origin of a concept. *Science, Technology, & Human Values, 35*(5), 601–617.

Nevejan C, & Sefkatli P. (2020). City Rhythms, an approach to Urban Rhythm Analysis. In *Rhythm and Critique, Technics, Modalities, Practices*, Paola Crespi & Sunil Manghani (eds.) Edinburgh University Press.

Nevejan, C., Sefkatli, P., & Cunningham, S. (2018). *City Rhythm, logbook of an exploration*, Delft university of Technology (The Logbook can be downloaded from: https://books.bk.tudelft.nl/)

Nevejan, C. (2018). *Urban Reflection: On diverse engagement in the networking city of Amsterdam*. Inaugural speech, 15th November 2018, University of Amsterdam.

Nevejan, C., & Brazier, F. (2011). Time design for building trust in communities of systems and people. In *ICORD 11: Proceedings of the 3rd International Conference on Research into Design Engineering*, Bangalore, India, 10–12.01. 2011

Nevejan, C. (2012). Time between Emergence and Design. In *Next Nature*, Koert van Mensvoort & Hendrik-Jan Grievink (eds.), Actar Publishers, Barcelona

Nevejan, C., & Gill, S. P. (eds.) (2012). Special issue: Witnessed presence, AI & Society. *Journal for Knowledge, Culture and Communication, 27*(1).

Nevejan, C. 2007. *Presence and the Design of Trust*. Doctoral dissertation. University of Amsterdam.

Oostveen, M. (2018). *Protecting individuals against the negative impact of big data: Potential and limitations of the privacy and data protection law approach*. Kluwer Law International BV.

Pamuk, Z. (2017). *Examining the Experts: Science, Values, and Democracy*. Doctoral dissertation, Harvard University

Raworth, K. (2017). *Doughnut economics: seven ways to think like a 21st-century economist*. White River Junction, VT: Chelsea Green Publishing.

17 Conclusions

Luca Bertolini and Nanke Verloo

What did we see and understand?

In this book, we have taken the patient reader through a variety of ways of seeing and understanding cities, each requiring a focus on different data, and different ways of collecting and analysing them. The variety was large. In succession, we have discussed what quantitative data and **surveys**, **participant observations**, **sensory** and **big data**, **interviewing** and **archival research** can enable us to *see* of the city, and how. From there, we have explored what **cultural analysis**, **institutional analysis**, **economic analysis**, **historical simulation**, **geographic information systems**, the study of **urban biodiversity**, **action research** and **research through design** can allow us to *understand* about the city, and how.

At the end of this journey, you might feel a little overwhelmed, and perhaps even a bit disoriented. But there is no way out. The city is a complex object, characterized by multiple and changing elements and relationships. It not only permits but *demands* that we look at it from multiple vantage points and understand it within multiple concepts. No single way of seeing and understanding can, by itself, penetrate the complexity of the city, and each way of seeing and understanding hides much more than it discloses.

Each way of seeing will reveal certain things but will hide others. Quantitative data, for instance, along with sensory and big data, can show – often in great detail – how many and what kind of people live in a city, or use its public spaces, and how that changes across different units of time, but will show little of what all those people feel, and why. Participant observation and interviewing can help us grasp some of the latter, but if used alone will make us lose sight of the overall picture, and therefore of the significance of all those individual observations and conversations for the larger whole. Furthermore, in most cases none of the data above will give us a view that stretches beyond the present or the proximate past, and we would have to dig into historical archives if we want to get at the far away sources of what we see in the here and now.

Similarly, each way of understanding the city will foreground some urban processes but at the same time relegate others to the background. For instance, institutionalist analysis will help us understand how practices in cities are shaped by institutions, such as formal legal regulations or informal social norms, and, in turn, how practices can affect institutions. Cultural analysis can add a layer of physical artifacts and **aesthetic** norms to the understanding of urban institutions and practices. However, even when used together, cultural and institutionalist analysis will give us no understanding of how the functioning of key systems, such as the economic and the ecological system, strongly shape urban form and condition the lives of the inhabitants of cities, both human and non-human. For an understanding of this, we need to engage with econometric or ecological analysis, and perhaps both. Were we to undertake *only* an econometric or ecological analysis, however, we would miss the key insight of institutionalist and cultural analysis – that economic and ecological systems are not just givens or neutral facts, but are rather constructed by human choices and values, sometime explicitly but often implicitly, and that these choices and values can be and are contested.

The picture emerging from the previous paragraph is already quite complex, and yet several key analytical dimensions of the city are still missing. Two of these are the basic analytical dimensions of historical time and geographical space. How does the fact that urban processes happen in space, often on multiple scales, and throughout time, often starting in a distant past, affect the way cities are and are lived in? In order to answer this question, we could engage with geographical information systems and historical modelling respectively. But there are even more key analytical dimensions missing. If our aim is not just to understand cities, but also to contribute to their improvement, all of the suggestions above are unlikely to suffice, or will only give very indirect and difficult to interpret indications. In order to address head-on the relationship between knowledge and action, between research and policy making, one would have to employ the tools of research through design and action research.

We could give many more examples, but the bottom line should be clear by now. The first conclusion is that choosing one way of seeing or understanding the city, or even combining a few different ones, though it is in practical terms inevitable, will immediately and inevitably also generate the question of what that way of seeing and understanding misses: what it *does not* see, what it *cannot* understand. This inherent limitation of any approach to seeing and understanding the city is also the source of the never-ending quest for *other* and *new* ways of seeing and understanding cities, and this is what makes the city such a fascinating object of study.

The second conclusion is that the only possible way out of this conundrum is the *combination of different ways* of seeing and understanding. Chapters 15 and 16 have articulated and illustrated how interdisciplinary and transdisciplinary approaches can help make these connections between different disciplines, and between academic and societal knowledge. They have also shown how to make these connections in meaningful ways – that is, in ways determined by the nature of the specific problem at hand. This meaningful combination of approaches is a very promising but also very challenging direction. In many respects, we are just at the beginning of the journey. Much has to be learned by those who believe in its promise, and many are still skeptical and need to be convinced. In the process, we will keep discovering possibilities, but also difficulties.

How did we progress?

Like any research project, the very production of this book was also a journey, rich in both possibilities and difficulties, as documented by the illustrative examples in chapter 15. We embarked on this journey with the intention of developing a network of scholars and practitioners who could start imagining new forms of inter- and transdisciplinary cooperation. We organized a series of workshops with authors and with the scientific board whom we invited to advise on the content of this book.

Bringing such a wide variety of scholars together brought about engaging and inspiring conversations, but at times also hilarious or painful confrontations. One conversation in particular stayed with us. When one scientific board member approached the city through the question 'Who is profiting from other people's misery?', a fierce discussion unfolded about the extent to which scholars should engage in political matters. Some believed that scholars ought to be 'neutral' and just provide the data to support political decision making. Others replied that there is no such thing as neutrality and that all research has an implicit or explicit bias, so it is better to make that transparent and openly engage in political conversations. No consensus was found and the divide between immaterial paradigms became a physical presence in the room.

One exercise that we used to overcome differences such as this was an inspirational exercise that required everyone to note down on a Post-it their answers to the question 'What does the city mean to me?'. The multitude of meanings ranged from the city as a historical process, to a palimpsest of different memories and layers that build on each other, to a knot of potential problems and solutions, to a complex socio-technical system. Others wrote down 'I don't know!' or 'I reject the word *city* because it refers to a physical appearance while I study a complex relationship which I call the urban'. Others demystified the concept and just defined it as 'a place I like to live in' or 'home'. These rather personal definitions provided us with a starting point for understanding how different people experience the city and relate that to how they study the city.

We found that there was a strong overlap between these personal experiences of the city and methodological approaches to studying the city. Using that relationship as a starting point for our discussion explains the rather fierce and sometimes even emotional responses to discussions about methodologies. Research, methodologies, and topics, but also paradigms and related ideas about the political responsibility of scholars, are as much personal as they are intellectual. Demonstrating that relationship and acknowledging difference is the only way forward in an inter- or transdisciplinary team. We were truly lucky to work with an open-minded group that was willing to step outside of existing belief systems and open up to different interpretations of scholarship and practice. Nevertheless, even in that context, exercises like the one described above, but also the boundary object exercise described in chapter 15, were necessary tools to constructively help the process of cooperation beyond disciplinary boundaries unfold.

What did we miss?

While already large, the variety of data and methods for collecting and analyzing data introduced by this book is far from exhaustive. It has already been argued that the complexity of the city as an object of study is such that the quest for different and new methods is bound to be never-ending. By definition, therefore, a book like this cannot be complete, and will inevitably miss some things out. But we can and must be more precise. We need to acknowledge some more specific limitations of the book and highlight at least those that are most directly relevant for addressing major, upcoming urban challenges. You should not be surprised by our preemptive disclaimer that even this list of shortcomings will not be in any way complete. We rather suggest you see these final notes as a trigger and an invitation to keep being critical, and always on the lookout for new needs and possibilities, even beyond the examples discussed below.

Chapter 12 of the book is focused on ecological analysis, in particular of the biodiversity of nature in cities. However, there is much more to the understanding of the city as a natural system than that chapter could cover. We have, for instance, no chapter discussing the data and approaches to the analysis of the metabolism of cities, of the flows of energy and matter being demanded, transformed, and produced by cities. Nor there is a chapter introducing ways of seeing and understanding the impacts of these flows on the life of people, animals, and plants living in cities. In response to the ever louder call to make urban economies circular and cities carbon neutral, and in general more environmentally sustainable, these are of course evident shortcomings.

Also missing from the book and related to the focus on the city as a living environment are data and analytical tools to see and understand the impacts of urban life on the physical and mental well-being of urban inhabitants. With an increasing share of the world population living in cities, many of them suffering from city-related illnesses, and large differences between cities in the quality of the physical and mental health of their inhabitants, this is becoming a major area of societal concern and academic research.

A striking group of omissions from the book are data and analytical tools with which to see and understand cities as technical artifacts: complexes of buildings and infrastructures, such as those for transport, telecommunications, energy, water, or waste. Cities are, in fact, the quintessential human technical artifact, and one whose nature is dramatically changing. A key area of change and related research is that of the impacts of developing digital technologies on the form, functions, and life of cities. Be it about artificial intelligence, the internet of things, automated vehicles, digital platforms, or other technologies, the debate is fierce. At the risk of oversimplifying, two extreme positions can be sketched. At one extreme are those who see technological development as largely exogenous to and uncontrollable by urban inhabitants and institutions. For them, the main challenge for cities and their residents is that of adapting to technological change. At the other extreme are those who instead stress the role of human agency, including the agency of urban inhabitants and institutions, to shape the course of technological development. For these researchers, the main task is conditioning technological developments to make them fit values that have been collectively and freely agreed upon, not the other way around. Wherever one stands – and there is, of course, also a lot in between these two extremes – the impacts are expected to be enormous and understanding the underlying dynamics, both technological and social, is becoming essential for any urban scholar.

The above are just some of the major emerging but missing themes, and more could be added. Beyond specific substantive themes, an area of enquiry that we had originally intended to include in the book, but in the end were not able to, is the modeling of cities as complex adaptive systems. The notion that cites are complex has been reiterated many times, but mathematical modeling and the definition of cities as complex adaptive systems add a more formal connotation to this notion. Given its abstract nature, mathematical modeling of cities as complex adaptive systems has the potential to provide an overarching analytical framework allowing connections and interactions between heterogeneous data and processes. Many are exploring this potential.

As anticipated, the list is not comprehensive. We are sure that if you asked yourself (and maybe you should!) 'what do *I* think is missing from the book?', you would come up with even more, and perhaps more striking examples. But comprehensiveness is beside the point. *Any* list of methods of studying cities should be seen as incomplete and being more indicative of what it does *not* help to see and understand than the other way around. The real point, and the one we hope this book has by now gotten across, is a different one. It is the message that different ways of seeing and understanding the city each have a distinctive value, and that each one contributes a necessary facet to the grasp of the exceedingly complex object of study that the city is. It is becoming increasingly important for urban scholars to be aware of these different and distinctive contributions and be able to selectively mobilize and combine those that seem most necessary to address a specific urban problem. This book has highlighted in some depth some of these different approaches and what they might distinctively reveal, but also what they might just as distinctively miss and conceal of the city. The book has further highlighted why combinations of different approaches are needed and how this can be done, particularly in chapters 15 and 16. In this sense, perhaps the most important lessons of the book are to cultivate an attitude of openness and to practice a process of combination. In order to learn these lessons, not just in abstract terms but also their application, a pretense or even an aim of comprehensiveness is not necessary, and might even be distraction.

Agenda for Urban Research

This book is not an end point, and some areas for future work are evident. One is expanding the range of data and ways of collecting and analyzing this data. Some of the absences highlighted in the preceding section might give a concrete focus to this future effort, which could perhaps be best hosted by a web-based, continuously evolving twin of this book. Along with expanding the range of approaches, there is a need to continue exploring ways of effectively combining different approaches in order to address specific urban problems. We are just at the beginning of this journey and far from mastering this ability, even with respect to the combinations of methods discussed in this book.

In some areas, there might even be the scope to do more than just combine different methods, but rather attempt to develop new, hybrid approaches by fully merging existing ones. One area where this is already happening is in the hybridization of methods from the natural and social sciences, working towards a science of the lived world that recognizes its 'more than human' nature: the human being as just one participant of nature among many, with plants and animals as citizens of human societies in their own right. Similar explorations are to be found at the intersection of the humanities and the development of technology, responding to the ever-expanding integration of algorithm-driven devices into human cognitive and emotional processes. On a more methodological level, the hybridization of analytical and creative knowledge development modalities (as we see in design and the arts), introduced by chapter 14 of this book, is also a rapidly developing area of research. It is in hybridization that many see essential routes to mobilizing the 'radical imagination' that is desperately needed to address daunting challenges such as climate change or rising social inequality.

If, by now, you feel even more overwhelmed or disoriented than at the beginning of this concluding chapter, you are not alone. These are very challenging and demanding times for urban scholars, we will not deny it. But we believe they can also be uniquely exciting and rewarding times, and especially for those urban scholars who are open to a diversity of disciplinary approaches and willing to explore new ways of combining them. The aim cannot and should not be the development of a unified, comprehensive 'science of cities'. We have explained why we do not believe this is possible, or even desirable, certainly not at the level of the individual researcher, nor arguably at the level of society. The complexity of cities is simply too great, or, more precisely, too borderless. Rather, the aim could and should be that of learning how to better realize the potential of specific combinations, which are inevitably partial but all the more targeted to real world problems and challenges that cities are facing. Like cities themselves, the aims of urban scholars are more akin to open processes than closed products. We hope you will become such a scholar!

Glossary[1]

Abductive reasoning. A form of reasoning or logical inference that starts with an observation or set of observations and seeks to find the most likely conclusion from those observations, a conclusion which is plausible but not proven. This differs from deductive and inductive reasoning. *(See chapters 1, 3, 15.)*

Abiotic factors. The non-living factors, such as soil acidity (pH), water level, nitrogen concentration. *(See chapter 12.)*

Action research. Refers to a research philosophy and methodology that aims at transformative change through simultaneously taking action, doing research, and reflecting on the process at hand. It usually includes both scholars and practitioners and is therefore a strategy of transdisciplinary research. *(See chapters 12, 13, 15, 16.)*

Aesthetics. Concerns beauty and taste, and is critically studied by examining the subjective and emotional values of natural and artificial objects. *(See chapters 3, 7, 14, 15.)*

Aggregate data. Coarse-grained quantitative or qualitative data that have been compiled into larger spatial units (e.g. postcode areas, regions etc.) *(See chapter 4.)*

Allele. A variant form of a given gene, i.e. one of two or more versions of a known mutation at the same place on a chromosome. *(See chapter 12.)*

Anonymization. The process by which the researcher makes respondents non-identifiable and their identities untraceable in order to ensure their privacy. *(See chapters 2, 3, 4, 5.)*

Archival research. A type of research in which the researcher selects, extracts, and sorts out archival records and evidences. *(See chapters 6, 8, 10.)*

---

[1]   We did our best to provide a glossary that is comprehensive and does justice to the various interpretations of these concepts within the various disciplines. These definitions are based on the texts provided by the authors and adapted definitions from Wikipedia.

Belonging. A complex concept that refers to the human emotional need to be an accepted member of a group, organization, neighborhood, city, etc. Closely related to **ownership** and also a topic of **empirical research** in the field of urban research, it requires **operationalization** in relation to each research project. *(See chapters 5, 7.)*

Big data. A term referring to very large sets of data, usually fine-grained, unstructured, and produced dynamically through interactions with technology and digital networks. The generation, storage, and analysis of Big Data involves tools and methods enabled by advances in computing. *(See chapters 2, 4, 10, 11.)*

Biotic factors. Concern those effects caused by live organisms, such as vegetation cover, herbivory/grazing pressure, trampling. *(See chapter 12.)*

Budget constraint. In economics, a budget constraint represents all possible combinations of goods and services a consumer may purchase, given her income and current prices. Used in combination with preference mapping to analyze consumer choices. *(See chapter 9.)*

Case study. A research strategy that aims for an in-depth and detailed examination of a particular case in which the **unit of analysis** may include individuals, organizations, places, or processes. *(See chapters 1, 3, 5, 15.)*

Census. The enumeration of the population of a defined territory through a complete sample. *(See chapter 2.)*

Citizen scientists. People from the public who non-professionally collect, or participate in the collection of, scientifically important data. *(See chapters 12, 13, 15, 16.)*

City Science. A container term that refers to research that happens in, with, and for the city and which is transdisciplinary through all phases of the research process and potentially affects all phases of the policy process. *(See chapters 1, 16, 17.)*

Close reading. A method of analysis that emphasizes the scholar's active role in constructing a detailed reading and interpreting the text or object actively. It is not receptive but productive; it is an act of writing. *(See chapter 7.)*

Co-create. Refers to the process of collaborative creation, decision making and implementation of projects that may be related to research, but can also be in the domain of policy making or design. See also **co-design**. *(See chapters 13, 14, 16.)*

Co-design. Refers to the process of collaborative designing, decision making and implementation of projects that may be related to the field of design, but can also be in the domain of policy making or research. See also **co-create**. *(See chapters 13, 14, 16.)*

Composite good. In economics, a composite good is a notional good that represents many goods, usually all of the goods in the relevant budget apart from the one that is the focus of analysis. *(See chapter 9.)*

Concave. In mathematics, a function is called concave if the line segment between any two points on the graph of the function lies below the graph. More specifically, if the second derivative of a variable is always negative on its entire domain, then the function is concave. An implication is that a function is increasing or decreasing with a decreasing rate. *(See chapter 9.)*

Constructivism. A **paradigm** in the philosophy of science that opposes objectivism and that maintains that knowledge is constructed through the human mind and the scientific community. See also **social constructivism** *(See chapters 1, 3, 5, 15.)*

Control variable. A control variable is a variable which is held constant in order to assess the relationship between multiple variables. Its unchanging state allows the relationship between the other variables being tested to be better understood. *(See chapters 2, 4, 9, 11.)*

Convex. In mathematics, a function is called convex if the line segment between any two points on the graph of the function lies above or on the graph. More specifically, if the second derivative of a variable is always non-negative on its entire domain, then the function is convex. An implication is that a function is increasing or decreasing with an increasing rate. *(See chapter 9.)*

Critical theory. A research **paradigm** in the social sciences and humanities in which critical reflection on and evaluation of society and culture are used strategically to reveal and question existing power structures. *(See chapters 1, 8, 15.)*

Cross-sectional. Refers to the study of (a sample of) a population at a specific point in time. *(See chapters 2, 11.)*

Cultural analysis. A discipline in which qualitative methodologies are used to collect and interpret data on cultural phenomena and processes in order to gain further understanding of a given culture. *(See chapters 1, 7.)*

Data mining. The process of finding patterns in a large data set, usually combining machine learning, database systems, and statistics *(See chapters 2, 4, 10.)*

Deductive reasoning. Contrasts **inductive reasoning** and starts from one or more premises to reach logical and certain conclusions. *(See chapters 1, 2, 4, 9, 11, 15.)*

Deep map. Refers to a digital map that goes beyond two-dimensional images of places, names, and topography, by adding additional layers of information. *(See chapter 10.)*

Designed data. A category of data such as **census**, **interview**, and **survey** usually designed and implemented by governmental authorities. *(See chapters 2, 4, 11.)*

Diary. A record with discrete entries that ethnographers tend to use to record their experiences, thoughts, feelings, and first interpretations of field research situations. Usually used in combination with **Fieldnotes**. *(See chapters 3, 5, 7, 8, 13.)*

Digital Mapping. The process by which a large amount of data is compiled, synthesized, and reformatted into a virtual image, most often in the form of a map. *(See chapters 4, 10, 11.)*

Digitalization. The process of leveraging digitized products, services and data to improve organizational processes. *(See chapters 4, 10.)*

Digitalized spatial data. Spatial data that has been converted into any digital format to be processed in a computer by a spatial data processing software, such as a GIS application. *(See chapters 4, 10, 11.)*

Digitization. The process of converting information into a digital format. *(See chapters 4, 10.)*

Disaggregated data. Fine-grained quantitative or qualitative data broken down in smaller units, sometimes even addressing individuals (e.g. a person's employment status). *(See chapter 2, 4, 11.)*

Discourse analysis. A method of analysis that compiles a representative set of 'utterances', which can be written, vocal, or visual, with the aim of revealing patterns, norms, or power relations. *(See chapter 7.)*

Driver. A key factor that largely determines a response variable. *(See chapters 2, 4, 9, 11.)*

Economic analysis. The study of production, distribution, and consumption of goods and services. *(See chapters 1, 9.)*

Empirical observations. Information that is received via the senses, particularly via **observations**, experiences, or documents, closely related to **empirical research**. *(See chapters 3, 6, 8.)*

Empirical research. Research that uses evidences based on records of **observations** and experiences that can be qualitative or quantitative in nature. *(See chapters 2, 3, 6, 8.)*

Endogeneity. Occurs in regression analysis when an explanatory variable is correlated with the residual. *(See chapter 9.)*

Epistemology. The study of the nature of knowledge and the conditions for a belief to constitute knowledge. Related to but different from **ontology**. *(See chapters 1, 2, 3, 15.)*

Equilibrium. In economics, equilibrium describes a situation in which economic forces such as supply and demand are balanced and in which, barring external influences, the (equilibrium) values of economic variables do not change. In general equilibrium theory, under the conditions of the 'perfect competition' the market reaches equilibrium at the point at which quantity demanded and quantity supplied are equal. If the market is not in equilibrium, as a result of the price being above the market price, there are natural forces at work (i.e. downward price changes) to bring the market back into the situation of a market equilibrium. *(See chapter 9.)*

Ethnography. A type of social research that relies heavily on **participant observation** and aims at the qualitative and holistic understanding of cultures, practices, people, and places from the points of view of the subjects of study. *(See chapters 3, 5, 13, 15.)*

False Positive. An error in data reporting in which, for example, significant effects are indicated improperly. *(See chapter 2.)*

Fieldnotes. Qualitative notes of the phenomenon under study recorded by the researcher in the course of field research. *(See chapters 3, 5, 7, 8, 13, 14.)*

Fixed effects. A model that refers to a regression model in which the group means are fixed. Generally, data can be grouped according to several observed factors (e.g. locations, households). In a fixed effect model each group mean is a group-specific fixed quantity. (See chapter 9.)

Gentrification. A process of change in the character, economic value, and demography of a neighborhood by the influx of more affluent residents and businesses. In the field of urban studies, gentrification is an important topic of **empirical research** and analyses. *(See chapters 2, 5, 6, 7, 11.)*

Geographic Information Systems (GIS). A framework for managing and analyzing spatial data. A GIS involves a set of methodologies and tools to capture, store, manage, analyze, and visualize data linked to geographic locations on the globe. *(See chapters 1, 2, 4, 10, 11, 15.)*

Geolocation. The linking of a feature to its real-world location through its latitude and longitude coordinates or other coordinate systems. *(See chapters 4, 10, 11.)*

Heterogeneous. While all units of a homogeneous product are identical (i.e. with regard to color, shape, size, weight, height, texture, distribution, architectural design, etc.), the units of a heterogeneous product can vary noticeably in these respects. *(See chapter 9.)*

Historical simulation. The process of using computational methods to create working representations of historical scenarios. *(See chapter 10.)*

Indifference curve. An indifference curve shows any combination of two or more products that will provide the consumer with equal levels of **utility**. The consumer has no preference for one combination or collection of goods over another on the same indifference curve. *(See chapter 9.)*

Inductive reasoning. A form of reasoning that starts with **empirical observations** and synthesizes general principles from these specific observations without claiming truth but by providing arguments for probability based upon evidences. *(See chapters 2, 3.)*

Institutional analysis. Data analysis strategy which studies how institutions behave and function in terms of **empirical** rules (norms) and in terms of theoretical rules (law). *(See chapters 1, 8, 15.)*

Interdisciplinary research. Entails the integration of relevant disciplinary contributions, which might involve the theories, methods, and/or the data of the participating disciplines. This integration leads to a more comprehensive insight, which is particularly relevant for complex and dynamic problems. *(See chapters 1, 2, 15, 17.)*

Interview guide. A tool for interviewing that directs the questions or topics discussed during the interview. It can consist of a pre-determined set of questions posed in a fixed sequence – referred to as structured interviews – or broad, open-ended questions in **semi-structured**, **open**, or **narrative interviews** with an additional item list for probing. *(See chapters 4, 8, 13, 14.)*

Interview. A guided conversation in which the respondent shares their expertise or experiences on a particular topic with the researcher. *(See chapters 1, 2, 3, 5, 8, 13, 15, 17.)*

Item list. Used in interview guides to list a set of topics, or themes to discuss. May be in the form of a **semi-structured**, **open**, or **narrative interview**. *(See chapters 5, 8, 14.)*

Kernel. A kernel is a weighting function used in non-parametric regression analysis. Kernel regression is used to estimate the expected value of a random variable, with the objective of identifying a potentially non-linear relation between two random variables x and y. *(See chapter 9.)*

Large-n dataset. A dataset with a large sample-size. Census data and register data are large-n datasets. May be contrasted with **Big Data**. *(See chapters 2, 4, 9, 11.)*

Locally weighted regression. Locally weighted regression (also known as moving regression) is used to model a relationship where a single functional form will be inadequate. The most frequently used methods, initially developed for scatterplot smoothing and later adapted for statistical modeling, are LOESS (locally estimated scatterplot smoothing) and LOWESS (locally weighted scatterplot smoothing). These are both non-parametric regression methods that place greater emphasis or weighting on closely neighboring data points. *(See chapter 9.)*

Log-linear. A log-linear model is a mathematical model that takes natural log values for its dependent variable while assuming that it is a linear function of the independent variables. The algorithm of this function equals that for a conventional linear regression which makes it easy to carry out multivariate analyses. *(See chapter 9.)*

Logbook. The record of events during fieldwork, usually used in qualitative fieldwork that combines various methodological activities. *(See chapters 3, 5, 7, 8, 13, 16.)*

Longitudinal. Refers to the study of (a sample of) a population at a multiple points in time. *(See chapters 2, 3.)*

Marginal willingness to pay (MWTP). The maximum amount of money a consumer is willing to pay for the last unit of a particular characteristic of a product she consumes. If the product is supplied on a market at a given price per unit, a consumer is willing to pay for another unit as long as her marginal willingness to pay exceeds the price. This is similar for characteristics of a heterogeneous commodity. For instance, a consumer prefers a larger house as long as her marginal willingness to pay exceeds the additional amount of money – the marginal price – that has to be paid for a house with one additional square meter floor area. *(See chapter 9.)*

Misspecification. Model misspecification refers to regression analysis using a model that is in error. This may be due to the choice of independent variables, functional form errors, or other factors that cause the model to misrepresent aspects of the true data-generating process. *(See chapters 2, 9.)*

Mobile phone data. Data generated by mobile phones, such as call detail records (CDRs) and user-generated application data. *(See chapters 2, 4.)*

Monocentric city model. Descriptive model developed by William Alonso in 1964, visualized as concentric circles with a single Central Business District (CBD) at its center, and surrounded by a residential region. This model may be viewed as a starting point for urban economic analysis. *(See chapter 9.)*

Multicollinearity. Also called collinearity. In regression analysis, multicollinearity occurs when one predictor variable in a multiple regression model correlates with another or several other predictor variables. In this situation, the coefficient estimates of the multiple regression may be disproportionately affected by or change erratically in response to small changes in the model or the data. *(See chapter 9.)*

Multidisciplinary research. Research that includes the theories, methods, or data from different disciplines. Disciplinary contributions might be presented next to each other, yet without leading to their integration. *(See chapters 1, 2, 15, 17.)*

Narrative interview. Interview technique that seeks to reproduce a storyline of idiographic experiences of the interviewee. *(See chapter 5.)*

Non-parametric. Sometimes called distribution-free. A non-parametric test is one that does not assume anything about the underlying distribution (for example, that the data comes from a normal distribution). This can be contrasted with a parametric test, which makes assumptions about the parameters of distribution (for example, that an explanatory variable relates linearly to a dependent variable). *(See chapter 9.)*

Nonprobability sampling. A sampling technique whereby respondents are selected strategically on the basis of particular shared characteristics, rather than randomly selecting respondents from the research population. This technique is based on the notion of **(theoretical) saturation** rather than aiming for statistical generalization. *(See chapter 1, 3, 5, 15.)*

Objectivity. A philosophical concept that proposes an objective truth independent from individual subjectivity. *(See chapters 1, 2, 4, 9, 15.)*

Observations. The active acquisition of information from a **primary source**. In social sciences and biology, they are usually done by researchers who employ their own senses, but new technologies allow for observations via sensory techniques. *(See chapters 3, 4, 5, 12, 13, 14.)*

Omitted variable bias (OVB). Occurs when a statistical model leaves out one or more relevant variables (known as confounding variables). The result is that the model will attribute the effect of the omitted variables to included variables that are correlated with the omitted one. *(See chapter 9.)*

Ontology. Refers to the philosophy of being, existing, and the nature of the world. Related to but different from **epistemology**. *(See chapters 1, 15.)*

Open access. Refers to the principle and practice of distributing research output online, free of charge and unconstrained by other access barriers. *(See chapters 4, 16.)*

Open interview. A type of **interview** whereby the interviewer raises broad, open-ended questions and then lets the respondent determine the direction of the conversation. Often used in exploratory research, when the range of possible answers is not yet known to the researcher. *(See chapters 5, 8, 14.)*

Operationalization. The process in the research design that defines the relevant variables so that they may be measured or analyzed. This enables the measurement and interpretation of a phenomenon that is not directly measurable, in order to make it understandable by **empirical observations**. *(See chapters 3, 5, 7, 8, 11, 15.)*

Ordinary least squares (OLS). The method used to estimate the unknown parameters in a linear regression model by minimizing the sum of squared residuals – that is, the sum of the squares of the differences between the observed and predicted values of the dependent variable. *(See chapter 9.)*

Organic data. A category of urban data that is generated either through technologies embedded in the urban fabric (e.g. sensors, cameras, etc.) or is the byproduct of people's online activities (e.g. tweets, blog posts, reviews, etc.) *(See chapters 2, 4.)*

Ornamental plants. Plants which are placed in houses, gardens, or parks for their aesthetic appeal. *(See chapter 12.)*

Ownership. A complex concept that refers to the exclusive right and control over a property, asset, land, or intellectual property. This could represent a legal entitlement, but it could also refer to an experience or feeling, e.g. the ownership over a place. The concept of ownership is an important topic of **empirical research** and analyses and should be **operationalized** in relation to each specific research project. *(See chapters 2, 3, 5, 6, 7, 8, 10, 11, 14.)*

Paradigm. Refers to a set of beliefs and concepts that shape a particular way of making sense of the world. It represents a worldview that defines, for its holder, the nature of the 'world'. It includes theories, research methods, and standards for what constitutes the quality of findings. *(See chapters 1, 2, 3, 15.)*

Participant observation. A data collection methodology that is typically used in qualitative or ethnographic research in which the researcher conducts longitudinal and in-depth fieldwork aiming to gain close and intimate familiarity with a given group, social situation, or place. *(See chapters 3, 5, 13.)*

Physical sensor data. Refers to data generated by miniaturized computer systems that can be embedded and deployed in the **urban fabric**. Sensors are new data sources that complement conventional urban data with real-time measurements of the urban environment. *(See chapter 4.)*

POI-based web data. Online data referring to a **point of interest (POI)**. *(See chapter 4.)*

Point of interest (POI). Digital proxies of real-world places (e.g. restaurants, theaters, squares etc.), represented as geometric point entities around which many user-generated data sources revolve. *(See chapter 4, 11.)*

Population. The typically unobserved set of units for which research aims to develop statistical and/or theoretical generalizations. *(See chapters 2, 9, 12.)*

Positivism. A paradigm that presents a worldview that assumes the world is an external objective reality that is apprehensible via objective findings that explain how things 'really work'. *(See chapters 2, 3, 11, 15.)*

Post-positivism. A paradigm that is critical of **positivism** and presents a worldview that assumes the world is an external objective reality, partially apprehensible via objective findings that explain how things 'really work'. Where positivists believe that researchers are independent from what is being researched, post-positivists recognize that what is researched is always influenced by the researcher. *(See chapters 1, 2, 3, 11, 15.)*

Primary sources/data. In the study of history, a primary source may be any source of information that was created at the time under study, e.g. artifacts, documents, recordings, etc., and is usually collected during **archival research**. A primary source is distinct from **secondary sources/data**. These are relative terms whose meanings depend on their specific usage. *(See chapters 6, 8, 10.)*

Probability sample. A sample (of a population) for which probabilistic statistics are used to generalize for the **population** of which it is a sample. *(See chapter 2.)*

Propagule. A dispersal unit (e.g. a plant seed). *(See chapter 12.)*

Purposive sampling. A sampling technique in which the researcher chooses the sample based on who they think would be appropriate for the study. Often used in **case study research** and small-n qualitative research; see also **nonprobability sampling**. *(See chapters 1, 3, 5, 15.)*

Questionnaire. An instrument to consistently gather data from respondents via a series of questions; see also **survey**. *(See chapters 2, 13.)*

Regression analysis. In statistics, a method for examining and estimating the relationship(s) between a dependent variable (the variable being analyzed, also called the 'outcome variable') and one or more independent variables (factors it is hypothesized may have an impact on the dependent variable; these are also called 'predictors', 'covariates', or 'features'). The most common form of regression analysis is linear regression, which a researcher uses to model a linear relationship between variables by finding the line (or a more complex linear combination) that most closely fits the data. *(See chapters 2, 9.)*

Relative abundances. The number of individuals in a sampling area relative to the numbers of other organisms. *(See chapter 12.)*

Representative sample. A sample that shares as many of the characteristics of the population as possible, in order to enable it to represent that population statistically within a certain margin of error. *(See chapters 2, 4, 8, 11, 12.)*

Research through design. A research strategy that is embedded in the process of design and redesign. *(See chapter 14.)*

Residuals. Capture the deviation of an observed value of an element of a statistical sample from its 'theoretical value'. More specifically, the residual is the difference between the observed value and the estimated value of the quantity of interest (for example, a sample mean). *(See chapter 9.)*

Ruderal plants. Plants that grow on places where the vegetation has been disturbed by humans. *(See chapter 12.)*

Sampling error. The mismatch between the sample and the population; usually only applies for the variables included in the analysis. *(See chapters 2, 9, 11.)*

Sampling variance. The variation in a measurement variable that is present in a sample from a population or community due to sampling date, time, year, weather, etc. *(See chapters 2, 8, 11, 12.)*

Sampling. Set or subset of observations taken from a broader population that can be representative for that population (see **representative sampling**), but can also be deliberately chosen (**probability sampling**), or can be random (**nonprobability sampling**). *(See chapters 2, 3, 5, 12.)*

Saturation. Describes a situation in which data collection or fieldwork no longer generates further empirical insights, indicating that the researcher can therefore stop collecting data. Also associated with **nonprobability sampling**. *(See chapters 3, 5, 15.)*

Scalar. A number used to indicate a variable. With a scalar you can express one value, number, or string. *(See chapter 9.)*

Secondary sources/data. In the study of history, a secondary source usually refers to a source of information that relates to or discusses information from **primary sources/data**. These are relative terms whose meanings depend on their specific usage. *(See chapters 6, 8, 10.)*

Self-reporting. Refers to the practice of letting respondents record data, usually through questionnaires or diaries, instead of direct observation or recording of the data on the part of the researcher. *(See chapter 2.)*

Semi-structured interview. A type of **interview** that combines a set of pre-determined questions with open-ended questions. *(See chapters 5, 8.)*

Semiotics. The study of sign processes that **social constructivists** use to interpret the production of meaning by breaking down a representation – be it a text, an image, or a space – into distinct elements and tracing what these elements mean. *(See chapters 3, 5, 7, 15.)*

Sensor data. See **physical sensor data**. *(See chapter 4.)*

Smart cities. Generic term related to policies aimed at using data monitoring and regulating to create efficiencies and improve productivity or quality. *(See chapters 2, 4, 10.)*

Snowball sampling. A **nonprobability sampling** technique in which existing research subjects are asked to recruit additional respondents among other people they may know. *(See chapters 4, 8, 14.)*

Social constructivism. In sociology, a version of **constructivism** that understands knowledge and reality as actively created by social interactions and relationships. *(See chapters 1, 3, 5, 7, 8, 15.)*

Social media data. Data generated from online social networking applications (e.g. Twitter, Instagram, Facebook, etc.) *(See chapters 4, 10.)*

Spatial data. A term that describes any data that can be related to a location on the Earth's surface, whether linked to a broader spatial unit or to a specific point. *(See chapters 2, 4, 10, 11.)*

Spatial patterns. A perceptual structure or arrangement of features – and the spaces between them – across space. For example, we can think of spatial patterns such as clustering, dispersion, linear arrangements, random distribution, etc. *(See chapters 10, 11.)*

Spatial unit. Basic building block for the analysis of location-specific attributes. Examples of spatial units include postcode areas, street segments, neighborhoods, regions, etc. *(See chapters 2, 4, 11.)*

Street-level imagery. Imagery of roads and roadside features. Street-level imagery is typically collected by car-mounted cameras. *(See chapter 4.)*

Streetlabs. A co-creative and collaborative approach to **Research Through Design** that creates a setting for different users to share their experiences and perspectives, in this case on using and redesigning a common public space. *(See chapter 14.)*

Structured interview. A type of interview that uses a pre-determined set of questions posed in a fixed sequence. *(See chapters 5, 8, 14.)*

Survey. A method to understand a social phenomenon in a population by looking at a sample of the population. *(See chapters 2, 13.)*

Taxonomic group. Taxonomy is the branch of science concerned with classification, particularly of living beings; taxonomists create orderly, hierarchical systems of living organisms. A taxonomic group (shortened to *taxon*, or *taxa* pl.) can be any level in this system: species, genus, family, order, etc. Examples of *taxa* are bees, vascular plants, the Fen orchid, butterflies, flies, hoverflies, lizards, the sand lizard, reptiles, and birds. *(See chapter 12.)*

Theoretical saturation. Refers to a situation in which data collection or fieldwork does not generate further conceptual insights and the researcher can therefore stop interviewing. Also associated with **nonprobability sampling**. *(See chapters 3, 5, 15.)*

Thick description. In the social sciences and specifically in ethnography, researchers use thick description to make detailed descriptions of human social interaction and human behavior within its context, with the aim of allowing outsiders to understand the situation. *(See chapters 3, 7, 8.)*

Total differential. The total derivative of a function $f(\cdot)$ at a point is the best linear approximation near this point of the function with respect to its arguments. Unlike partial derivatives, the total derivative approximates the function with respect to all of its arguments, not just a single one. In many situations, this is the same as considering all partial derivatives simultaneously. *(See chapter 9.)*

Transcribing. The activity of producing a written **transcript** of a completed oral interview. *(See chapters 3, 5, 13.)*

Transcript. A written record of a completed oral interview. *(See chapters 3, 5.)*

Transdisciplinary research. Occurs when researchers collaborate with extra-academic stakeholders, who contribute experiential knowledge, values, and interests. Integrating these with academic insights, transdisciplinarity affects all research stages: from problem definition to implementation of a solution. *(See chapters 1, 2, 15, 16, 17.)*

Transect. An array of samples placed along a line that follows an environmental gradient or crosses several habitat types. *(See chapter 12.)*

Triangulation. The strategy of using multiple sources in qualitative research to develop a comprehensive understanding of a phenomenon of study and to test the quality of outcomes via the convergence of multiple sources. *(See chapters 1, 3, 14.)*

Unit of analysis. The entity that is being analyzed within a study, or the entity that is studied as a whole (may be qualitative and quantitative). *(See chapters 2, 3, 8.)*

Unit of observation. A subset of the unit of analysis. *(See chapters 2, 3, 8, 12.)*

Urban biodiversity. Refers to the variety of living organisms that can be found in the ecosystems of a given city. *(See chapters 1, 12.)*

Urban commons. The collective management of common resources by an urban community of stakeholders. *(See chapter 13.)*

Urban fabric. The physical urban environment (including aspects such as streetscape elements, urban blocks, materials, configuration, density, networks) in conjunction with its socio-cultural, ecological, managerial, and economic structures. *(See chapter 4.)*

Urban green spaces (UGS). Any space in the urban ecosystem that consists of living plants or bare soil. *(See chapter 12.)*

Urbanization. Refers to the population shift from rural to urban areas and the way societies adjust to that change. *(See chapters 2, 3.)*

User modeling. The process of creating and updating a user model (i.e. a data structure that characterizes a user, such as a person using a social networking application, at a certain moment in time), by deriving user characteristics from user data. User data is either data provided explicitly by the user (e.g. through an interview) or as a byproduct of a user's online activities (see **organic data**). *(See chapter 4.)*

Utility. A concept used to model worth or value in economic analysis. Initially introduced within the ethical theory of utilitarianism, where it represented a quality or property producing pleasure or benefit, the term has evolved and been adapted within economics in the concept of **utility function**, which represents preference ordering with regard to a set of consumer choices. *(See chapter 9.)*

Utility function. In economics, a utility function is an important concept that represents a consumer's preferences with regard to a set of goods and services. **Utility** refers to the satisfaction the consumer receives for choosing and consuming a product or service. *(See chapter 9.)*

Vector. Contains multiple numbers or scalars. In the context of hedonic price function, it means that one house contains multiple housing characteristics. We may summarize this in a vector $k = k_0, k_1, ..., k_l$. *(See chapter 9.)*

Velocity. Refers to the speed by which Big Data are created and analyzed. *(See chapters 2, 4, 10.)*

Veracity. Refers to the unreliability of Big Data, amongst others due to the uncertainty of the boundaries of the population and sample. *(See chapters 2, 4, 10.)*

Viable (meta)population. Formally a population or network of populations that has an acceptably low (1–5%) risk of going extinct in the next 100 years. In normal terms, a robust population that can survive on its own. *(See chapter 9.)*

Volatility. Refers to the lack of structure in **Big Data**. *(See chapters 2, 4, 10.)*

Willingness to pay (WTP). Indicates the maximum amount a consumer will definitely pay for one unit of a product. This can also be expressed as the consumer reservation price. See also **marginal willingness to pay.** *(See chapter 9.)*

List of contributors

Arundel, Rowan is Assistant Professor in the Department of Geography, Planning and International Development at the University of Amsterdam, specializing in Geographic Information Science (GIS) and housing research. His research examines dynamics of housing inequalities and interactions between housing, labor, and welfare, as well as more broadly spatial analysis and macro and micro quantitative methods. His current research focuses on the interaction between growing spatial divides in housing markets and divided housing access in driving wealth inequalities.

Bertolini, Luca is Professor of Urban and Regional Planning and Academic Director of the Institute of Interdisciplinary Studies at the University of Amsterdam. His research and teaching focus on the integration of transport and urban planning for humane, sustainable and just cities, concepts and practices to enable transformative urban and mobility change, and ways of enhancing collaboration across different academic disciplines and between academia and society.

Boterman, Willem is a senior lecturer in the Department of Geography, Planning and International Development Studies at the University of Amsterdam. He works on a wide range of urban issues, using different methodological approaches. The themes in his work lie at the intersections of class, race, and gender in the production of urban space.

Dijk, Geke van is co-founder and Strategy Director of STBY (www.stby.eu). Her experience working in Design Research spans more than 15 years. She has a background in ethnographic research, user-centered design, and service strategy. Her passion is bringing people into the heart and soul of innovation processes. Her strong drive to contribute to positive change in society has shaped the direction of STBY's portfolio through work on topics such as community participation and inclusivity, as well as sustainability and circular economy.

Keestra, Machiel is a philosopher of science at the Institute for Interdisciplinary Studies and a researcher at the Institute for Logic, Language and Computation, University of Amsterdam, focusing on philosophy of cognitive neuroscience and philosophy of interdisciplinarity. He is a past president (2016-2018) of the international Association for Interdisciplinary Studies and founding board member (2019) of the Inter- and Transdisciplinary Alliance, and has co-published *An Introduction to Interdisciplinary Research: Theory and Practice* (Amsterdam University Press, 2016) and edited a special section on 'Interdisciplinary Collaboration' in Issues in Interdisciplinary Studies (2017).

Koster, Hans is full Professor of Urban Economics and Real Estate in the Department of Spatial Economics, Vrije Universiteit Amsterdam. Hans is also a Leading Research Fellow at the Higher School of Economics in St. Petersburg, affiliated as Research Fellow with the Tinbergen Institute, and affiliated with the Centre for Economic Policy Research. Hans's research concerns the economic analysis of cities, regions and the environment. His interests lie in understanding the functioning of housing and land markets, the agglomeration of firms and people within cities, the consequences of place-based policies, income inequality and segregation within cities, as well as the functioning of retail and commercial property markets within cities.

Majoor, Stan is an urban planner and political scientist and is Professor in the Coordination of Urban Issues and Director of the Centre of Expertise Urban Governance and Social Innovation at the Amsterdam University of Applied Sciences. His fields of interest are local governance innovation, public participation, and integral urban development projects.

Meerkerk, Joachim is a researcher and PhD candidate at Centre of Expertise Urban Governance and Social Innovation, part of Amsterdam University of Applied Sciences. His research continues with the theme of his work as a program maker for New Democracy at Pakhuis de Zwijger: the innovative and democratic power of social initiatives and co-creation between stakeholders in the city. Joachim works as an action researcher and focuses on urban commons as a model for collaborative governance.

Nevejan, Caroline is Chief Science Officer of the City of Amsterdam and holds the chair in Designing Urban Experience at the Amsterdam Institute for Social Science Research of the University of Amsterdam. Her personal research focuses on the design of trust in an era where mediated architectures change our performance of presence significantly. In this context she now focuses on Designing Rhythms for Social Resilience, which is funded by the National Science Foundation of the Netherlands.

Oostermeijer, Gerard is Assistant Professor in the Evolution and Population Biology department of the Institute for Biodiversity and Ecosystem Dynamics. He is a passionate conservation biologist, specializing in the effects of habitat fragmentation on the population viability of endangered plants and animal species. In addition, he focuses on biodiversity assessment in relation to conservation management in various ecosystems, ranging from coastal dunes to the urban landscape. Evolutionary adaptation of organisms to the urban ecosystem is a new topic. His personal mission is to integrate more population biology and genetics into conservation practice, which he achieves through the Foundation Science4Nature, which he co-founded and currently chairs.

Pinkster, Fenne is Associate Professor of Urban Geography in the Department of Geography, Planning and International Development at the University of Amsterdam. Her research focuses on the geography of everyday life in cities, examining how residents experience, use, and appropriate urban space and how they are both affected by, and contribute to, broader processes of urban change, such as segregation, gentrification, social mixing, and urban tourism.

Psyllidis, Achilleas is Assistant Professor of Location Intelligence and Spatial Analysis at Delft University of Technology (TU Delft). He is also an affiliate of the Amsterdam Institute for Advanced Metropolitan Solutions (AMS Institute), where he leads the Social Urban Data Lab (SUDL), and of the Leiden-Delft-Erasmus Center for BOLD (Big, Open, and Linked Data) Cities. He holds a PhD in Spatial Data Science from TU Delft, as a scholar of the Onassis Foundation and the European Social Fund (ESF) of the EU. His research focuses on the development of computational methods and tools that give insight into people's activities, behaviors, and interactions and the places they occur.

Raijmakers, Bas is co-founder and Creative Director of STBY in London and Amsterdam (www.stby.eu), established 2003. STBY specializes in creative research for considerate transformation towards more human, just, and sustainable societies. Bas has worked for clients in industry, government, and the public sector for more than 25 years. He holds a PhD in Design Interactions from the Royal College of Art in London. Bas co-founded the Reach Network for global design research (reach-network.com) in 2008.

Rasterhoff, Claartje works as Assistant Professor of Cultural Policy and Management at Maastricht University and as project leader of the Culture Monitor at Boekman Foundation (the Netherlands). In her research she integrates approaches from digital history, arts and culture studies, and urban studies to understand the organization of cultural life, past and present. Until 2020 she worked as Assistant Professor in Urban History and Digital Methods and acted as coordinator of the Amsterdam Time Machine at the University of Amsterdam.

Rouwendal, Jan is a full professor in the Department of Spatial Economics, VU University Amsterdam. He graduated in spatial economics at Erasmus University Rotterdam in 1983 and received his PhD at VU University Amsterdam in 1988 for a thesis about discrete choice models and housing market analysis. He is also affiliated as a research fellow with the Tinbergen Institute, Amsterdam School of Real Estate and Netspar.

Savini, Federico is Assistant Professor in Environmental Planning, Institutions and Politics at the University of Amsterdam. He combines approaches from political sociology, urban planning, and critical geography in the study of institutions and socio-spatial change in cities. His expertise ranges across the areas of land policy, land regulations, social innovation, environmental justice, and urban politics. In his works, he studies the politics that drive institutional change, focusing on the different sets of regulations that shape city regions.

Stegeman, Nina works as a Design Researcher at STBY Amsterdam (www.stby. eu). She is fascinated by social interaction and likes to dive deep into the lives of the people she is researching. She asks lots of questions and is a compassionate listener by instinct and experience. Prior to her work at STBY, Nina worked as an independent writer and researcher, mostly in civil society and the creative sector. She studied Journalism and Cultural Anthropology and uses both disciplines in her current work as a Design Researcher.

Verlaan, Tim is Assistant Professor in Urban History at the Amsterdam Centre for Urban History. His main research interests concern post-war urban renewal and gentrification in Western European cities. As an associate editor of *Urban History and Failed Architecture*, and a lecturer at graduate and postgraduate levels, Tim examines our built environment as the product of contemporary political, economic and social conditions.

Verloo, Nanke is Assistant Professor in Urban Planning in the Department of Human Geography, Planning and International Development Studies at the University of Amsterdam. Her research and teaching take an interdisciplinary and ethnographic approach to planning for inclusive cities. Her current research is focused on situations of conflict in participatory planning and other efforts to democratize urban development processes. She is on the editorial board of the journals *Tijdschrift voor Sociale Vraagstukken* and *Beleid en Maatschappij*.

Wesselman, Daan is a lecturer in Literary and Cultural Analysis at the University of Amsterdam and a researcher affiliated with the Amsterdam School for Cultural Analysis. His research explores material-discursive interfaces between the body, the city, and everyday life, seeking to bridge divide between the humanities and urban studies with a focus on issues like heterotopia, the right to the city, and the aesthetics of gentrification. Recently, he co-edited – with Simon Ferdinand and Irina Souch – the volume *Heterotopia and Globalisation in the Twenty-First Century* (Routledge, 2020).